UNTOUCHABLE

UNTOUCHABLE

THE UNDEFEATED, UNSCORED UPON 1964 RIDGEVIEW PANTHERS

Interviews, Essays, and Articles about the monumental 1964 season

Robert Canipe, Publisher and General Editor
Richard Eller, Research and Composition
Tim Peeler, Editor
Patty Thompson, Project and Permissions Coordinator

Redhawk Publications
2550 US Hwy 70 SE
Hickory, NC 28602

ISBN: 978-1-952485-29-9

Library of Congress Control Number: 2021943810

Printed in the United States of America

GO RIDGEVIEW!

Table of Contents

This book is Dedicated to:

William Heard
Ollie Parks
Willie Byrd
Allen Burch
Edward White
Frank Abernathy
Jerry Johnson
Charles Thompson
Edward Cunningham
Hubbard Morrison
Xenophon Lutz
Harrison James
Dwight Thompson
Douglas Bumgarner
Johnny Hodge
James Thompson
Craig Wilfong
Mitchell Anthony

Samuel Davis, Coach

Allen Pope
Tillis Rendleman
Hamp Davis
Eddie Corpening
Lewis Collins
Detroit Rhyne
Danny Carter
Charles Redman
John Thompson
Douglas Thompson
Jimmy Shade
Larry Williams
Tommy Yearby
Anthony Parks
Curtis Cunningham
Elbert Little
Bobby Bivens, trainee

Roger Scales, Assistant Coach

1964-1965 STATE 2A CHAMPIONS
"THE UNTOUCHABLES"

Front row (left to right): Lindsey Parks (not pictured), Hubbard Morrison, Mitchell Anthony, James Thompson, Xenophone Lutz, Douglas Bumgarner, John Hodge, Allen Pope, Dwight Thompson, Edward Cunningham, Craig Wilfong, Harrison James. Second row: Coach Sam Davis, Detroit Rhyne, Roosevelt Corpening, Danny Carter, Curtis Cunningham, Charles Thompson, Tillis Rendalman, John Thompson, Louis Collings, Tommy Euby, Coach Roger Scales. Third row: Jerry Johnson, Hamp Davis, Allen Burch, Willie Boyd, Carroll Carter, Douglas Thompson, Elbert Morrison, Frank Abernethy, Pete Heard, Ollie Parks, Edward White (not pictured), Anthony Parks, Ronald McKnight, Trainer (not pictured).

HICKORY DAILY RECORD 1964

Panthers Take State Title, Finish Season Unscored On

By ELLIS JOHNSON

The amazing Ridgeview Panthers of Hickory set a record at Lenoir Rhyne College Field Friday night as they shut out the Monroe Avenue Tigers of Hamlet, 16-0.

The 1960 team went through 11 games but this team has completed 12 games and ended a perfect season. In it they won the Northwestern Conference, District Class AA (District Two and defeated the District One champion) and defeated the District Three champions for the Western Class AA title Friday.

The Ridgeview Panthers became the North Carolina Negro Class AA champions for the second time. In 1962 they defeated Edenton for the crown on College Field (LR). For Coaches R.W. Davis and Roger Scales it was a happy ending to a dream.

Lost Toss

The Panthers lost the toss and had to kick off to the Tigers. It was returned to the Tigers 35-yard line. Deep in their own back yard the Tigers pulled a quick kick on third down. The ball was put in play on the Panthers 29-yard line behind excellent blocking, halfback Lee Bumgarner carried for 27 yards and again behind excellent blocking halfback Lee Bumgarner carried to the Tigers 14-yard line.

At this point Lee Bumgarner was called on again and carried to the four-yard line. The Panthers attempted to score on three tries but were pushed back on fourth down from the three-yard line. A Panther fumble was recovered by the Tigers. The Panthers defense soon made the Tigers kick and the Panthers took over on their own 31. A long penalty forced the Panthers back to their own 16-yard line where the Panthers had to kick. The gun sounded ending the quarter.

Halfback James Thompson got off a fine kick to start the second quarter. It was taken on the Tigers 46-yard line. The Tigers moved the ball well, picking up two first downs. On the Panthers 25-yard line, defensive guard Edward White recovered a fumble. Guided by quarterback Allen Pope, the Panthers moved the ball to the Tigers 45.

Plagued by a 15 yard penalty which set the Panthers back to their own 40-yard line, the stout defense of the Tigers pushed the Panthers back to the 36. Once again the Panthers had to call on James Thompson, their fine punter. The punt was returned to the Tigers 30-yard line. The fine offense of the Tigers began to click, picking up two first downs. The Tigers found themselves on the Panthers two-yard line, first and goal to go. The Panthers defense, led by Captain John Hodge, Xenophone Lutz, Charles Redman, Allen Pope and others, stopped the drive of the Tigers on the one-yard line as the gun sounded to end the scoreless half.

The second half kickoff to the Panthers own 15 yar line. Once again the Panthers were moving as fullback Edward Cunningham carried for eight to the 23, but this fine defense of the Tigers forced them to kick once again. James Thompson's kick rolled dead on the Tigers 14 yardline. The Panthers defense held and forced the Tigers to kick, which was taken on the Panthers 40 yardline.

At this point fullback Edward Cunningham raced fro 15 yards and a face mask penalty give the Panthers a first down on the 10 yardline. The hard hitting Tigers hit halfback Allen Burch, who fumbled the ball on the Tigers six yard line. The happy Tigers moved the ball down to the Panthers 34 yardline and were pulled down from behind.

The Tigers pass was intercepted by halfback Frank Abernethy and a penalty set the Panthers back to the six yardline.

Pass Intercepted

At this point halfback Lee Bumgarner brought the crowd to their feet as he raced for 59 yards behind good blocking. He was pulled down from behind on the Tigers 35. At this point the explosive Panthers called on halfback Allen Burch, who, behind excellent blocking, raced 35 yards to score a dtouchdown. Halfback Frank Abernethy added the two pointer.

The kick was returned to the Tiger 30. The Tigers picked up a first down on their own 40 and had another on the Panthers 45 yardline as the third quarter ended.

In the final period the Tigers were on the Panthers 31 yardline as a result of a 15 yard penalty. Then the Tigers fell back to the Panthers 46 yardline due to a fifteen yard penalty. Halfback Frank Abernethy intercepted another Tiger pass on the Panthers 38 yardline.

Once again Panthers quarterback Allen Pope got his team rolling as halfback Allen Burch carried for eleven yards after a nine yard loss. Pope hit Burch on the Tigers 35, then Pope hit Bumgarner on the 10 yardline. An offside penalty against the Tigers was refused. It gave the Panthers first and goal on the 10 yardline where fullback Edward Cunningham, behind excellent blocking, raced ten yards to score. Quarterback Allen Pope added the two pointer.

From this point the Tigers tried to score. The Stout Panther defense stopped their drives on the Panthers 35 yardline. Quarterback Pope fumbled on the Panthers 46 as the final gun sounded. The untouchable Panthers ended a victorious perfect season.

Ellis Johnson

ALMA MATER

By the Ridge of Blue Top Mountains,
Stands Dear Ridgeview High,
Whose Fame and Honor Ev-er Mounting,
Nev-er Nev-er will die.
Ridge-view, Ridge-view Al-Ma Mater,
Your Sons and Daughters are True.
Long as the Sun Sinks O'er Yon Mountain,
We'll Cheer the Orange and Blue.

FOR JUST SUCH A TIME AS THIS
BY JEREMY WILSON

"Yet who knows whether you have come to the kingdom for just such a time as this?"—Esther 4:14 NKJV

Ten years after the Supreme Court's decision in *Brown v. Board of Education* (1954), not much had really changed. The country had learned a few things about human nature in those ten years. For example, if you give people a task, but not a deadline, they tend to procrastinate, especially if the task is one they have no real interest in completing. Also, people will almost always put up some kind of resistance to a task they don't want to do. The Court had ordered in 1954 that public schools were to be desegregated "with all deliberate speed." Whatever they had in mind by using that phrase, many schools in the South were still segregated ten years later. The Civil Rights movement was in full swing by 1964. The Montgomery Bus Boycott, the Woolworth's Sit-Ins, and the March on Washington had all proven that African-Americans were determined to force the country to change and to give them their rightful inheritance as citizens of a free nation. In the summer of '64, President Johnson signed into law the Civil Rights Act, which forbade discrimination based on race and intended to get things like school desegregation moving along at a faster clip. Things looked to be going better, if not yet just the way they should be.

During that same summer, about a month after President Johnson signed the Act, the Ridgeview High School Panthers football team began training camp for their fall football season. Their coach, Samuel Davis, felt as though he faced an enormous task in getting his players ready for the season. He had lost some key players from a very good 1963 squad and was wondering how (or if) he would be able to replace them and field a successful team. His primary worry was that his team was young, with sophomores expected to start at several positions, including quarterback. It looked like the Panthers might be a year away from repeating the success of the previous several years. Whatever Coach Davis thought about them during camp, Ridgeview's 1964 squad proved to be the right team at the right time. The Panther offense was very good. They averaged 37.2 points per game against competition Coach Davis described as troublesome going into the season. The defense, on the other hand, was... what's the word... untouchable. The scoring average of Ridgeview's opponents was a little easier to calculate. It was zero. It didn't matter if the games were played at home in the Dust Bowl or on the road. It didn't matter if they were regular season games or playoffs. It didn't matter if the game was against faraway Spindale High or their previously-undefeated crosstown rivals from Central High in Newton. The Panthers not only completed an undefeated season, they also didn't allow any of their opponents to score a single point. They won a state title and redefined the term "perfect season." They stood as an example of black excellence in a time when it was not typically acknowledged by the wider community. They showed the community what they could do when they were allowed and encouraged to excel. It was perfect timing. The young men who made that team so special then headed out into a world that would be suspicious toward them, if not outright hostile. The toughness, resiliency, and determination shown during their perfect 1964 season would go on to serve them well through the next few years of chaotic change at home and throughout the country.

While the story of the Untouchables is certainly one of athletic excellence, it's also one of community pride and togetherness in a time of difficult transition. Ridgeview was a vibrant community with a great deal of pride in their football team. They showed that pride by showing up to support the team on Friday nights. They encouraged the players. They "coached" from the stands. They let the players know that they were admired by their families, friends, and neighbors. And, they policed the players' behavior off the field so that they could stay in good shape and continue to excel on the field. Their teachers, coaches, family members, friends, and neighbors realized that the players would be at the forefront of a transitional period and that they needed to be ready for it. The encouragement and education the players received helped them to be ready when the changes came. Those players were well-equipped to help lead their community into the future in a variety of roles. They were prepared to serve as examples for those who would follow them as students and as members of the Ridgeview community. The Untouchables came together just when they were needed by their school and by their community

Just two years after the 1964 season, the Hickory Public Schools began the process of integration and Ridgeview High School closed. The football players who had made the Ridgeview teams great became part of integrated teams at Hickory High School. Sadly, school integration allowed the legacy of the Ridgeview Panthers to fade somewhat over the years. Telling their story after so many years has allowed people to see that the Untouchables came along at just the perfect time to serve as a bridge from one period in Hickory's history to another. Their ascent to the state championship and their completion of a perfect season gave the players and the Ridgeview community the confidence that they could move forward into whatever an uncertain future held. They truly were community heroes at just the right time.

2001 LOCAL STORY ABOUT COACH SAMUEL DAVIS' INDUCTION INTO THE CATAWBA VALLEY SPORTS HALL OF FAME.

SENIOR Accents

published monthly by HICKORY NEWS

Vol. 7 - No. 7 | Complimentary Issue | May 10, 2001

INSIDE

Puzzling passion

Entertaining hobby of working crosswords puzzles featured, page 8.

Gridiron great set for Hall induction

Barbara Burns

Senior Accents staff
bburns@hickorynews.net

At the golden age of 78, he's still known as Coach.

After a lifetime of sports, civics, and athletic honors, Samuel William Davis, Sr., will be anointed with one of the highest accolades of his career when he is inducted into the Catawba Valley Sports Hall of Fame.

Coach Davis, who began his coaching career at age 23, is one of four inaugural inductees who has distinguished himself and made significant contributions to Catawba County sports heritage.

He earned recognition as head football coach of Hickory's former African-American Ridgeview High School for 14 years in the 1950's and 1960's.

Under Coach Davis, the Ridgeview Panthers captured 13 straight conference football championships, winning five state titles, including three consecutive by winning 36 games in a row.

His last three teams were not only state champions but also unbeaten and unscored upon.

A native of North Wilkesboro and a graduate of Winston-Salem State Teachers College (now University), Coach Davis came to Ridgeview in 1952 and coached football and basketball, and later taught at College Park Middle School where he retired in 1982.

— Barbara O. Burns

COACH Samuel William Davis Sr. will be inducted into the Catawba Valley Sports Hall of Fame.

Coach Davis moves a little slower now, but he jumps at the chance to reminisce about his years in athletes and academics.

He has the voice, mannerisms, and wit of Bill Cosby, and loves to talk about his years of coaching.

"When I came to Hickory in the school year of 1951-52, we played 17 or 18 boys on the football team," he said. "We started a little winning season," he laughed, "and played 500 ball that year."

The next season the Panthers started with close to 40 players. From that point on, they were always in contention in the old Northwest Athletic Conference.

"We had a training program that most coaches wouldn't dare try," he said with a smile.

For the first seven days of practice, the players would run, and run, and run. They ran until they could run five miles in less than 20 minutes.

"When most teams were giving up, we were just getting ready to play," Coach Davis said. "We never lost a game because we were out of condition."

Coach Davis said he watches the high school boys playing football now.

"They come out and fall down with cramps in their legs, and the coach has to take them out because they don't have that stamina to go any longer," he commented.

Coach Davis said that during those years they had many coaches.

"I was head coach, but everybody that had a boy on that team had several coaches. I set a 9:30 pm curfew for my boys," he said. "If one of them

See page 2 ➤

Coach Davis to be inducted into Sports Hall of Fame

— From page 1

wasn't in the house by then, his mother or father would call me. The boys never knew how I knew when they weren't in, because the parents wouldn't say anything, and I wouldn't either.

That's how close we worked together and it paid off for us."

Coach Davis' last three teams at Ridgeview won consecutive state championships and were unscored upon.

They were called 'the untouchables' because no one could beat them.

After a prep session and prayer, the players would come out onto the field loudly chanting, "Let's go down and get it over with."

"They just got that habit of wanting to win," he reflected. "You've got to want something bad enough to fight for it in order to get it."

Little did Coach know that 1966 was the end of his coaching days at Ridgeview. It was also the end of the Panthers.

Ridgeview High School was closed to carry out the community's goal of racial integration.

When asked to comment on that, Coach Davis replied, "It was a smack in the face, it really was.

Had we been told ahead, it would have been better, but they waited until they were ready to just pull us out, and nobody knew.

Nobody knew it until it was announced at the end of the season."

Coach Davis said that was the year that they gave a championship team to head football Coach Frank Barger at Hickory High School.

"A championship team was handed over to them, and they couldn't push it over," Coach Davis said. "I wondered about that many times until I worked with him for a few times."

Coach Davis said he stayed at Hickory High off and on for quite a while.

"Finally I got tired of being pushed down and I told Dr. Wishon, the superintendent, just to send me to College Park Junior High and let me stay," he said quietly.

Coach Davis would call plays when asked, only to have the call changed right before the play commenced.

Coach Davis said it was hard on the players, not to be able to play the position they normally got to play.

"I know you can't have everybody doing what you think they ought to be doing, but the thing about it, you've got to be fair with those boys," Coach Davis said. "I notice the coaches now, they're fair with all the boys. As long as you're fair with them, they're going to work their hearts out for the coaches, and they'll keep working for them."

When Coach Davis went back to College Park he was assigned to work with Joe Rhyne.

"We worked together for 17

See page 4 ➤

SENIOR Accents

Editor/General Manager - David Threshie
Advertising Director - Mickey Price
Production Director - Jeff Isenhour
Marketing Director - Angie Pooley
Advertising Assistant - Nicole Miller
Advertising - Karen Pless, Hal McPherson, Allison Beach, Roger Brooks
Production - Pat Decker, Debbie Smith
Reporter/photojournalist - Barbara Burns
New Media Director, Bookkeeping - Melanie Zimmermann
Reception - Peggy Barrier • Circulation - Vickie Price

Telephone (828) 328-6164 - Fax: 322-6398
newsxtra@hickorynews.net • www.hickorynews.net

Senior Accents, a publication of The Hickory News, is published monthly at 270 Union Square, Hickory, NC 28603. P.O. Box 2650.

Team

From Page 1A

of our physical play. The grass was destroyed."

There was also some showmanship on the field, said 'JoBo' Lutz. "The late Mitch Anthony who centered the ball for the Panthers would excite the team, opponents and fan by turning a flip before he centered the ball."

The closest an opponent came to scoring on Ridgeview happened in the championship game against Monroe Avenue of Hamlet. They made it to the 5-yard line before getting turned back.

"The score was 0-0 at halftime. We won the game on a miss-direction play, a nervous experience," said Lutz.

Lutz said he was surrounded by great players. "Pope was a great quarterback who played intelligent and hard," said Lutz. He also mentioned players like Allen Burch, who scored two touchdowns in the championship game.

Edward Cunningham was a great player as well as Dwight Thompson and Curtis Cunningham. They all played a valuable role in helping the team be as successful as it was.

Because of their undefeated and unscored upon season, the team was labeled the Untouchables. Their main rival was Central High School in Newton.

Bobby Rowe, who played at Ridgeview in the early 1950s, coached at Central. "They were a good football team," said Rowe. "The community and families supported them and that is one of the reasons they were so successful."

The Untouchables' season ended at Lenoir Rhyne College Field with a shutout of the Monroe Avenue Tigers of Hamlet, 16-0 to win the state title. "The last game, I had mixed emotions playing," said running back Lee Bumgarner. "I realized it was over and now comes the real challenge facing the world."

Several of the Untouchables went on to play college football at Winston Salem Teachers College and NC A&T College. They included Lutz, Bumgarner, Johnny Hodge, Johnny Thompson, Anthony Parks and Mitch Anthony.

The team's legacy as Ridgeview's greatest team is the pride, respect and support the community has always given it, and the fact that those Panthers players stand as role models for other players.

Coach Davis is recognized as one of Catawba County's best coaches. He was inducted into the Catawba Valley Sports Hall of Fame in 2001, in its first class.

Davis, also athletic director at Ridgeview from 1952-1967, coached the Panthers to 13 straight conference football championships, winning five straight titles from 1962-1966. His last three teams at Ridgeview were state champions.

"You can achieve the impossible with faith and hard work," said Cunningham. "We got the respect from people all around the city, and after winning the state title, we all got steak dinners."

Other members of the team:

James Thompson, John Hodge, Craig Wilfong, Harrison James, Detroit Rhyne, Roosevelt Corpening, Danny Carter, Charles Thompson, Tillis Rendalman, John Thompson, Lewis Collings, Tommy Euby, Jerry Johnson, Hamp Davis, Willie Byrd, Caroll Carter, Douglas Parks, Ronald McKnight, Elbert Morrison, Frank Abernethy, Ollie Parks, Edward White, Anthony Parks, Hubbard Morrison and Lindsey Parks.

LOCAL STORY CONCERNING COACH SAMUEL DAVIS AND HOW SCHOOL INTEGRATION LED TO HIS BEING "SIDELINED," ASSISTING WITH THE HICKORY TEAMS, A "COP" KEEPING PLAYERS "IN LINE." DAVIS ASSISTED FRANK BARGER, SAYING, "YOU CAN'T HAVE TWO BOSSES IN ANYTHING, AND HE WAS THE HEAD MAN."

SPORTS

School integration sidelined winning coach

By By DENNIS BENFIELD
Special Correspondent

Quick now, who's the last high school head football coach in Catawba County to end his career with a winning streak?

No, not him. Think back a few years. Give up?

Samuel William Davis, 68, of Hickory coached the Panthers of the former all-black Ridgeview High School for 14 years in the 1950s and 1960s, and his last three teams were undefeated state champions, 36 wins in a row.

After playing "50-50 ball" his first year at Ridgeview, the Panthers settled into a tradition, winning the old Northwest Athletic Conference championship 13 straight years.

His last three teams, nicknamed "The Untouchables," not only were the undefeated state champions — but no one even scored on the Panthers. Overall, Davis' teams captured five state titles in 14 years.

"We went three years without anybody crossing our goal line," Davis says proudly.

Secret to winning

Davis' coaching secret was in being unpredictable on the field.

"I believe you have to keep a defense honest, so if they'd look for us to run, we'd pass. If they looked for a pass, we'd run," he said. "We had a play out of punt formation where we'd snap to the fullback and run straight up the middle."

But all that gridiron glory came to an end after the 1965 season, when Ridgeview High School was closed in 1966 to further the community's goal of racial integration.

Sam Davis was transferred to College Park Junior High (now a middle school), where he coached, and taught eighth-grade science, math and physical education for 16 more years.

"The kids lost something in that, but they gained something, too," Davis said. "Black teachers had a different slant. We first wanted to show them that they were loved. We just went to College Park to help children to get what they needed to be successful.

"You still have to show them you care. The years that I was there, I enjoyed it, and we had several doctors, lawyers and judges we turned out, too."

On to Hickory High

For about five years, in addition to serving as an assistant football coach to College Park's Joe Rhyne, Davis assisted with Hickory High teams. He says he was "the cop who kept (the players) in line."

About his secondary role to the late head coach Frank Barger, he simply shrugs: "You can't have two bosses in anything, and he was the head man."

Davis retired in 1982.

He still substitute teaches, and he doesn't especially like what he sees.

"The one thing that scares me most," Davis says, "is taking away the discipline in schools. Teachers don't have the support of parents like they used to, and the principals are running scared. They're afraid if they try to get strict with discipline, somebody's parents will want to sue."

He believes problems with drugs, alcohol and casual sex among youngsters stem from neglect or lack of guidance from parents.

"Nobody's telling these children what they can and can't do," he said. "In my day, a teacher could set the boundaries, and the parents would back you on it.

"Now, (discipline) has got to come from the home, 'cause home is where the problem is. The family's got to take over and know what their kids are doing."

And teachers are too busy to teach nowadays, he said.

"Look at what all they have to do, besides teaching," Davis said. "They've got all that busy-body book work, staff development, and too many other things that take up their time. We need to go back to giving teachers time to teach."

His college days

Davis, a native of North Wilkesboro and graduate of another former all-black school, Lincoln Heights, went to Winston-Salem State Teachers' College (now a university) on an athletic scholarship, playing both football and basketball.

One of his coaches was Clarence "Big House" Gaines.

Davis graduated from Winston-Salem in 1946 and worked at his alma mater for a couple of years before teaching at a training school in Pender County. He came to Ridgeview in 1952.

After his retirement from the schools, he turned full-time to his skills as a chef, working first for eight years at Service America and then adding three at Piedmont Vending. He was a chef at Hickory's Charolais Steak House for eight years and has cooked at the Hickory Moose Lodge for several years. He also does catering.

Davis is still active as a volunteer in the community, serving as an assistant football coach at Grandview Middle School and as a neighborhood commissioner with the Piedmont Council, Boy Scouts of America.

Being a team player

Davis says he learned volumes from his high school and college coaches, including Al White and Brutus Wilson, about human relations. At Ridgeview, he teamed with coaches Burrell Brown and Thomas Penn, now memorialized in the name of Ridgeview's Brown-Penn Recreation Center.

"We understood that, to get kids to play for you, you had to be fair with them. Quite often, we'd gather the kids together at the beginning of a game and say, 'All right, now let's get some points here. Let's let everybody play.' "

Later, working in the desegregated Hickory school sports program, he saw himself as part of another team — of coaches.

"There was a great deal of unity with all the coaches at Hickory High. We all worked together — we were a team ourselves. They seemed to like me, and I liked them. There was a lot of mutual respect."

Davis says his own coaches always helped him to understand that "the only way to having a winning team is to have the players on your side."

"You've got to show them you intend to do right by them. You don't browbeat them. You work with them and help them," he said. "You try to make them understand that you've got to be as good a person in the classroom as you are on the football field."

JEFF WILLHELM/Staff

Went out a winner: Samuel Davis, 68, of Hickory coached the Panthers of the former all-black Ridgeview High School for 14 years. His last three teams were undefeated state champions.

Samuel Davis

- **Age:** 68.
- **Family:** Three sons, Sam Davis Jr., 28, of Hickory; Ernie Davis, 25, of Williamsburg, Va.; and Neil Davis, 21, of Charleston; granddaughter, Ashley Lee Ann, 2, who lives with him.
- **Philosophy:** "You have to be fair with people. That's how you get their respect, a lasting understanding. It's the same thing for black people or white people."
- **Quote:** "Parents need to support the teachers and put the discipline back in schools. Somebody needs to set limits on what kids can and can't do."

RECREATION AND SPORTS

Wrestling event is Jan. 18

NEWTON — Smoky Mountain Wrestling is coming to the Newton Parks and Recreation Center at 8 p.m. Jan. 18. The event will be for television taping.

Wrestling stars scheduled to participate include the Rock-N-Roll Express, Tracy Smoothers, Jim Cornette and the Heavenly Bodies, Kevin Sullivan, Tim Horner, the Fantastics, Paul Orndorff, Dutch Mantell and Robert Fuller.

Tickets are $6 at the Newton Recreation Center, South Brady Avenue and East A Street.

Center hours are 8 a.m.-8 p.m. Mondays through Thursdays and 8 a.m.-5 p.m. Fridays. Details: 465-7470.

Basketball league to meet

NEWTON — Teams registered for the East Newton Recreation Center's men's basketball league must have at least one representative at a 6 p.m. organizational meeting Monday at the Newton Recreation Center, at South Brady Avenue and East A Street.

Line-dancing classes slated

MORGANTON — Western couple and line-dancing classes start Tuesday at Liberty Middle School, 529 Enola Rd. The six-week class on Tuesdays will meet 6:30-8 p.m and costs $25 per person. Larry Whetstine is the instructor. To register, call 433-4255, 8 a.m.-5 p.m. weekdays.

Sports news?

Catch that record fish? Finally sink a hole-in-one? Proud of a son or daughter who excelled on the playing field?

Catawba Valley Neighbors wants your sports results, achievements and activities from Alexander, Burke, Caldwell and Catawba counties.

You can drop sports items by at 261 2nd Ave. S.E. in Hickory on N.C. 127 South, 9 a.m.-5 p.m. weekdays. To fax, call 327-3480. Or mail to:

Catawba Valley Neighbors
P.O. Box 2492
Hickory, N.C. 28603

We want you on our team.

Photo by Robert Reed, courtesy *Hickory Daily Record*

Photo Courtesy of Beverly Snowden, Hickory Public Schools, courtesy *Beverly Snowden*

A RESOUNDING "YES!" BY KATHRYN T. GREATHOUSE

In April of 2018, a grant panel appointed by the United Arts Council of Catawba County was meeting around a table, hearing funding pitch after funding pitch from area arts, science and history groups. As usual, we were hearing about some great projects, but it can make for a long day.

Our twelfth presenter, at 1:10 pm, was a group from Catawba Valley Community College led by historian Richard Eller. While I knew some about what they were proposing, it took just a short time before I, and the entire grant panel, became enthralled with the story of "The Untouchables," the 1964 undefeated, unscored upon football team from Ridgeview High School.

Did we want to fund animation for a documentary about this incredible group of young men? A resounding yes to that!

Later that year, I was persuaded by a top level arts supporter, Kimberly George, to watch a webinar put on by the Z. Smith Reynolds Foundation about a large grant for public art. Because Kimberly asked, I did it, and it became clear that a public art piece about "The Untouchables" would check every single box that Z. Smith Reynolds required for the grant. A story not often told? Check. About a diverse community? Check. The possibility of a $50,000 grant for a public art project to honor "The Untouchables"? Check.

But was the community interested? After all, it was a painful time when the all-black Ridgeview High School was closed in 1966 and local schools were integrated. The Ridgeview students were bussed across town to the formerly all-white Hickory High School. It was a loss to the community. So we asked. And we heard a big enthusiastic yes. So, check and double check.

Next came the process of a Letter of Intent to the Z. Smith Reynolds Foundation. This involved a great deal of planning and we knew we could get hopes up and then be let down at the end. This was of special concern after meeting some of the amazing and charismatic members of the team. Xenophone Lutz, Hampton Davis, Tillis Rendleman, Douglas Bumgarner and Larry Williams were along every step of the way and the thought of their being disappointed kept me awake at night.

Throughout the fall of 2018, we conducted listening sessions and canvassed residents in the Ridgeview community to determine what shape the final piece would take. The ideas began to narrow down to murals, sculpture or possibly some type of structure.

One thing was clear. Whatever form the public art took, it had to be located in the heart of the community.

At one meeting, Margaret Pope, a highly regarded Ridgeview resident, suggested an archway at the Samuel William Davis Sr. Field, known as The Dust Bowl, where the team played its home games. At that point, we knew we had our project. By the end of that meeting, we had talked about the archway having wings spreading from each side featuring murals – one about "The Untouchables" and the other about Ridgeview High School.

If we heard nothing else, we heard loud and clear the pride the Ridgeview community feels in the school that closed 55 years ago. The faculty, the band, the glee club, the debate club, the cheerleaders, and, of course, the teams, are still fondly remembered and revered. Local resident Vickie Scott heads an active alumni association and her contributions and insights were invaluable.

To make our grant more compelling, we needed an artist who was rooted in the community. We learned about Adele James McCarty, a talented local muralist whose parents went to Ridgeview High School. We saw right away she would be the perfect person to bring our ideas to fruition.

We had the bones of our grant, but we were a long way from getting it. We submitted our Letter of Intent and learned we were among 82 vying for what would in the end be 10 grants. Not great odds, we thought.

Of course, we knew nobody had a better story, but it all boiled down to another grant panel – this one at the Z. Smith Reynolds Foundation. Not surprisingly, in November of 2018 they named us one of 20 semifinalists.

As a semifinalist, we had a 50-50 chance of getting the grant, still not the kind of odds we liked. Z. Smith Reynolds provided a very helpful $5,000 planning grant so we spent a great deal of time fleshing out our proposal, holding further meetings with the community, making sure we had permission from the City of Hickory for the project and working with local architect Ernie Sills to design the project. We found we could just squeak in the cost of the project with the potential grant, so after more paperwork for the foundation, we sent it off in April of 2019 and we waited.

At that point, we were practically shovel ready, and we knew it would be a crushing blow to the community if we were not selected.

Finally, in June of 2019 we were notified that the United Arts Council of Catawba County was one of 10 winners of a $50,000 grant. We celebrated and then we got to work on our "Untouchables" project.

We broke ground and began construction in August. One of our goals, from an idea by then Arts Council President Jill Towery, was to have the name of every team member inscribed on a brick that would surround the mural about "The Untouchables." We had a photo of the team and used that to make sure we included every member.

While construction continued, we worked with Adele McCarty on the mural designs. We had a very engaged committee who met with us regularly to monitor the progress and offer suggestions. The location of the archway and murals had the added advantage of being in a highly visible location right on the City of Hickory's proposed new Ridgeview Walk, part of a system of pedestrian walkways under construction in the city.

We worked closely with the City of Hickory, the City Manager Warren Wood, Mayor Hank Guess, and City Councilperson David Williams all of whom enthusiastically followed our progress and offered help at every turn. The City of Hickory Appearance Commission was involved and encouraging. Richard Eller documented our project and continued to work with his colleagues at Catawba Valley Community College on a documentary about the team.

Incoming Arts Council Board President Danielle Cannon and the entire Board of Directors remained strong proponents of the project. The Z. Smith Reynolds Foundation and liaison Brenda Miller Holmes offered not only funding, but experience and guidance.

Writer Kevin Griffin of the *Hickory Daily Record* helped get the entire town excited about this historic team and its legacy. The team appeared at the Hickory Rotary Club and at Hickory's Ted X event to standing ovations. It seemed it was the year of "The Untouchables."

We looked forward to a finished product and a celebration event in 2020. Then Covid hit. It just didn't seem right to hold a celebration the whole community could not attend. The new celebration and unveiling of the murals is scheduled for September of 2021.

One more thing. When I first met the members of "The Untouchables," one of them told me they would love to be named a Team of Distinction in the Catawba County Sports Hall of Fame. The fact they have not been was quite an oversight in my opinion, though their beloved coach, Samuel William Davis Sr., was in the first class. I nominated them for the 2019 class and they were not chosen. However, they were considered again in 2020, were voted in, and will officially be inducted as a Team of Distinction in May of 2021.

Being around these humble and gracious guys has taught me the value of pride in community, hard work, and loyal friendship. I will never forget "The Untouchables" and their story, one that is unique to our town and unique to the time.

Thanks to Z. Smith Reynolds Foundation, the United Arts Council of Catawba County, and Catawba Valley Community College, the story will live on and will continue to inspire all who hear it.

ALLEN & AGGIE
A TEAM WITHIN THE TEAM
BY DESMOND, GRANDSON OF ALLEN BURCH DOUGLAS & DENYSE, CHILDREN OF EDWARD DOUGLAS WHITE, SR. AKA "AGGIE"

Allen and Aggie (uncle and nephew) would have been 75 years old this year—born only a month apart. Allen's touchdowns were made possible by Aggie's offensive and defensive mastery through quick and aggressive blocking.

Bonded like brothers, these two souls were born to play together, make sense of life together, and ultimately to make history. The Panthers did the unthinkable at a time when Black people were not thought of.

Our dads were passionate, talented men who poured the best of themselves into their families. What they learned on the field became our life lessons. We know they are proud of who and what we have become—an Entrepreneur, a Police Detective (retired), and an Entertainment Executive. Their relentless drive for excellence is the wind beneath our wings.

Desmond, Entrepreneur, ShopKurij

Allen Franklin Burch, my granddad was wise. He was a mathematician with a business mindset. He saw that in me. It was like he knew something about me that I didn't know about myself. Resourceful, honest, and moral, Daddy was made for greatness. The Panthers gave him a chance to share some of that greatness on the field.

The Untouchables were an important part of his life. He told me that they trained and worked and worked and trained. Daddy scored 13 touchdowns in this historic year. But from what he told me, this was not the only championship year. Either way, if he were playing football today, he probably could have gone pro, if he wanted to.

Growing up in Hickory, those championships are as much a part of his story as they are my own. My brother Darrien and I both played football, carrying on his legacy. Our Daddy was at every game. And whenever my uncle Aggie was in town, he was on the sidelines coaching us from his wheelchair. Breaking state records runs in the family. Darrien is fourth in the State for scoring seven touchdowns in one half of a game.

Daddy really wanted us to succeed. I brought home a "D" in art. It was the first and last time. He called a conference with the teacher and myself to make sure it would never happen again. The man and father I am today are because of the father he was to me and the unwavering example he set.

If Allen Franklin Burch were here today, he would be glad to see the team honored for the role they played in Hickory's history. With his legendary smile and straightforward honesty, he would tell the stories that only he could tell. People would not forget.

Douglas, Retired Detective

My father, Aggie, was a brilliant, humorous, and complex man. Maybe that's why he understood the architecture of football so well. Growing up on "F" Avenue, his childhood friends loved to play marbles. His nickname came from the aggie marble—small, strong, sleek, powerful, and fast.

Football was always a part of our lives. Some of my first toys were a G.I. Joe and a football. It would be a part of my future whether I knew it or not, whether I wanted to or not. Watching the games and learning about the sport was as common as breathing air.

Gifted with similar athletic ability, like my father, I was an incredibly swift runner. I ended up playing football in High School in New York. My father was invited to join the coaching staff. Because he became disabled at an early age, this was an important outlet. He loved the game, and coaching gave him the ability to relive the glory days of Ridgeview. His drive and sacrifice despite his disability is a model of grit that I will never forget.

Beyond sports, we are both Black Men in a country that both celebrates and fears us. Living in the tension between the two realities, my father's passion, persistence, and anger had gifted me with resilience and insight that has served me no matter what field I played on—from the football field to the field of academia or the field of justice. He was a walking example of relentless determination.

Denyse, Entertainment Executive

I am a sportless soul. Once I remember running into the living room after hearing my dad yell. He and my brother were huddled around the television watching football. Rolling my eyes, I walked out of the room, thinking, when is football season over? Ugh.

Like Des and Doug, I can't remember when I did not know that our dads were a part of something great, something historic. The children of celebrities often have no idea who their parents are. It was clear that people revered my dad. They respected the legacy. Whenever I visited Hickory, I was Aggie's daughter, and that meant something. It is one thing when someone tells you their stories. It's another when others repeat those stories, making them lore.

My aunts and uncles talked about sneaking into those unforgettable games. It sounded magical. Mom and Dad were High School sweethearts. She, in the marching band. He was on the team. For me, it was like imagining the Black version of Archie comics.

Beyond the romance, I saw another story. The story of a young Black man who went to school whenever he could. He worked to feed his mom and siblings as the de facto provider when his father was away working in another town. In one interview, Dad told me that football saved his life. He needed something to ground him. Being a Panther helped to shape his identity.

I saw the story of a young father who, despite having a third grade reading level, moved to New York to build a life for his young family. I remember a man who purchased encyclopedias instead of toys and taught me to read at the age of three. I saw his pride when I graduated magna cum laude from college.

Forever tactical, he told me that there was a time when a person is running, and both legs are in the air. He would wait for that moment and tackle them, laying them out—that sounded incredibly rhythmic, sinister, and strategic. Stories like these taught me how to analyze and think on micro-levels.

Whether I understood it or not, I was raised by a champion. As my father's sidekick, I learned to engage with life like a game—to play, strategize, push through the tough times, move forward despite difficult circumstances, and to find the essence of resilience.

If my dad were here today, of the Panther recognition, he would simply say, "*It's about damn time.*"

THE ICONIC LETTER
JACKET OF THE 1964
RIDGEVIEW PANTHERS.

A SEASON IN TUNE
BY RICHARD ELLER

The moment had come. As players stepped onto the field they knew this game was the most important one they might ever play. The stadium where they had earned the right to compete for the state championship was just across town from their home field, but in terms of its grandeur, the two gridirons were a study in contrasts. The team practiced and played on their home turf so much, overuse had turned the field to dirt. In fact, everyone knew Ridgeview's arena as "the Dust Bowl." Senior lineman Xenophone Lutz remembered there was "very little grass. At halftime you could see dust in the lights, so you knew Ridgeview was playing football."

Now the Ridgeview Panthers walked onto a surface so cushioned by grass, they all took notice. "Other teams had grass, we didn't have grass," recalled senior halfback Douglas Bumgarner, so when the team won their semifinal game at the Dust Bowl, the field at the local college was deemed to be a more appropriate place for the State 2A Negro League Championship. The choice of Lenoir-Rhyne College as the site of the game was an ironic one since the school at that time did not allow African-Americans as students.

As a team, the Ridgeview Panthers had seen this moment before. In 1960, the team ran the table, refusing to let any team score on them on their way to the big game. However, when the earlier team played for the championship, they not only allowed Lincoln High from Chapel Hill to score, they lost, 38-6. That was the year before any of the current members of this team were old enough to play. The following year, as many of the now seniors were freshmen Panthers, they again lost to Chapel Hill in the state championship.

The bridesmaids did not take the losses cheerfully. In 1962, they worked hard to return to the championship. That year they faced Edenton, thankful it was not Chapel Hill, beating them for the state crown. But the year after they lost in the playoffs in the semi-finals to Lexington Dunbar. As rising senior Tillis Rendleman said, looking back on that loss, "that left a sour note in our mouths and made us feel really bad."

The playoff defeats were especially painful given the winning ways of the team throughout the regular season. They never lost. Winning conference championships became a regular occurrence for the Ridgeview Panthers year after year. Always a formidable team, the streak of consecutive regular season wins began in 1957 and continued until integration finally occurred after the 1965 season. As of 2020, the team still holds the record of consecutive regular season wins at 74. The problem had been the playoffs where they lost to Dunbar in semifinal games before what looked like a perfect season in 1960, one that went down to defeat in Chapel Hill.

Losing to Dunbar affected the team profoundly. Feeling themselves a better team, Tillis and his teammates made a pact not to let it happen again. "We decided amongst ourselves, the future seniors coming up, we were going to do something special. We were going to get in shape, we were going to stay in shape," ready to meet whatever any other team threw at them during the 1964 season. "Conditioning and confidence," that's how fellow senior Xenophone Lutz described the team as they prepared for one last campaign. The confidence was there. Almost a decade of dominance had given the Panthers a reputation as winners; now they just needed to be able to outlast any opponent.

"Our coach was big on running," said Tillis Rendleman. "When he said run, you ran," and they did. Noticing the hunger with which his leaders, the seniors came back for preseason work, Coach Samuel Davis loaded his team up on a rickety old bus, taking the team out to some of the most rural country Catawba County could offer. There he ordered his men off the bus and drove away. They knew the drill. The entire team was expected to run back to school, a distance of five miles. During the summer the bus pulled out of the high school parking lot at 5:00am. Every team member was expected to be there and they were. In addition to endurance building, the runs were also team building exercises. No one was left behind, although some of their most excellent runners, like Hampton Davis was always at the head of the pack. They nicknamed him "Rabbit."

No Panther who ever stepped off that bus forgot those runs, or what it did for the team to build their stamina. During the fourth quarter of every game, these young men were eager and ready to play, conditioned for anything the other team might throw at them. Those 5am mornings paid off on Friday nights when opponents were dragging late in the game. The Panthers were as fresh as if it were the first quarter, quite a feat for a team where many of them played both sides of the ball, offense and defense. John Thompson, who gained college fame at the University of Minnesota and played for the NFL's Houston Oilers, asserted "high school superseded anything we did as far as physical training in college." He went on to favorably evaluate his playing days at Ridgeview against his professional career, saying "Even the conditions there, professionally with the Houston Oilers was nothing like we had in high school."

For the players who did not live near the high school, their running regimen was even greater. Douglas Bumgarner and several other teammates lived in East Hickory, several miles from the school. They ran in the predawn stillness to get to school to ride the bus so they could start the formal workout. Washington Forest, the neighborhood where Hamp Davis lived was even farther out. One might think such exertion would leave him at the back of the pack, but instead he outran them all.

By the time Hamp Davis and his teammates came along, football was established as the premier sport for young men in and around Ridgeview. "That's the way our community worked," said Mac Rowland, senior quarterback for the team in 1963. "First through the eighth grade, your main thing was to be good enough to make Ridgeview's football team." Pickup games were common. Douglas Bumgarner recalled, "when I was a kid in East Hickory we were out there playing football in the snow. It was around Christmas time. Somebody got a football for Christmas." He added, "If you've got a football, there was going to be a game somewhere."

"If you had a football you was a king," Hamp Davis said, only half joking. Football became a rite of passage for boys. Several important developmental milestones were occurring in those games. First, the physical activity of running, passing, catching, and defending against each of those provided exercise and developed skills that would become part of the fundamentals necessary to make the team. "We'd choose up teams, pick up players and start a game anywhere. We'd play till dark," recollected Douglas Bumgarner, who also mused, "sounds crazy but we enjoyed it. It paid off."

Playing a variety of positions in games gave youngsters some idea of their strengths. Senior quarterback Allen Pope described selection for a pickup game. "You kind of find out how good you are, because when they picked the two captains, the captains would then start choosing guys and the guys would be standing on the side. You could kind of tell how good you would be based on how fast you were chosen. So as long as you were chosen in those first five or six guys it's like, 'oh, I'm pretty good huh'."

But the process of improving your skills could be rough. Larry Williams, an underclassman for the 1964 season also remembered the impromptu games. "When I was like twelve years old before I started playing for Ridgeview, I was playing football with guys who were 35 and 40 years old." Larry wanted to get into those games to be able to show his developing skill as a football player, saying "you had to be real good to get picked." Even though he admitted, "I got run over by a guy who was 40 years old," he didn't complain. Whatever bruises he sustained were all part of the training he sought to improve his skill, which he hoped would eventually lead to making the team.

Not all games were brutal combat, but they were always helping to develop the skill of participants. Allen Pope commented on games that occurred just about every day, he recalled. Playing on the "field where the community center is. We used to play on that field all the time. Wherever we could put a game together, it could be two hand touch or it could be tackle, depending on what kind of mood we were in." Those pickup contests served to substitute for what later would be little league and junior varsity type games.

Before many neighborhood kids were ready for organized games, there were variations. The popular activity of 'keep away' offered less structure and more tackling. In Ridgeview, they called the game, "hot grease." Xenophone Lutz described it as an "initiation," adding "guys would gather and surround the football and throw it in the ring, so to speak. And whoever was brave enough to pick up the ball, everyone ganged up on them and tackled them." It was one of the ways kids showed each other how tough they were. "Everybody had their own little hot grease," declared Douglas Bumgarner.

In addition to getting young men ready to play for Ridgeview, the almost daily activity of football games gave them an activity to play and become proficient. Senior William "Mickey" Heard pointed out that, "if you didn't have much you created your own games to play with and stuff because we were always doing something." Teammate Lewis Collins, who later became an accomplished musician agreed. "We took our sports seriously because that was something that kept us busy." While the games were fun and most thought only occasionally about how the experience might help them, they were actually training for a place on a far grander stage.

Before the 1964 season began, Coach Davis had strong words for his team. He felt the loss of his seniors from the previous year very strongly. Gone were his quarterback William "Mac" Rowland and pounding fullback Franklin Derr. In a pre-season interview in the pages of the *Hickory Daily Record*, Coach Davis lamented, "everything we've got is as green as grass, we're going to be hurting just about everywhere." He started with the quarterback position. Declaring that senior Allen Pope was "somewhere in Pennsylvania," the coach wondered aloud if he was coming back to play, ten days before the season was to open. Placing strong emphasis on who his starting QB was going to be, Coach remained pessimistic. "If we find somebody that can throw the ball, we'll be a passing team, but otherwise we'll stay on the ground," he said. Neither was he convinced that he had a running game. Predicting that he planned to use a varied backfield that included a T-formation, he grimaced that "we might even use a single wing if we can find someone to run it."

The only place Coach Davis seemed to feel comfortable was with his line. Since most of his senior members played both sides, he seemed to feel they could handle whatever was thrown at them, offense or defense. Mitchell Anthony anchored at center, while Xenophone Lutz and team captain John Hodge next as guards. Craig Wilfong and Charles Redman were first string tackles, Dwight Morrison and Hubbard Morrison starred as ends.

The backfield remained a puzzle. Ed Cunningham had seen action in the previous two seasons and was expected to hold down the job of fullback. Halfbacks Douglas Bumgarner and Allen Burch were also experienced at their positions and with Ed Cunningham's younger brother Curtis, they formed the core of the ball carrying offense. If Allen Pope really was gone (he wasn't), quarterback duties fell to two sophomores, Danny Carter and Willie Byrd. Most of the young men Coach Davis slated for the backfield were estimated in the 125- to 150-pound range.

It was hard to tell if Coach Davis was really down on his team or if he has some other purpose in mind. As Tillis Rendleman pointed out, other teams "read the same newspapers we read." He believed that the coach was giving false confidence to the other teams by lamenting the weaknesses of the 1964 team. Instead of allowing his men to become overconfident, he wanted the opponents to think, as Tillis characterized, "the coach at Ridgeview says these guys are not ready, they're too small, not fast enough. They lost too many seniors." The article would lead rivals like the Newton Central High Hornets to believe, "we got you now," said Tillis. He added his own evaluation of that view. "Bad choice."

Standout lineman Xenophone "Jobo" Lutz had a similar view of the coach's words. Believing that Coach Davis actually knew he has "something special" in his team, Jobo thought the coach was sending a message, not to the other teams but his own. "He used those words as a caution," said senior Lutz. He believed Coach Davis was speaking directly to him and his teammates, relaying in a codified way, "remember what happened to you last year. Those words. He was just downplaying the situation." Maybe the coach saw overconfidence in the downfall of the team in last year's playoff. If Coach Davis actually did recognize the talent he was guiding in his squad for '64, he vowed to remain silent until they proved themselves.

The summer of 1964 had been a tumultuous one in the United States. While the football Panthers focused on getting ready for the season, news about race relations in the country promised a better future, while still reporting tragedy. In August, three klansmen were indicted for the murder of Lt. Colonel Lemuel Penn. While driving back to his home in Washington, DC, from summer training at Ft. Benning, the Army Reserve officer was gunned down on a rural road in north Georgia. The death of Lt. Col. Penn came on the heels of passage of the 1964 Civil Rights Act. In fact, that act helped convict the attackers. After the three were acquitted in state court, federal officials brought charges under the act. Two years after the slaying, two of the Klansmen were convicted. The Civil Rights Act had been one of Lyndon Johnson's signature accomplishments during his time as president.

1964 was a landmark year in the struggle for Civil Rights. With numerous groups like the Student Non-Violent Coordinating Committee headed south to register African-Americans to vote, local racists lashed out. In Macomb, Mississippi, a family's home was bombed. An African-American school in Mount Sterling, Kentucky, was burned to the ground after protests over integration plans. Mobile, Alabama, leaders were charged with promoting segregation, ten years after the Supreme Court declared the practice unconstitutional.

Closer to home, a more subtle battle raged. In adjacent Alexander County, a pastor discussed the goal of integration with a reporter from the *Hickory Daily Record.* Using the Golden Rule as a standard, the pastor acknowledged the rights of African-Americans as the same as his own. But he argued that "to mix and mingle in our schools" was unwise. "Fair treatment for all, and all in their places, is best," was his published position. The pastor wrestled with the same issue that engulfed the nation. In the wake of the Brown v. Board decision of 1954, where the Supreme Court said 'separate but equal' had no place in our land, the Hickory Public School system remained segregated.

Members of the team, in all likelihood did not overtly concern themselves with the problem of race relations in the U.S. They had more immediate challenges. As Xenophone Lutz confided, "I interacted a lot with whites. Some positive, some negative." While his parents and grandparents sought to help him come to terms with the state of race relations, he also credited Coach Davis with part of that education. "He reminded us of the way society is and we needed to be disciplined and learn as much as we can, so that we can take our rightful place one day in society."

Coach Davis had a very simple philosophy, which he conveyed to his team. "Eat football, sleep football, live football." As head coach, Samuel Davis oversaw the entire program. By the 1964 season, he was in his early 40's. His emphasis was defense. He left much of the design of his offense to a much younger coach, Roger Scales. At Ridgeview, Coach Scales also handled duties with the school's basketball and track teams. But it was his work as, what player Larry Williams called "an offensive genius" that the assistant coach made his most impressive mark.

The first opponent of the '64 season was Huntersville, a town just north of Charlotte. At the Dust Bowl, the Panthers kicked off to a crowd of enthusiastic football fans. As several members of the team have remarked, spectators were both black and white. Once described as the most integrated event in Hickory, Ridgeview football was ready to accommodate all who came to see what the team planned to execute on the field. Stadium seating held up to 2,000 spectators, and with the lights and the dust rising up from the field's surface, the atmosphere was electric.

Even before the game, the team put on a show. The year the Panthers first lost to Chapel Hill, they noticed their opponents sauntered onto the field singing an intimidating song. Quickly the team adopted the same song as their own. To the rhythm of their clacking cleats as they walked down across the street from their gymnasium, the team singing in harmony, "*Let's go down and/ get it over with/ get it over with/ get it over with/ Let's go down and/ get it over with/ we're gonna win this game*!" It wasn't the only song the team would sing, but it would be the first and loudest one heard by their opponents, unnerving whoever dared to take on the Panthers.

The team sang the song every time they hit the field, in games home and away. It gave the young men a swagger they knew they would need to back up with superior play in the game. Fortunately for them, such a performance was no problem. The men sang together as a team often. For example, when on the bus to an away game one favorite was a variation on the Claudine Clark song from 1962, called "Party Lights." Referring to the stadium lights of the opponent as they came into view, the team would joyously sing, "I see the lights, I see the party lights, red and blue and green..." The music no doubt lightened the mood of team members who looked forward to proving themselves on the gridiron.

Both sides of the ball came to play when Huntersville came to town. On its first offensive series, Huntersville gained just three yards in three plays. When they attempted to punt, a high snap lost possession of the ball. Hubbard Morrison secured the fumble and the Panthers were in business on their opponent's 13-yard line. It took just one play to score as halfback Allen Burch got the call and ran it in.

Kicking off to Huntersville again, the Panthers repeated their feat. This time another fumble on the 21-yard line was recovered by star senior lineman Xenophone Lutz at the 13 again. Allen Burch got the call again, this time carrying for two yards. When the handoff went to Douglas Bumgarner, he ran it in from the 11.

During that era, the practice of kicking for an extra point was not practiced by the Panthers, or most any other team for that matter. Extra points consisted of bringing the ball back out to the two-yard line and bringing it across the goal line again. On those plays the Panthers hit pay dirt again about one-third of the time. Huntersville finally put a drive together, but James Heard recovered a fumble on Ridgeview's 24-yard line. Penalties sent the Panthers back to their own three. What looked like a Ridgeview punt turned out to be a fake as James Thompson threw a pass to Douglas Bumgarner, who ran it back. The half ended with the Panthers ahead, 18-0.

Half time activities were considered by some as dazzling as the game. The Ridgeview High Marching Band took the field as aggressively as the team. Every performance was hailed with words like "great" and "high stepping." Starting the season marching at an already jaw-dropping 280 steps per minute, band director A.V. Evans hoped to ramp up the pace to 300 steps. Mary Cornwell, Patricia Coates, and Betty Foster led the 40-piece procession as majorettes, winning cheers and admiration for their performance.

The second half fared no better for Huntersville than the first. Fullback Ed Cunningham ran back the kickoff 69 yards to the Huntersville 11, when he was pulled down from behind. Douglas Bumgarner carried it the rest of the way for a score. Ed muscled his way in on the extra point, giving the game a 26-0 score. It looked like the Panthers were having their way when Danny Carter intercepted a pass but quickly Allen Pope threw an interception to even out the activity. Substitute halfback Frank Abernathy added another score, a 35 yard run. Then with less than four minutes left to go, guard Ed White recovered a fumble that put Ridgeview on the Huntersville 26-yard line. Penalties pushed the Panthers back, but quarterback Allen Pope eventually ran it in for the night's final touchdown. The scoreboard at the final gun reported that Ridgeview had won its first shutout of the season, 40-0.

The victory set a standard for the new season. Even with a few mistakes, the Panthers dominated. Pressbox announcer and reporter Ellis Johnson credited both the offensive and defensive line for the "ripping" Ridgeview gave Huntersville. "The Panthers looked like old form as they received good blocking for the scatbacks (a reference to the speed and agility of the runners) and played good defensive ball as the Panther line stood out," he wrote to recap the game.

Next came a "Battle of Panthers," as Wilkesboro's Lincoln Heights High School traveled to Hickory. Remarking that both the offense and defense "stood out like shining armor," Ellis Johnson again filled readers of the *Hickory Daily Record* in on the dominance of the hometown Panthers. Like the Huntersville game, an early mistake by their opponents resulted in Ridgeview points. As announcer Johnson reported, "a high pass from center was picked up by the punter in the end zone but was hit hard by a host of orange jerseys for a safety."

If anyone doubted the Untouchables were earning their name, all doubt was erased when Danny Carter as quarterback threw to Allen Burch on Wilkesboro's 30-yard line, where he "raced the distance to score, untouched." With extra points added by fullback Ed Cunningham, the first quarter ended with a 10-0 advantage for the hometown Panthers.

After a punt return of 35 yards by Ed Cunningham and a Douglas Bumgarner score from 15 yards out, "a host of Ridgeview Panthers" forced a fumble on the ensuing kickoff that raised "a cloud of dust." Soon Allen Pope, back in as quarterback, connected with Ed Cunningham for the touchdown. Frank Abernathy added the extra point. Ridgeview was once again on a roll as Douglas Bumgarner added a 19 yard run for a TD followed by Ed Cunningham tacking on the extra point.

The second half started with Allen Burch taking the kickoff at the three, running it out to the 28. From there, Douglas Bumgarner did the rest. He romped 72 yards "behind excellent blocking" to score. The points kept piling up as another mistake by Wilkesboro gave Ridgeview the ball on their opponent's 25-yard line. Fullback Jerry Johnson followed the lead he had witnessed all night. He produced his own 25-yard run to extend the Ridgeview lead.

The scoring frenzy just would not stop. Curtis Cunningham, halfback produced his own 25-yard run for a score. By the end of the game a couple of new faces got their turn to produce a touchdown. Willie Byrd "tossed to lanky End Detroit Rhyne, Jr. who gathered it on the 2-yard line and fought is way to the end zone." As time ran out, Hickory's Panthers were driving again after defensive end Harrison James recovered a fumble on the Wilkes 40.

The game gave Ridgeview the crown of top panther. It also produced the most lopsided victory of the season, a 56-0 drubbing of Wilkesboro. The Panthers were on top of their game, a sharp contrast to the white Hickory High School who that same night lost their season opener. If football fans wanted to see a dominant, disciplined and determined team, they needed to come to Ridgeview.

The third game of the season promised more of the same. The Carver High School Eagles from Spindale arrived to see if they could stop the Panthers from successful and high scoring season. The game started like those before, with Ridgeview losing the toss, putting its defense on the field first. Even worse than the Huntersville performance in their first possession, Spindale's opening set of downs gained them one yard. The Eagles at least got the punt off when the Panther offense took over. An evenly balanced run attack ground to a halt when a fumble on the five-yard line turned the ball over, but they got it back after Spindale fumbled on the ten, thanks to Ed Cunningham on defense. Allen Burch had a touchdown but a penalty called it back. Douglas Bumgarner not only carried the ball in for a score, he also caught the point after touchdown giving the Panthers an early 8-0 lead.

The defense was awesome that night. Xenophone Lutz sacked Spindale's quarterback and recovered the fumble setting up the offense again, this time on the 11-yard line. From there Ed Cunningham took it on in. The passing game had started to crank up with Allen Pope hitting his fullback for 28 to end the first quarter. At the start of the second, Coach Davis replaced Allen Pope with Danny Carter. It only took a quick interception to switch back. At that point the defense became their own worst enemy with penalties pushing Spindale down to the Panther 35-yard line, but the drive stopped there. The defense held when it needed to.

All cylinders began to fire for the Panthers. Once the offense got the ball back, Allen Pope, back behind center, handed off to Allen Burch, who raced for 20, then hit Douglas Bumgarner who scored "standing up." He also ended the next series for Spindale, intercepting a pass, then catching one from his quarterback for the score. Halfback Frank Abernathy added the extra point. After an exchange of punts tackle Craig Wilfong recovered a fumble on the Eagles 30-yard line. Allen Pope dropped back to the 40, threw a 38-yard pass that was tipped, but Hubbard Morrison pulled it in with a tremendous second effort. Allen Burch poured it on with the two-point PAT.

The big runs made by the Panthers were possible thanks to the offensive line. Time after time, Ellis Johnson used the phrase "behind excellent blocking" to explain to readers how Ridgeview carved out such big chunks of yardage. Once the high flying Panthers got the ball back, it took only one play for Douglas Bumgarner to go 34 yards and another

TD. John Hodge ended the third quarter with an interception, but while the Panthers couldn't hang on to it that time, a fourth quarter drive saw the team move the ball consistently. Allen Pope went for 18 yards on a run, before Danny Carter came back in, advancing to the one. Halfback Allen Burch carried it in for the score with Danny gaining the extra point.

The well oiled machine that was the Panthers proved "untouchable" in their contest with Spindale. Scoring not quite as much as they did the previous week, the total was nonetheless substantial, 52-0. Fans saw quite a show. Never letting up, the team followed another of Coach Davis' favorite sayings: "How do you kill a gnat?" They knew the answer. "With a sledge hammer."

It had to happen. Sooner or later there would be an off night. Following the stratospheric performances of the first three weeks, where they averaged almost 50 points a game, a challenge came from the Newbold Panthers of Lincolnton. The defense showed up as usual with Douglas Bumgarner intercepting, ending Lincolnton's first drive. But a fumble, a mere seven yards from the end zone ended Ridgeview's first drive. However, pinned back close to their goal line, the Newbold Panthers could not get out of the hole. The defensive line smothered Lincolnton's punter and "a host of orange jerseys rained in on the kicker to block the kick, which was recovered by tackle Xenophone Lutz out of the end zone for a safety." The game took on a very un-Ridgeview characteristic with a series of punts on both sides until Douglas Bumgarner broke out for an 80-yard run. Then both teams lost their ability to hang onto the ball for most of the second quarter, but again Douglas Bumgarner, now becoming Ridgeview's top scorer, shifted the momentum. He intercepted a Lincolnton pass and switched back over to his role as left halfback. Ed Cunningham drove for 22, Frank Abernathy for 17, and Douglas added to his season total with another touchdown, ending the first half.

The Panthers took the kickoff to start the second half with a 16-0 lead. Any other team would have been thrilled to be up by such a margin, but the Panthers knew the performance was not their best. During an error-filled third quarter, Ridgeview's newest member made himself known. Tillis Rendleman had joined the season late. He already had his time occupied as a bus driver and student. But compelled to play, he threw "a beautiful key block" that gave Allen Burch the room he needed to get down to Lincolnton's ten-yard line. After a few tries and a penalty in Ridgeview's favor, Allen Burch punched it in to cap Ridgeview's scoring for the night. At 22-0, the final score indicated that the Panthers had been in a tougher battle than any they had faced so far in the season. But the important thing was the shutout. They walked off the field with their record intact.

Then the team got lucky. Scheduled to play Shelby, their first away game, rain "washed out" the affair. The story in the press said the match would not necessarily need to be rescheduled since conference rules stated that a team only needed to play seven opponents within the Northwest Athletic Conference to qualify for the playoffs, and since the ten game schedule covered the spread, the game would not need to be rescheduled. Some said that Shelby had used the weather to duck playing Ridgeview with its reputation and shutout streak on a roll. As it turned out, the game was not cancelled but postponed until the end of the season. Perhaps more importantly, the break gave the team a period of rest, that after the performance against Lincolnton, they could use to recharge and prepare for the anticipated struggle against Reynold High School in Canton, which ended up being Ridgeview's first away game.

The headline might have given some fans a fright. It read "Hot Ridgeview Panthers Melt Canton Tigers, 42-5." It sounded like their opponent west of Asheville had done what no other team that season had accomplished; they scored on the Panthers. But the 42-5 was not the score of the game. It was instead the average number of points scored by the team up to that point. As Ellis Johnson put it, "It was a cold Thursday night at Canton High stadium, but a hot Ridgeview High Panthers of Hickory completely smothered the Reynolds High Tigers, 44-0."

The Tigers punted twice (the second one was blocked by John Hodge, recovered by Craig Wilfong) and on a third offensive series threw an interception (James Thompson caught it) which only began the defense's dominance. On offense, the Panthers scored on its first three possessions. Quarterback Allen Pope ran the first one in from 25 yards out, Douglas Bumgarner took it from the 10-yard line to score on the second, and Allen Burch ran thirty-five more yards for the third. Add in the extra points of Ed Cunningham and Ridgeview displayed a very balanced attack. All that activity came in just the first quarter. At 22-0, the Panthers had equaled the points they put on the board in the entire Lincolnton game.

Ridgeview's defense just kept forcing turnovers. After Douglas Bumgarner scored his second touchdown of the night, he then recovered a Canton fumble. The Panthers converted with a strong 22-yard run by Ed Cunningham. The defense would not let up. The Tigers found themselves on their own ten-yard line on fourth down and smelling opportunity "the on rushing orange jersey" forced the punter to shank the kick ten yards down the line. Allen Burch carried the ball in for his second score of the night. The PAT was a quarterback keeper with Allen Pope adding two to the score.

Then the game went from boring to a nail biter. The third quarter passed with no score. The highlight was a Tillis Rendleman fumble recovery that led to the last quarter. Substantial runs by Frank Abernathy and Allen Burch got the team to the 15-yard line. Then it became a brothers affair as Ed Cunningham score the touchdown, and his younger brother Curtis added the extra point. However, Canton was not done. Beginning at their own 35-yard line, the Tigers drove down to Ridgeview's five. The win was never in doubt, but as Xenophone Lutz once commented, "The reality was teams knew they were not going to beat us. If somebody could just score, that would be their victory." Canton almost did. After a penalty that took the ball half the distance to the goal line, the Tigers came closer than any team up to that point of ruining the shutout streak. Unfortunately for Canton, the defense stiffened, pushing the Tigers back to the 6-yard line, denying the opponent of at least scoring once on the Panthers.

At this point in the season, the streak became very real. Everyone could see what was happening. It was possible, five games in, that the Panthers could run the table on every team they faced. The school's reporting team, who wrote regular columns for the *Hickory Daily Record* said it out loud: "Try as they may, it seems that no team can open a pathway to score a touchdown through our linebackers. These boys act as an impenetrable brick wall." Reporters Alivana Curry, George Derr, and Jacqueline Rendleman boldly advanced the team's goal of "an undefeated and unscored on season for the year." The players were thinking about it too. Coach Davis stressed the importance of remaining focused on winning, not the possibility of shutting out the remaining teams. He seemed to think such a quest might backfire, short circuiting what he now realized was a playoff contender.

In their "Ridgeview School News" column of October 10, the reporters first associated the team with the title of "Untouchables." The term had been around for a while, first coined by the television crime drama about Eliot Ness. When the 1962 team was on its way in their own succession of shutouts, Elllis Johnson dubbed them "the Untouchables." When the team ended the season with a loss, reportedly Ellis quipped, "the Untouchables have been touched," a line that got him in all kinds of trouble with fans. Now the team was on another streak. Would the name stick this time? As Xenophone Lutz said, an opponent's victory would be simply *scoring* on the Panthers.

Rain kept Ridgeview's Homecoming from happening when originally scheduled, but the following Monday night, the school held its annual festivities in the middle of the Panthers' match-up with Freedman High School of Lenoir. The ceremony was marked by the crowning of Joyce Ann Pope as homecoming queen, crowned by team captain John Hodges. Also that night the Veterans of Foreign Wars instituted the Ridgeview Football Hall of Fame. The Eugene Sadler Post (#9881) of the VFW selected four players from the Panthers storied past to be the inaugural entrants into the Hall. Remembering the glory years of the early 1930s when Ridgeview first became a powerhouse football program, the committee presented plaques for Guilford McCall Derr, James Fisher, James Whitner, and Elmore Eckard. Coach Davis accepted the plaques from E.T. Moore, post commander and renowned Catawba County educator, for placement at the school. The presentation demonstrated a recognition of football as integral to the school's reputation.

The Freedman High Blue Devils sent notice early that they intended to move the ball. With a couple of first downs on the opening drive, they pushed the Panthers' defense back. When the drive stalled, the Panthers took the punt back into Blue Devil territory. From there, the backs ground out yardage until Ed Cunningham crossed the goal line. Allen Pope added the extra points, playing what Ellis Johnson called "his finest game of the season."

The Blue Devils from Lenoir felt the Panther defense when Dwight Thompson stopped the visitors "cold on a brilliant tackle." The rest of the defense muscled up to deny Freedman any yardage on a fourth and one on their own 42-yard line. Leading the charge was "Tillis Rendleman, Charles Redman, Edward White, and William Heard.

When the Panthers got the ball back, they marched down the field once again with Ed Cunningham scoring for a second time in the game. Halftime activities only slightly interrupted the scoring frenzy as Douglas Bumgarner broke loose for 55 yards on the opening drive of the second half. Allen Burch topped that with his own 85-yard touchdown run for an exciting third quarter.

This game marked a shift. Early in the season Danny Carter had substituted occasionally for Allen Pope at quarterback. With Quarterback Pope clearly in control of the offense, Coach Scales moved Danny Carter to receiver. In the fourth quarter the two quarterbacks connected, on a Pope to Carter pass for substantial yardage. Another pass to Douglas Bumgarner got the ball in the end zone. Underclassman Ollie Parks gained his own scoring opportunity at halfback, adding the PAT to the touchdown. The team took the win "with ease," as Ellis Johnson described it, 38-0.

Prior to homecoming, the Panthers had played only two games in four weeks. The Shelby washout and the delay of the game with Lenoir had given the Panthers a break. But they had to pay for it. Just three days after the homecoming game, Coach Davis packed up his team in an old bus and traveled to Mount Airy, a 2+ hour drive toward the Virginia border from Hickory.

Most remember the bus ride more than the game. Apparently, Ellis Johnson did not accompany the team because the report of game was short and not under his byline. The article in the *Hickory Daily Record* announced the score, 30-0 and the scorers, "Lee (Douglas) Bumgarner, Ed Cunningham and Allen Burch, left halfback, fullback and right halfback, respectively. The only other detail concerned an additional score by the Panthers that was called back on an illegal procedure penalty. However cold and bumpy the ride might have been to Mt. Airy and back, it continued the roll the Panthers were on. Next came Morganton.

The Olive Hill Yellow Jackets were also in the midst of a stellar season. They couldn't match the shutouts accomplished by the Panthers, but the Morganton team felt they had a chance to topple Ridgeview and began the game in a "highly spirited" mood on their home turf. For the first time all season Ridgeview won the toss and took the opening kickoff almost to mid-field. Coach Scales wanted to strike early. Allen Pope let a pass fly that reached the fingertips of Hubbard Morrison. Unable to pull it in, the offense went back to its ground game. Despite crushing penalties, the Panthers took over five minutes off the clock, getting the ball down to the ten-yard line, but turned it over.

Ridgeview's defense backed up only to Morganton's 45 before they shut their opponent down. Once the Panther offense took over again, they didn't make the same mistake. Allen Pope threw to Danny Carter for a 14-yard TD and the scoreless game was no more. An Ed Cunningham interception brought the ball back to Ridgeview who scored again on a Douglas Bumgarner run of 21 yards. Allen Pope ended the half by first intercepting a Yellow Jacket pass, then throwing to Hubbard Morrison for his second chance at a touchdown. He pulled this one in and the half ended with Panthers holding a comfortable lead, 20-0.

In the memories of the players the Morganton game held a noteworthy place. In the second half, the team scored twice more on runs by the Cunningham brothers, Ed and Curtis. But the main reason for remembering the game was the palpable frustration that seemed to grip Morganton as the game slipped away from them. Ellis Johnson noted, "The Yellow Jackets were the Western North Carolina District I Champions and had a good chance at the Northwestern conference championship until the Panthers went to Morganton and pulled the championship rug from under them." When the Yellow Jackets made a mistake, the Panthers were there to capitalize on it. Frank Abernathy and Ed Cunningham both grabbed fumbles in the game.

Finally, it was too much. Though it was not reported in any newspaper account, members of the Morganton team threw off their helmets and wanted to fight. The confrontation brought fans to the field too and a brawl looked imminent. Panther players credit the quick thinking of Coach Davis for deescalating the melee. He ordered his men to head for the bus. Still in their uniforms, they complied, leaving Morganton in a hurry, but still with a 32-0 win.

"We may not win the game but we'll win the fight." That was how Xenophone Lutz characterized the attitude of the Yellow Jackets by the last quarter of the game. With everything clicking in Ridgeview's game plan, the Morganton team could mount no viable defense. Tillis Rendleman placed the anger elsewhere. "The fans just got mad," he said, "and they run us off the field." Either way, with playoff hopes so high for Morganton and watching them dashed as the Panthers had their way on the field, the loss must have been a hard one for the Yellow Jackets as they watched Ridgeview cruise to their eighth consecutive shutout of the season.

The game had another unfortunate event for Douglas Bumgarner. This was the first game he could convince his mother to attend. Skittish about the violence of the game, she had to be coaxed to come see her son play. It just so happened that during the game (an indicator of how rough Morganton played) the leading rusher for the Panthers got knocked out and had to be brought back with ammonia. When they got home she announced, "I won't be back to no more games." She did not want to see her son get hurt and informed him that "I'll just wait and let them tell me what happened when you get home."

At this point in the season, the local paper printed some amazing stats. Douglas Bumgarner had already run for over 1000 yards, with 19 touchdowns to his credit. He was followed by Ed Cunningham and Allen Burch, both with over 600 yards in their column. Quarterback Allen Pope called it a triple threat. "Little do people know that we had three backs with double-digit touchdowns," he said. "Ten touchdowns a year is a great season. But we had three. And they all had more than ten touchdowns. That's part of the reason that they became untouchable. Once they get past the line, none of them has ever been caught from behind."

The dashed hopes of one playoff contender was followed by another as county and conference rivals Central High from Newton came to the Dust Bowl. Like Ridgeview the Central Hornets were undefeated going into the clash that would decide the conference championship. "We were supposed to beat them," remarked Milton Johnson, a Hornet. "Out of four years in high school, we lost four games. I was on a team that lost four times. One game a year. Ridgeview." It seemed that no matter how good Newton was, Ridgeview was always a step ahead. In fact, the Panthers had not lost in a contest with the Hornets since 1958. Of those six games, the Panthers had shut out the Hornets in three of them.

Because of the rivalry and the connections, it was always a special game when Ridgeview played Newton. Allen Pope confided, "yes, Newton was our biggest rival and we always talked trash with Newton." For the 1964 matchup "there was an overflowing crowd," which meant more than 2,000 spectators came to see how the game would play out. As Milton Johnson noted, "you had to get there early."

"I think after the first series when Cunningham intercepted the pass and took it all the way back, I said 'its over,'" observed quarterback Allen Pope on the start of the game. "It was good, hard football" Ellis Johnson commented in his report of the game. An exchange of punts and penalties kept the clock moving, but the Panther defense slowly pushed the Hornets back until Ridgeview put a drive together that netted Edward Cunningham his second rushing touchdown of the game. On both scores, the Panthers tacked on extra points, the first by Douglas Bumgarner, the second from Allen Pope. As the game went to the half, Ridgeview carried a 16-0 lead into the locker room.

Another competition took place at halftime as both the Central High band and the Ridgeview marching band took the field to display their abilities. Newton "displayed a showboat style playing hit numbers of present and past," reported Ellis Johnson. Not to be outdone, the 46-member Ridgeview band "also put on a 'big show.'" No winner was declared, but on their home field, the Panther band likely got more cheers than their cross-county rivals.

Play got off to a lively start in the third quarter as the Panthers fumbled on their own 21-yard line. The misstep gave the Hornets a chance. But Allen Pope, who had lost the fumble, redeemed himself by intercepting a pass and returning Ridgeview to offense. They could not convert, but punt exchanges improved field position for the Panthers. With their unusual, solid running, Panther backs opened the door for Allen Pope to take the ball in for a score.

As with all their opponents the Panthers did not let up. With Coach Davis' "sledge hammer" philosophy, the defense pressed Newton to the point that Ed Cunningham ran back an interception for six points. Douglas Bumgarner ran another back to the Hornet 30. After Danny Carter sacked Newton's QB, things got sloppy. Ridgeview dropped a punt return to give life to the Hornets, but they in turn fumbled. After Newton did the same, the Panthers threw an interception. With yet another interception by Ed Cunningham, his third of the night, he set up little brother Curtis for a run to the end zone. With Jerry Johnson adding two more points in the PAT, the Panthers capped off a glorious night as they were crowned the conference championship. "Wallops" was the word Ellis Johnson used to describe the victory in the press. Milton Johnson of Newton admitted, "that game was nowhere near close." Looking back on the beating his Hornets took, he added, "they (Ridgeview) came at you hard."

The Newton game was intended to complete the regular season. However, the Shelby game was rescheduled for the following Friday night, rounding out a ten-game schedule. Like the Newton game, Ed Cunningham drew first blood on defense with a "pick six" on the Cleveland High Tigers first drive. Ridgeview did not expect the ferocity with which Shelby mounted its second possession. Pushing steadily down field, the Tigers got to the Panther eight-yard line before the defense woke up and put a stop to the progression. When the front line forced a fumble, Dwight Thompson grabbed it on the 10 to turn things around. The Panthers lost a few yards on a "missignal" then Douglas Bumgarner gained some breathing room on a short run, followed by Allen Burch busting loose for 87 yards and a second touchdown of the night. With the quarterback running in the extra point, the Panthers were off to a 14-0 lead.

Douglas Bumgarner characterized the backfield for Ridgeview as "all basically equal." He said, "we all had the speed; it was just in different moves. Mine was short and quick, Cunningham's fast and long. And Burch was hard to touch. He just kept moving and that was a good thing. An easy target is easy to hit." As in most games, the Ridgeview run game was a balanced attack. One example was the next score by the Panthers. Ed Cunningham fielded a punt, bringing it back thirty yards. Then Douglas Bumgarner carried it another thirty for the score.

The Tigers got to mid-field with their next drive before the Panthers forced another turnover. Frank Abernathy grabbed a fumble and the game was once again fully in the hands of Ridgeview. Coach Scales then put in Lewis Collins as quarterback. He used his halfbacks to take them down the field with Allen Burch crossing the goal line for his first touchdown of the game. Even with a good return on the kickoff, Shelby could not keep the ball. Ed Cunningham snatched another pass, allowing Frank Abernathy to get past the line for 73 yards and another TD.

Great defensive play by the Panthers often put the offense in prime position to score. After pushing the Tigers back to their own 16, thanks in part to a 60-yard punt by James Thompson, tackle Xenophone Lutz recovered a fumble that gave the offense a first and ten on the Shelby

12-yard line. Allen Pope, back at quarterback, ran it in himself. Forcing a punt that went bad got the Panthers a safety, followed by another run by Ed Cunningham with Allen Pope adding the points after.

When the final gun sounded, Ridgeview had finished a perfect regular season, not one point against them. Like the team of 1960, when these players were in the eighth grade, hopeful to make the team one day, the '64 version had matched the record. However, as youngsters they had also seen the elder team take it all the way to the championship only to lose in a way that many saw as tarnishing all they had accomplished to that point. These Panthers vowed not to repeat history in that manner.

Their first opponent in the playoffs was the one who sent them home the year before, the Dunbar Tigers from Lexington. They had not had the season Ridgeview had, but their only loss came from a 3A opponent. The Tigers had beaten another 3A team and blanked the rest of their foes, minus one—a season opener against Belmont.

Halfback Douglas Bumgarner called the game the most "tense game I've ever played because everybody was banking on that." He knew losing would repeat their heartbreak of 1963. If the Panthers did win but let Dunbar score, the shutout record would be gone. "Every time they'd get the ball or we fumbled or something like that you know, ahhh." The cry of the night was "get him, get him, get him, get him," as each team member tried to cover for the others by being in "on every tackle."

Losing the toss for the tenth time in eleven games, defense hit the field first. On the second play from scrimmage, John Hodge and Douglas Bumgarner combined to recover a fumble and the offense once again was set up in good position. The run game banged out yards until Allen Pope hit Douglas Bumgarner on a pass to the end zone. Allen Burch got the points after touchdown. The second drive went no better than the first as another punt put Ridgeview back on offense and Douglas Bumgarner struck for the second time that night, a 42-yard run for TD to go with his pass reception.

Smothering the Dunbar Tigers with a crushing defense, the Panthers snagged a fumble, taking it to their opponents' 13-yard line. Another score looked imminent, but Ridgeview ran out of downs and gave the ball back to the Tigers. Fortunately, they did the same, unable to gain much of anything. The two Allens, Pope and Burch, connected for a thirteen-yard TD pass. A blocked Tiger punt held promise for another

Panther TD, but time ran out in the half before Ridgeview could cash in.

Holding onto the ball proved tough for both teams, but the Panthers lost it at a particularly bad time. After Douglas Bumgarner pulled in a pass and ran for 70 yards and another score, things got sloppy. "During an exchange of punts late in the quarter, a bad pass from center and the Tigers took over on the Panther 22-yard line," wrote Ellis Johnson. The treat gave Lexington a good position from which to strike; however, they could do nothing with it. As the newspaper continued, "Aided by a long penalty and fine defensive play, the Panthers got out of trouble."

Ridgeview got into trouble again in the fourth quarter. Their punt was blocked and Lexington took over on the Panther's 15, their best field position of the night, seven yards better than the last try. Once again the Panther defense forced the Tigers to cough up the ball. This time Craig Wilfong recovered the fumble.

As if to put a coda on the game, a late game drive found the Allens, Pope and Burch again connecting for a TD with quarterback Pope putting a bit of icing on the cake, hopping across the goal line for the extra points. The final tally gave the Panthers a 28-0 victory and one last hurdle to mount in their quest for a perfect season. So far, Ridgeview had scored 430 unanswered points. Their dominance had persisted down to the championship game. If they could continue the streak for one more game, they would have to combine the feats of the 1960 and 1962 teams, a state championship, and shutout record that would earn them the title of "Untouchable."

Excitement for the clash grew all week, even as the team faced a short week to get ready. With Thanksgiving coming up the game was scheduled for the night before, but rescheduled for the night after, giving them a bit more time to prepare. Once again, like the year of the 1962 championship, College Field at Lenoir-Rhyne College would host the event. The location wasn't much better than Ridgeview's field in terms of the number of fans it could accommodate, but the field itself was all grass and drew the admiration of the players. As Xenophone Lutz remembered, "If the team had a nice field, that's all we talked about at first. 'Man look at this field. Man, this is nice, ain't it, man." The Lenoir-Rhyne field provided the nicest surface the team would play on all year, appropriate enough for what the Panthers hoped to accomplish there.

After a "long and hard" practice on Monday, the team strolled onto the campus of Lenoir-Rhyne ready to face one more challenge, this time from the eastern division winner Hamlet, a small town about as far southeast of Charlotte as Hickory was northwest. Facing another team nicknamed the Tigers (as their two previous opponents had been, this time from Hamlet) the Panthers lost the toss yet again and began the game on defense. Ridgeview was surprised by a "quick kick" on third down that gave the Panthers the ball on their own 29. Pushing forward with back to back gainers from the legs of Douglas Bumgarner, the Panthers got down to the three-yard line of Hamlet. The Tigers took a lesson from Ridgeview's usually stout defense and refused a score. On fourth down, the Panthers tried again only to lose the ball on a fumble. Holding the Tigers to one set of downs, Ridgeview got the ball back on its own 31 to round out the first quarter.

Even with some good efforts by regular contributors like Edward White, who pulled in a fumble and James Thompson who punted well that night, the Panthers found themselves backed up against their own goal line. The Hamlet Tigers were two yards away from a score, threatening to erase the mark all 34 men for Ridgeview hoped to achieve. The moment of determination had arrived. Collectively, the crowd at Lenoir-Rhyne held their breath, on their feet to see if Hamlet could do something no other team had achieved, a score.

The situation drew out the intensity of Xenophone Lutz. The star, senior lineman could keep his emotions in check no more. He blurted out to the Tigers, "You're not gonna score," repeating it with emphasis. Lineman Lutz had been a spark plug for the team throughout his career at Ridgeview, a fierce competitor, fixated on helping his team to win. Captain John Hodge thought the outburst too emotional. He chided the player beside whom he had lined up all season. "Shut up and play some ball" was the response. It settled Xenophone Lutz down to focus on the task at hand, refusing Hamlet a score.

If the defense ever needed a stop, it was now. Getting into their three-point stance the line waited for the hike. When it came the Tigers progressed to the one-yard line. From there the Panthers took over, driving back the Hamlet offense time after time. When the gun sounded to end the half, the Panthers had successfully defended their goal and escaped tragedy. The score remain tied at zero.

A game this big would not have been complete without a performance by the Ridgeview marching band at halftime. Offering a salute to all the football team had, and they hoped were to accomplish, the band dedicated their show to the "Panther coaches and football team and to the many fans for their support this year." No one ever reported if the band got to its stepping goal of 300 steps per minute, but every account of their presentation by those who saw it expressed admiration and amazement for the dazzling show the band put on with their music and marching.

In the second half, the Panther scoring machine slowly cranked up to put some points on the board. The first two drives ended before hitting pay dirt, the first a punt, the second a fumble on the Tiger six-yard line, a heartbreaking turn of events much like they did in the first quarter. But the Panther running game still had juice. Douglas Bumgarner ran for 59 yards, then Allen Burch added another 35 to get across the goal line and break the scoreless tie. Frank Abernathy added the extra two. Penalties hurt the remaining Tiger drives and the Panthers put together another winning drive. Ed Cunningham took it the last ten yards for a score with Allen Pope exercising a quarterback keeper for the extra points. The Tigers got back as close as the Ridgeview 35-yard line, but the defense rose up one last time. Quarterback Allen Pope lost the ball, but it didn't matter. The final gun sounded and the Untouchables had proved themselves truly worthy of the name. With a 16-0 win over the best in the state of North Carolina, Ellis Johnson wrote, "The untouchable Panthers ended a victorious perfect season."

THE UNTOUCHABLES INTERVIEWS BY RICHARD ELLER

The incredible history of the Untouchables became known to me in August of 2015. A colleague, Steve Hunt, told me this astounding story, and when I asked, rhetorically, why I hadn't heard of this before, he gave a baleful look. I understood. I was white, and the legend that was this team was largely unknown beyond Ridgeview and its inhabitants. I immediately sought to change that.

With a few introductions, I was allowed to bring my camera to the Ridgeview Community Center and set up in the weight room, during the Ridgeview Reunion, a gathering of alumni that happened every other year. There I got to talk to some incredible people. Rev. Xenophone Lutz, Douglas Bumgarner, John Thompson, Robert "Mac" Rowland, and Allen Pope. That weekend I also interviewed Jessie Walker, who was president of the Alumni Association and not only went to Ridgeview High but also taught there. I talked to Frank L. Suddreth, Lewis Collins, Pete Oglesby, and Wright Cade, Jr. I thought at the time I had enough to start a documentary on the team. I even got the chance to ask a player what it was like to face the Untouchables. Milton Johnson from Central High in Newton, married into the Ridgeview High family and was candid in his description of the Panthers that year.

However, this story was much like an onion. Peel back a layer and find much more to learn. I waited another two years, and with more questions, I went at it again, this time asking to speak again with Rev. Lutz, Mr. Bumgarner and Mr. Pope. The discussion ranged farther than ever. More questions answered. More history explained. I needed more though.

In 2018, we found more players, some willing to talk about their experiences during that championship year. Tillis Rendleman, Larry Williams, and Hampton Davis took part in these sessions. All of the players were most gracious with their time; some of the interviews went on for hours. Also interviewed were a number of other people who either saw the team play or were familiar with the story.

Then in 2019, the CVCC Office of Multicultural Affairs honored the Untouchables at their annual Black History Month Celebration. Surviving members (or a family representative) were awarded with limited edition medallions, designed and created by CVCC's computer-assisted-design program, headed by Stephen Rhoads. It was a great night and a fitting tribute. But as usual in this journey, there was more to understand.

Meanwhile, we came up empty in the search for film footage of the team in action. If there ever was film on the team, it was lost to history. Instead, we approached the United Arts Council of Catawba County to fund a series of animations to help portray some of the most revered tales about the team; their formative playing of a game called "hot grease,"the five mile runs, the championship game where they were backed up to their own two-yard-line, when team captain John Hodge told Rev. Lutz to "shut up and play some ball" to get Lutz's head back into the game and focus on the problem at hand. The Arts Council then took the story in a whole new, exciting direction of their own.

Often, I would call Rev. Lutz and ask if he would get a group of team members together because one media outlet after another wanted to talk to them. UNC-TV, WBTV Charlotte North Carolina, *Our State* Magazine all came calling. Each time, I would be there with my camera to see if I could get a detail left out earlier.

In January of 2020, I conducted my last interview with a group on the heels of their appearance on the TEDX stage, where they received a standing ovation for their exploits on the ball field and their entertaining tales of that astounding season.

Then Covid-19 hit. We planned to debut everything, the documentary, the public art all that summer, but quarantine kept the screening and unveiling from happening. In 2021, after being elected into the Catawba County Sports Hall of Fame and other notoriety, the team and their story has a much wider audience. On September 4, Hickory Mayor Hank Guess proclaimed it, *Untouchables Day* in Hickory. Finally, the monumental feat that was the ***perfect season*** will be known to everyone. Next stop, a feature film about the lives of these extraordinary men and their journey.

Allen Pope

The quarterback of the Ridgeview Panthers during the Untouchable year, Allen Pope guided the offense, regularly scoring himself. He also played defensive back, several times forcing turnovers by an interception then throwing the ball on the very next play. Mr. Pope was interviewed both in 2015 and 2017. The longer and more substantive interview from 2017 is first, with the 2015 conversation second, which is noted. Both interviews were conducted during reunion weekends.

Interviewer: Where did you grow up and how did you start playing football?

Allen Pope: I lived on 2nd street, Southwest. It's probably a mile away. We all walk to school, pretty much. We played football, pretty much every day, pick up or tackle or two-hand touch and what gave us a lot of experience, we got to play with the guys that were already playing football for Ridgeview. We weren't quite ready to play because we hadn't reached the ninth grade, but we would still play with them and it would be out here on the field or there was a field where the community center is, that we used to play on that field all the time. Wherever we could put a game together, it could be two-hand touch or it could be tackle, depending on what kind of mood we were in. When you guys are talking about junior football and that kind of thing, that was our junior football.

We got to play with guys who were having experiences at where you're playing for Ridgeview, so you kind of find out how good you are because when they pick the two captains, they would choose... the captains would then start choosing guys. The guys will be standing on the side. You can kind of tell how good you would be based on how fast you were chosen, so as long as you were chosen in that first five or six guys, it's like, oh, I'm pretty good, huh? You didn't maybe get down to the last two or three and say, "Oh well, we'll take him."

Interviewer: I'm guessing you were chosen first or second.

Allen Pope: Yeah. Well, I was a defensive player then, before I was... I got to play a little quarterback every now and then, but I would play with guys that played quarterback. Ultimately, that's what I wanted to be, but I played a lot of defensive back as well.

Interviewer: So that's how it got started?

Allen Pope: It was Doug, it was Cunningham and myself, basically played defensive backs. The one thing about this team, even though sometimes we were smaller than teams we played, speed is everything. Speed makes up for a lot of mistakes that you might be able to make, but we had linemen that were seriously fast. Our linebackers were unbelievably fast, so if they missed anything, Cunningham and myself would clean up. We did very well there. The other thing is that when he started talking the racial experience, you really don't know. See when you're young, you really don't know you're being discriminated against because this is my neighborhood. Everybody in this neighborhood treats me great. Everybody in this neighborhood is black. A neighbor can discipline your child, but they discipline with love. But if a neighbor had to discipline you, you'd have to... they'd tell your parents. If they tell your parents, now you got disciplined twice. If you went to school and gave your teacher a hard time, all you could pray was that don't tell my father.

Otherwise, that's why you basically never had any real trouble because neighbors were raising, the whole neighborhood was raising the kids. Sundown, you need to be in the house. I mean, you really couldn't be out after dark until you actually got to be a football player in the ninth grade. It was great. I think I was discriminated against a couple of times. When I was really young, I'd try to go buy a hamburger or something like that. You go through the front door and you buy a hamburger, and the guy say, "Well, you got to go around the back to pick it up." I didn't know. That's what we got to do. I went to North Carolina A&T, where those guys actually did the first set in at Woolworth. That's really where you start to say, "That's a real difference here." But still, it didn't bother you so much because you were still a part of your own neighborhood, a part of your own growing groups, but you look sideways now at the other people.

Interviewer: Tell me more about what you mean about sideways.

Allen Pope: Sideways means you start to say, "oh, these are the people that discriminate against you" or something like that. Not so trusting anymore, but after a while, once you learn that there are good people on both sides, then you can deal with whatever you had to work with.

Interviewer: Did A&T have a big effect on you?

Allen Pope: Yeah, A&T had a big effect on me in terms of understanding, gosh, you're supposed to be able to do this without consequences. That's when the separation started in terms of being cautious, being prejudice or things like that. You've thought sometimes, when your parents say work hard and you be successful, but success in their mind, pretty much was that you get a job, you go to the factories pretty much and get a job. You do all right. Dream was basically a professional job was, man if you were a teacher, you were at the top, as far as we were concerned, but when you actually started being, dealing with teachers, some of them would have a little more foresight. They say, "Well, you might be a doctor or you might be able to do this or that." That's what started to broaden our outlook. I used to say, "Well, everybody don't have to be a teacher to be successful. You could be other things." We had teachers come to our school because of out athletic program.

We had one teacher, name is Mr. Miller, who's a science teacher. Mr. Miller knew about us before he ever came to the school. He knew about the football team. We were sitting on the block one day, and a block for us is right there by the community center. We sat there and we talked and Mr. Miller walked through and there was grocery store, a little grocery store around the corner. He said, "I heard about you guys. That's one reason why I wanted to come to this school and teach." He said, "The people that are putting out these kind of athletic programs, you have to be putting out some great students here." In class, he would talk to us sometimes. He would mention Edward Cunningham. He said, "Cunningham, I can write a letter today and get you in Michigan State," he said, "But you're not ready." He would give you that kind of vision because he said, "I know the presidents of these universities." He was something, but I think we kind of beat him down.

Interviewer: Okay. So Mr. Miller was one of those people at Ridgeview High, who was trying to help say, "You can do this, you could do that?"

Allen Pope: Writing your vision about what's possible. And he was great. As a matter of fact, he talked to us one day about the dance ballroom. He said, "You guys not the ballroom." Don't miss the ballroom?" "Nobody balling around here," Mr. Miller. It's kind of a cultural thing, so I think he took us to the gym one day and he said, "I'm going to teach you guys how to ballroom." Really, nobody really liked it, but that was Mr. Miller. He taught us a lot of different things, so to me, he was one of the guys that made an impression on me. Another instructor was Mr. Penn. He was a band leader, big guy, hot complexion. Now, he was tough. You never gave Mr. Penn a hard time.

If you were not going to make the football team, and (Coach) Davis said you're not going to make the team, he said why don't you go play for the band director. Basically, he'll leave your pass in the dressing room, and you go on to join the band, you're not going to make it. It was necessary. I know we spoke about "Jap" Davis. He was also called "Ace."

Interviewer: Do you remember any great stories about him that would help us have a sense of what he's like?

Allen Pope: Ace was a disciplinarian. If you know about college clubs, where you volunteer to be a part and they have a bat, he had a paddle, so if you did something wrong, play wrong, (indicates swinging) with that big paddle. That was Ace's discipline, but we did all we could not to get that paddle. He only had to hit you one time. It hurt.

Interviewer: Was it more the shame or more the pain?

Allen Pope: It was pain. I mean, shame went with it, but it was pain. But to me, Ace was more of a defensive coach. The coach that really, really made the offense spring was Roger Scales. He was the offensive guy. Now, he made a heavy impression on me. We ran all kinds or formations. Most high schools ran a full back field. It might have had a split back every now and then, but most of the time, we had split back. We ran double wings, we ran single wings, we ran something called the belly series. If you watch the professional teams today, that have the mobile quarterbacks, they run what you call, well, they say, "We going to read the defensive man and if he dives down, you pitch it out." We call that our belly series. We ride the fullback into the line. If the defense up in, block down or came in at an angle, we pitch it out to the halfback floating around and he's gone.

A lot of teams couldn't handle the formations that we put before them. As a matter of fact, I heard one, a couple of comments say, "We never seen no formation like you guys run." I said, "We don't run that." Even when I went to A&T, they ran a full back field. I said, "Nobody run full backfield no more." I didn't get a shot to play for A&T, but I went there to get a shot to play. I didn't get a shot to play because I didn't have a scholarship. You have to give your scholarship guys... I did get a scholarship to Allen University, but I didn't want to go there. I wanted to go to A&T and play, but their coach came up. He actually told me to come down, but when I went, of course, it all changed. It was okay. You learn a lot.

Roger Scales put the offenses in that we ran and our 44 Cross Back was one of the major things that made Douglas Bumgarner great. He was a super back. He is the guy that did the 21 touchdowns and left to almost 1,200 yards, but little do people know that we had three backs, with double digit touchdowns. Now, so you might have one running back that has double-digit touchdowns and 10 touchdowns a year is a great season, but we had three, and they all had more than 10 touchdowns. That's part of the reason that they became Untouchable. Once they got past the line, none of them have ever been caught from behind. Not any of them.

Jobo (Rev. Lutz), he made that clear in terms of Bumgarner being the fastest. Once he got through the line, it was over. Cunningham had the smoothest or he didn't bounce. He was just fast. He looked like a streak. Allen Burch had more moves. When he starts wiggling, he was gone, a couple of wiggles, he was gone. That was it. We learned a lot of stuff, it was good.

Interviewer: Did you all have any trick plays?

Allen Pope: Yes. We had one special trick play. This trick play involves, when you set the ball down, we huddle about 10 yards to the right or the left of the ball. And when we broke the huddle, we made sure the guys were on the line, they were over here, but they were on the line with their backs, like I'm giving them instructions. All right, so doing that, they looked like they were already on the line. The center would break out and Bumgarner would break out and they would go over to the ball. We'd be calling them back. Center would say, "What? What? What?" And he would go over, and by the time he gets over the ball and snaps it, then they just throw it over to the back. Now, it worked for a touchdown a couple of times. It always worked for a big play. Always worked for a big play. That was the biggest trick play we had, and it was an excellent play too. It was an excellent play.

Interviewer: That must have really confused the other team.

Allen Pope: Oh, yeah. Now, we had other stuff. Forty-four crossbar was the main thing. We played in games where actually we had a team that said, you're not going to score on us anymore. That was like, oh, okay. We need to go ahead and shut these people down, so we might score a couple more touchdowns after that conversation.

The other thing was Newton, yes, was our biggest rival and we always talked trash with Newton. They were undefeated, just like we were for the first six games. Now, we did practice a longer time before we were to meet them because they were unbeaten also, but I think after the first series and Cunningham intercepted a pass, took it all the way back, I say, it's over. It's over. We went on and beat them 36 to nothing. We didn't hear no more talk about Newton then, being competitive with us. One of the things that made it that way was Bobby Rowe was an ex-Ridgeview player and he was good. He went to Newton and made them somewhat recognizable. That was it.

Interviewer: Did you guys have an aura about you for other teams? Just like Alabama these days, Alabama's on your schedule, you sort of think you may not win that one?

Allen Pope: Well, I got to say that we had an aura and sometimes it was created by the cheers. We cheered so loud one time, before a game in the gym that, because it was thundering lightning they delayed the game and the team forfeited the game. Was that Shelby?

Interviewer: They did.

Allen Pope: One of the games, they decided not to play us because it was just no sense going out there and get beat like that in the rain. It was thundering lightning, so they had to. They delayed the game, so they actually forfeited the game to us.

Interviewer: Did you all have cheerleaders?

Allen Pope: Oh, yes.

Interviewer: Do you remember any of the cheers?

Allen Pope: I only remember the chant that we did on our way to the field. We would be singing out something like… "Let's go down and" We beat our pads. "And get it over with." So we'd do that all the way all the way to the field. When we leave the gym, they hear us coming. That was our chant, when we hit that door, headed to the field. Going down to get it over with. Let's see what else.

Interviewer: Do you remember anything about your equipment, what it was like? Did you feel safe in it?

Allen Pope: Well, we felt safe because we didn't know any other way to feel. When you have something, sometimes you don't know there's better stuff because that's what we got. We just played with whatever we had, but we do know this, the first team had the best pads. The first team had the bast pads because they get a little worse as we get down to the guys on the second team. So yeah, we had pretty good pads. At least we thought they were. Every now and then we have some white ones, so that was just great. A lot of them are red. So we know they're getting really old. But yeah.

Interviewer: Did you ever think about what it would be like to play someone like Hickory?

Allen Pope: We constantly had conversations about playing Hickory High. We kind of wanted to play them, but that never came off, especially when we were winning like we were. They were a great team too at that time, but that never happened. We wanted to play Hickory High to see who's the best in town.

Interviewer: They had everything they wanted, in terms of a stadium, and equipment and everything else. I'm just curious to how you all felt, because they were still supposed to be separate and equal, but the black schools in Catawba County were not.

Allen Pope: Had we known how great their equipment was, we probably would have been. We didn't know. We played with what we had. You really didn't find out. We knew when we got issued books, they were never new. There were always somebody else's name in them. But we never really had conversations about it because that's the way it was. We never really thought about it. And since we pretty much stayed in our own neighborhoods, you don't know how bad off you are, as long as you're getting something to eat and a place to sleep. You don't really know how bad off you are. If you ask us, we'd say, "We not poor. We're doing great. We get to eat, we get to go home to mom and dad. At least it ain't raining on us when we go to sleep." Something like that, so you don't know how bad it is until you actually learn it, but if you're in the circle and you're growing up in this circle, and you're shielded from what's going on outside. Your parents knew. It also starts to kick in.

Actually, my father was one of the first black policemen in North Carolina and his instruction was you can't put white people in jail. He said, "If you have a white person that's drunk, you call us. You can't put them in jail." But, my father said, "If I put mine in jail, I'm going to put yours in jail." So every time he would arrest one, he had to go see the chief about it. I think he stayed in the job for about five years and that was it.

Interviewer: Did he leave out of frustration or just because he wanted to do something else?

Allen Pope: I don't remember exactly, but it was probably frustration because the rules were different. Now, within the neighborhood, he had a couple of tough battles, and I mean fights. He was cut with a razor across the chest, but this guy had a tough reputation anyway. He had put certain people in the hospital. After that, my father took him to jail, but after that they called him the Head-knocker. If you were around Johnny Hodge, he said, "Did the Head-knocker tell you to go home? You better get on home." He would give a person the chance to go home, say, "If you're here by the time I come back, I'm putting you in jail."

You don't know about those things until you've actually spread out and see what the rest of the world is about, and then you start to figure out, this is not right. This should be better, but when you're in that box, you actually don't know you're being discriminated against. You just think that's the way life is.

Interviewer: Did you guys have a social life outside of school? Did you have a hangout where you all went?

Allen Pope: Yeah, we had what we call the block and that block was mostly right there, where the community center is. That's where we would go talk about football and sing or whatever we needed to do. That was our hangout or the other block. When we got a little older, we'd go to the big block, where you can shoot some pool or maybe have a sneaky drink or something like that.

Interviewer: What about girls? Did you all do stuff with dating?

Allen Pope: Well, we all had girlfriends.

Interviewer: Not much money to spend on them.

Allen Pope: Not much money to spend to take them nowhere. You go visit them at their house of something like that, and you sit in and talk for while, and then you'd go home. There's a few guys that might have had a little money, but most of us, we didn't have any money to take anybody anywhere or buy anything. Yeah, everybody was pretty much in the same situation. Nobody minded.

Interviewer: Did any of you all have cars?

Allen Pope: No. A few of them, but no, we didn't have. I didn't have a car.

Interviewer: So everything was walking distance?

Allen Pope: Walking distance. Yeah, we were walkers, when we were coming up.

Interviewer: Did people walk uptown much?

Allen Pope: Oh, yeah. My first job at summer time was walking from 2nd street to the downtown area, to work, but it was construction. As a matter of fact, I worked with my neighbor. He mopped tar on the roof. I carried up some rocks, so he could put rocks on the roof where he mopped hot tar. I would walk with him to work in the morning. Then my next summer job was construction, where you go up and you wait on somebody to come by and say, "We need a couple of workers to come out and work construction." A couple of times, I had to go back home because I didn't get a job that day, because if you live with my father, you are going to work, okay. You get a few days off, but you're not going to hang around here and not be working. He'd say, "Well, it's been three days, if you can't find one, I'll get you one." A couple of days later, he said, "I got you one." I said, Okay."

This job was cutting back lots for the city. You go to these empty lots and you had to cut them back, seven to 10 feet from the curb. That meant briers, grass, trees, whatever. Well, I got poison ivy the second day, stung by bees. He forgot to pick me up, so I was walking to go home. He got me about half hour later, he drove us, “I forgot all about you all.” I said, "Well, I can't do this. I found my own job." I got a job in the sock factory, shipping socks and that kind of thing, so that was a great job, before I ever went off to school. Those were some of my summer jobs. Of course, we were paper boys until we couldn't carry anymore papers. I probably carried papers for seven years and my father had the paper rounds for, pretty much, the black area. Almost all the kids had worked for him at some point, carrying papers. If you grew up anywhere in the neighborhood, you probably carried papers for my father, at some point.

He would say, "Well, if you're old enough to ask for some money, you're old enough to ask for a job. Those are our memories. They're good memories because we actually were raised in a condensed area. We didn't get a lot of the worldly prejudice things. We found out about them later on, of course, that starts to shape you in a different fashion, but if you had a strong background, if you had football like we had, you know you build a team relationship and you can always go talk to these guys. That's really what made us great. We were a great team with a lot of good players. There's been a lot of great players that come through Ridgeview, but they were not necessarily as good a team as we were. The difference is we played together, we covered your back. We covered your mistakes and we keep pushing.

Interviewer: I may have got this wrong, but weren't some of the factories segregated or were they integrated where it was pretty much, if you can work there, you got a job?

Allen Pope: The ones that I worked were segregated, your job was restricted, pretty much, in the certain areas. There are just certain jobs that you're not going to get in. You basically put on your boots and you're going to get the crappy job. That's just bottom line, but it's a job.

Interviewer: It's so impressive the way you all didn't have resentment or maybe you did have resentment, but you dealt with it in a way you didn't let it eat you up.

Allen Pope: Yeah. I think we've actually dealt very well. We didn't have a lot of talk about heavy discrimination, even though we knew it existed. The thing was that when your parents treat you right, tell you what you need to do, you follow these things that they tell you because they've already been through it. There's one thing that hit me when I was later on in years, where your older parents would always say, "Boy, save a dime out of that dollar" because they'd lived through having nothing. They understood what to tell you to do, but they didn't know where to tell you to put it. But they could say, "Save a dime out that dollar" and I think everybody that's grown up and had grandparents and older people, they heard them say that because their life was rough.

I did learn to save. I learned where to put it and how to go about it, and so I teach that also I had that license to go teach mutual fund investments and things like that. That's where I learned, go put it right here. It ain't much, but you go put away $25 a month. Time is everything.

If you get started right out of high school, say you do $10 a month, great. Why? You got 40 years for that to work from you. Now we learn where to put it. They already gave me the advice, it's just, where do I put it. Most of them put it under your pillow, which didn't do well, or most of them didn't trust the banks, so they buried it in the backyard. Just got to learn it.

Interviewer: Do you remember if most people in Ridgeview, came from intact, strong families during the '50s and '60s?

Allen Pope: Most of the families in our time, they stuck together and they recognized that they all had hard times, and they would help each other. For some reason though, that kind of got away from maybe their kids thought they were entitled to something before they actually worked for it or their parents work so much, they didn't have an opportunity to instill certain things in them because most of the time, the father would be the one working and the mother would very rarely have a job. She would take care of the household. That was pretty much true on all and very rarely did the mother go out and get a job, but when they did, they were maids or they were ironing clothes. Or if they had a job in the house, they would iron your clothes. People would bring their clothes to the house. I remember my mother doing that for people she worked for. They would bring their clothes and she would iron their shirts and pants, and stuff like that. That's how she made a little money. My father might get a truck and go buy green beans, and peaches and stuff, and my mother would can that stuff. That's what would bring you through the year. Canned foods and that kind of thing.

Interviewer: You had two-parent families living on one income and you were okay. That sounds pretty solid.

Allen Pope: It's okay because you could get things. They had gardens, they had side jobs, that kind of thing, so we were okay. I mean it was hungry, but never really starving or anything so.

Interviewer: Was there an outcome of that teamwork ideology that you were talking in the football team that actually permeated to the neighborhood, that this person put up green beans and this person's beets did well. They trade the green beans for some beets, so it's like a team in the neighborhood as well?

Allen Pope: Part of the reason the team is great is because they came from that situation. They came from listening to what the parents had to say, so it was easy to listen to what the coach had to say, because theoretically, when you're in the company of the coach, he is now your parent. That's what you're taught in the household. If you're in the company of a teacher, that teacher is currently your parent because if your parent has to come to me and tell me something about you, my real parent, then I'm in trouble. See, it don't work that way anymore. The teachers now, they're disciplining a child and the parent's ready to kill him. Or you can't even discipline him now. I think that's one of the worst things that's happened in terms of, you can't discipline your child, even if you're the mom or the daddy.

If they know that, they sometimes use that against you, but old parents would say, "You can call them if you want to, but you better be ready to go with them when they come because you ain't staying here no more." Old parents would do that. You don't butt my head, you don't butt me. I'm your father. I'm your mother. When I tell you, that's what goes. You don't go call some stranger, talking about this and that, but today, I hear it a lot. Kids call the police on their parent. You can't hit me. You're in the wrong household buddy.

Interviewer: Could you tell me a little bit about how you got ready every week for a team? This was the years before there were films, right?

Allen Pope: We mostly worry about what we were going to do because we didn't have the film on the other team. Now, the only time we actually did something extra was we played teams that we knew were winning just like we're winning right now. In other words, they weren't winning exactly like we were winning, but they were winning games also, so we'll know. Of course, Newton was the best team that we faced most of the time. Canton was a surprise to us, when we went up and beat Canton because I think Newton had beat that team 40 something. Newton was picked to beat us by a few points, I think. They came and they lost 36 to nothing. Actually, I think the fact that they beat Canton with more points than we had, gave them a little more confidence that they could come into our backyard and beat us.

Interviewer: What was a Friday night game like?

Allen Pope: Friday nights was the thing. Everybody in town come to our games. Our games were packed.

Interviewer: And you had bleachers brought in or did you have stands?

Allen Pope: We had bleachers. Fortunately for us, we had a hill that

went up like this, so if when the bleachers were full, the people would start lining up in the hill that went up like... and just stood. It was almost like bleachers because they just stood up in the hill and watched the game. And we played Newton, nobody else could get in. It was just packed. Then you'd have guys that dug holes, trying to get in, dug holes under the fence. They would come out every week and try to close all the holes up.
Interviewer: In reading the newspaper about the season before it began, I read you were going to maybe not play quarterback. You were going out of state to play quarterback elsewhere. Is this accurate?
Allen Pope: No. I was always going to play.
Interviewer: How did you get the quarterback position?
Allen Pope: Actually, I didn't get to play my freshman year because I wasn't decided on that. I was more moved towards the halfback scenario and I really never would have wanted to be a halfback. I always wanted to be the quarterback, so the next year I came out, I made the team and I played defense. I was defensive back, sophomore year, and so I played defensive back the next year as a junior. I saw a little bit of action as a quarterback, as a junior, but then my senior year, quarterback all the way and then still defensive halfback. It was wonderful.
Speaker 3: Was it hard playing both ways?
Allen Pope: That was condition. We ran till we dropped, so we were conditioned more so than probably anybody. No, it wasn't difficult to play both ways at all. Not at all.

2015

Interviewer: Can you describe how the environment you grew up in helped create the men you and your teammates became?
Allen Pope: Got to have that environment. Got to have that, either family, or friends, or cousins or somebody with a solid background who can walk you through things.

Just like a parent tells his child, "Look, if you do this dope, you may end up right here." Now if the child didn't have a parent, it's like, you got somebody, "Oh, so you'll be all right. You can handle it. You're tough." "Oh, okay, I'll try it." Now he's hooked. He doesn't know what happened. But if you've got that support background, you're in good. You got a good family background, you're good. I got to say that most of us had good support background. That's why we made it to where we are today. That's why we made it.

Interviewer: Anything else you want to say about, either your time here in high school, or the ball team?

Allen Pope: Love coming back. To this day, we brag about the untouchables. I feel the love when I come home. It's great to see all your other teammates, even if we can't remember their names. Somebody lets you know who they are, even though they remember your name. "Oh... Who are you?"

We have kind of a family environment, as far as when we come for a school reunion, it's excellent. Everybody participates. Nobody has to be perfect. Just do what you do. Have a good time. Talk about old times. And knowing that this will almost never be duplicated. So you always have something to talk about and talk trash about. And we do talk it.

Interviewer: Did you ever think people will be talking about that season 50 years after it's over?

Allen Pope: No, not to this extent. Not at all. Not at all. I thought they would sweep this under the rug, just go on. But when you bring it up, see nobody believes that. I can bring it up to anybody in Florida, and they say, "Nah, that ain't true. That ain't true. Somebody scored something."

I say, "Okay." But then you give them the paper that said. But then they want to make it something like, "Well, what A (division) was it?" I say, "It doesn't matter." I said, "If you were a Pop Warner team, and you won all your games, and nobody scored on you, you were great. I don't care. Whatever your level is, that's the level you conquered, to that degree." So it doesn't matter what, I say, "It doesn't matter." Then they say, "Oh, well I guess you're right. It doesn't matter." That is a piece of history that may never be duplicated. I want to say never, but I'm going to say, may never. Okay. But we say it's never. All right.

The Bleacher Interview

Four members of the Untouchables gathered at the Hickory High School stadium for an interview. Xenophone Lutz, Douglas Bumgarner, Hampton Davis, and Doug Thompson were introduced to the 2018 Red Tornado football team, who sang the Ridgeview theme song, "Let's Go Down and Get It Over With." They met and talked with Head Coach Russell Stone, then sat down to talk about their recollections.

Interviewer: What was it about football that made you work so hard to get good at it?

D. Bumgarner: So we just loved football and that was just in us, that was our DNA for us. And I didn't look at it as other teams feeling the way about football that we did. Okay, we were the masters at it. We knew what we were doing. We'd been doing it for years.

Not to sound better than they are or anything like that.

D. Thompson: Well, we were.

D. Bumgarner: But we just felt it and I think that's what made us better.

Interviewer: Were you guys ever that age (referring to high school team on the field)?

Rev. X. Lutz: Absolutely, yes sir.

D. Bumgarner: We still are. Sometimes we still are.

Interviewer: What was the game atmosphere when you guys came onto the field? What would that be like?

D. Bumgarner: Well, to me, it was like heart palpitating. A lot of emotions. It was jittery. Excitement. Crowd's hollering. Everyone's out there hollering and you're coming down to the field and you hear the cleats and the guys cheering their cheers and all so forth. Built you up a lot. Got you ready.

D. Thompson: Excited. Feel like you're going to bust, you're excited.

Hamp Davis: There's a band playing.

D. Thompson: When they do that cheer, it helps build it up. Push it, build up inside you and you ready to play then, man.

Interviewer: You can't wait at that point.

D. Thompson: You can't wait at all.

Rev. X. Lutz: And again, the backup the song, "We going to win. We going to win this game." We were always confident we were going to win. No doubt. No doubt. We knew we were going to win the game somehow.

Interviewer: Well, that's the thing I got from other interviews and talking to you guys, is it's all about conditioning and confidence. Those two things. Is that true?

Rev. X. Lutz: Absolutely, yeah. Conditioning. Confidence. We believed we had the ability. We always believed we had what it took to win. 100% confident.

Hamp Davis: We didn't have stuff like these boys (reference to the 2018 Hickory High players). Gatorade and all that. They didn't let us have any water. When we had practice. Caused us cramps and that's why we was so in condition all the time. We was in good condition.

D. Thompson: You had to be elite to get on the team, because when you got there, from my experience as a freshman coming on, was Mr. Lutz and Mr. Bumgarner were seniors and I come out as a guard. And Johnny Boy Hodge and Jobo (nickname of Rev Lutz), they took me under their wing. "We're going to teach you something." And they put you in front, two on one. And buddy, you had to do what you could do to stay there.

Now out of my whole class, I think about eight of us went out and I think only two made it, so you had to be, it was elite. It was something else.

Interviewer: You had a whole tradition going, because you hadn't lost a regular season game, the high school hadn't, since '57.

D. Thompson: Right.

Interviewer: That season, once you figured out, "Okay, nobody's scored on us and we're going to try to do this for the whole season," it ever make you nervous to try to keep that going?

D. Bumgarner: Yeah. It put pressure on you. And like all this other stuff that's been said, conditioning and determination and the love of the game, we can't forget, before every game we had prayer, so we had faith in God and asked Him to lead us, protect us and guide us. All that emotion inside of us helped us do what we did to carry on the legacy.

Rev. X. Lutz: Personally, I never had any doubts. Personally, I never feared that we would lose. I always had that mindset, "We were going to win." Whatever it takes.

Interviewer: Even when they had you down on the one-yard line in that championship game?

Rev. X. Lutz: Absolutely. I never thought one minute about losing.

D. Thompson: That was even more so.

Rev. X. Lutz: I just felt that more motivated and confident. You might call it crazy, or wishful thinking or whatever, but never one thought crossed my mind that they would. It did not cross my mind that they would score that time. I just felt confident.

D. Bumgarner: Even though they were down that close, you got to remember, we come from a team that has had a winning streak for years. And we lost once or twice since I was playing, but like Joe said, you just don't think of losing. We're going to win. We're better than they are.

Rev. X. Lutz: We are Ridgeview. We are Ridgeview Panthers. You are not going to score. You are not going to win.

D. Thompson: When we go to the (away) games, everybody else in town knew we were coming, because they heard us coming. And we was hollering, raising cane on the bus. And when we got off, we was pumped up, buddy.

D. Bumgarner: You see, a lot of times, that right there, alone, itself, sort of cripples the opponents. When you get somebody that comes into their town, talking trash and all that noise coming in here and the reputation that they had? Some of them was already beat. We just loved football and that was just in us. That was in our DNA. I didn't look at it as other teams feeling the way about football the way we did. We were the masters at it. We knew what we was doing. We had been doing it for years. Not to sound like we were better than they were or anything like that, but we just felt it and I think that's what made us better.

Rev. X. Lutz: And again, if someone did score, that just means we going to just reach down and do whatever it takes to come back and win. That was the mindset. Regardless of whatever situation we were in. We just felt that we were going to come back and win. Particularly that year, we done it. Even the years back, that was the same mindset. Even though we lost, I think, two games while we were in high school and we weren't really playing that much on those losses, especially that first one when we were freshman. We got this from the other guys. The other guys always thought that they would win regardless of the situation.

But again, it didn't matter what the situation was. Ahead or behind, we were going to win. Two years before we set that record our last year, two years before that, Newton Conover led us twice at halftime by a couple of scores sometimes. But we never felt that we would lose and both times, we came back and beat them. Again, we just considered ourselves a second-half team, because of our conditioning, because of our experience, because of what we had accomplished in the past. We know that we felt that somehow, we were going to come back and win.

Interviewer: Talk about practice.

Hamp Davis: It was physical. People got hurt. I saw legs broke. Teeth knocked out. And that's the way they practiced. And you imagine, we did it to ourselves, imagine what we we're going to do on the field to our opponent.

Rev. X. Lutz: There was a lot of pride in practice. If you made a guy look bad, it was going to be a fight or you going to be in for a struggle. You going to get the hardest competition you ever had. Practice could be pretty rough at times, yes sir.

Ed White, Aggie. One time in practice, he got knocked out and started talking out of his head and coach come over and tried to bring him through. "Aggie, you all right?" and stuff like that. And then he start talking out of his head. Actually, he said some choice words. But he was out of his head.

At times, a few fights would break out. Some guys get bloodied. We'd have to, what we call, throw the bone on them. When it gets real rough, somebody get the best of you, your last resort is, what we call, throw the bone.

D. Bumgarner: It's just like family. Family, you fight each other. And growing up, on the weekends, when we went to play teams, we were family together. We protect them from the other team. Just like our own family, your brothers and sisters fight, but you can't let nobody in the community jump on your brothers and sisters. That's when you go to war with them. All in all, we got along real fine.

Rev. X. Lutz: Absolutely. Oh yeah.

D. Bumgarner: After we left the field, everything was okay.

Rev. X. Lutz: I was going to say, after practice, no matter how rough it got, we would get together and it's all forgotten and we just go.

D. Bumgarner: We tired and hungry and wanting to go home and someone might hit you the wrong way or something like that, on purpose, accident or whatever, a thing like that just happen, but we all loved each other. We all enjoyed the sports.

Interviewer: Could you talk about a couple of the guys who are no longer living that you remember on the team? Guys like Allen Burch and those guys?

D. Bumgarner: Yeah, Allen was from East Hickory, the side of town that I grew up in. His whole family was known for speeding. He'd had, I think, two other brothers before him, not that they were him, but they were all just fast. Allen was the fastest. And when he'd run, he'd run sort of like he was sideways.

He had a unique style of running, but he could be going full-speed and stop on a dime. Go one way and back the other, he could really fake you out. He was fast and he was strong. He was a good player, football player. I tell you what, he contributed a lot to the team that we had in '64. And he was just great. A great ballplayer.

Interviewer: What about the Cunningham brothers?

Rev. X. Lutz: Edward was a senior along with Doug and I that year. He was fast and strong. Ran low. Ran with a gallop. He kind of galloped as he ran. His senior year, he had a great year, but he probably had a better year his junior year. But he was an excellent back, great back. But Doug, that senior year, Doug was out-of-sight, Allen Burch was out-of-sight and Edward Cunningham, we called him Zs. We had three backs that anybody would love to have.

Those guys could play college ball anywhere. Ed Cunningham. And Curtis was a good back. But nothing like Edward. If that's all right to say. He wasn't a Zs, but he was good, but yeah, Ed was a class act.

If you don't mind me letting me say it, let me mention Johnny Hodge, our captain. Johnny was the heart of the football team, in my world, in my thinking. He was the heart of the football team. Very aggressive player. Very funny, always kept things going. Always had a joke. But yet, when it come down to playing ball and being serious, again, he was the captain. He kept things in order. Like I mentioned that time when the team was on the five-yard line with a first down at Hamlet, and

Johnny's the one who said, "Hey, man, shut up. Play ball." That's the way he was. He kept his head in the game. I believe he was really the heart of the team. Defensive tackling, offensive blocking. He was special.

Interviewer: What do you think you had? A better defense or better offense?

D. Thompson: It'll be hard to say. We had the same players playing both ways. Let me put it this way, when they were needed, they came to the occasion. Defense, offense, I couldn't say which is best, but they're both good, is all I can say about that. I don't think one was any better than the other. I know a lot of people said the offense was better because they put the scores on the board, but you can't put the scores on the board if the defense doesn't stop the opposite team. I'd say they was about equal. That's my opinion.

Rev. X. Lutz: And I agree with you to a certain point, but I think because of the uniqueness of what we accomplished, the defense had the edge. Offense was great, but the defense was greater. I'm just, like I said, we're speaking our peace.

D. Bumgarner: That's your opinion, though.

Rev. X. Lutz: Like I said, my opinion. The offense, the guys were just outstanding, but what we accomplished on defense, that gave us the edge. A lot of people scored touchdowns. A lot of other teams scored touchdowns. But defense was special. It was a discipline, continuity. And the talent. And the drive. I would give the defense an edge, personally.

D. Bumgarner: I can't disagree with you, because I played defense too.

Rev. X. Lutz: Like Doug said, we played both ways.

Hamp Davis: In the East Spencer game. I don't know if y'all remember Bull Jackson?.

Rev. X. Lutz: Yeah.

Hamp Davis: They said they were going to run all over us. So they got an automatic first down and I think Dwight Thompson was holding. They still stopped Bull. End of the game, Bull wanted to fight the whole team because he couldn't get over the goal line. He was thinking he's going to run over us.

D. Bumgarner: They built him up.

Hamp Davis: They built him up.

D. Thompson: They had that big old picture of him.

Rev. X. Lutz: Yeah, we ran into some guys that played and went off and done well in college. Like this Bull Jackson. Big, big back too. We put him in his place.

D. Thompson: Put him down.

Rev. X. Lutz: Put him in the place. Stopped him cold. And nobody had done that.

Interviewer: Could you talk a little bit about the coaches? Coach Davis and Coach Scales? What it was like to play for them?

D. Bumgarner: I enjoyed playing under both of them. They were very good coaches. Caring. Sensitive. They knew what they were doing. They knew about football and they were good teachers. Patience. And they knew how to put certain people in certain positions and they also were good at bringing in the substitutes when you got in a position where you could bring in the substitutes, let them get out there and play, get some experience. It wasn't about just running up numbers on the board and make the other team look bad, he wanted to build a whole team. Not only just first team, but his second team too. And that's what he accomplished. And a lot of time, because when the first team had to come out, get hurt or get tired, he could go to his bench and he could get some guys out there that can do the job. They had it together, both of them.

Interviewer: I've heard about Coach Scales being something of an offensive genius. What do you think about that statement?

Rev. X. Lutz: I think that's pretty accurate. He brought things, introduced some things to our offense that just made the guys really confident and some things we really loved and things that complemented our team. Speed pass 100, y'all remember that? Maybe Doug can remember. Was it a double wing? Anyway, he introduced a lot of different plays that really opened up the game for us.

Interviewer: And he had a trick play, right?

Rev. X. Lutz: Yes, okay.

Hamp Davis: The Faggart play.

Rev. X. Lutz: Okay, they said it.

D. Bumgarner: They said it on TV.

Rev. X. Lutz: Yeah, we called it the faggot (Faggart) play. Of course, back then, that name was attributed to guys that were sissies. But upon study, Ridgeview had a coach whose name was Faggart. If I'm not mistaken, seem like somebody said he had a play something like that. It could have come from that. In my immature mind, back then, I took it as something else.

But yeah, it was a wonderful play, diversion play and it made a difference a couple times while we were playing games. A couple of years, it made a difference. Especially that last game, that championship at Lenoir-Rhyne. After halftime, the score was 0-0, and we called the Faggart play and it worked beautifully. We threw the pass to Doug Bumgarner. It was a diversion play. Part of the line was on one side of the field and the other side was on the opposite side of the field, but everybody was lined up on the line of scrimmage legally. And the ball was snapped. The center would say, "Y'all come down here," and then, in between that time, the ball was snapped, the quarterback would throw the ball up to the group on the other end, Doug caught the pass and ran it for... How far did that go, Doug?

D. Bumgarner: It was about 60-something, but they said I ran out of bounds on the sideline.

Rev. X. Lutz: Did you go all the way for a touchdown?

D. Bumgarner: What happened was, on this side, when you're going down the field, my lineman's up front and I'm running behind him. I can only go as fast as my linemen are going. And they're coming across the field this way (indicating at an angle). And so, we got sort of messed up over there. I think that's where they said I went out of bounds. I couldn't go any faster because my linemen was in front of me. But we got it down close to the goal line.

Rev. X. Lutz: You trying to say we was too slow.

D. Bumgarner: Right. One is faster.

Rev. X. Lutz: Yeah, that was it, you're right.

D. Bumgarner: And so he said I stepped out of bounds a couple yards back that way, I don't know. The play was good. It could get you a touchdown easily, but the thing of it is, you could only use it one time in a game, right?

Rev. X. Lutz: Absolutely. It made a difference though. During the course of the game, because I think that broke any-

D. Bumgarner: Ambition?

Rev. X. Lutz: Broke any doubts, or fears, that we might have had. It broke the ice, so to speak. Put it that way. I think that made you realize that, hey, we're going now. We really got down the field on that one.

Interviewer: Anything else you want to say about the team? All that running that you guys did? Five miles out when the coach dropped you off and all that? Did you appreciate it at the time?

Rev. X. Lutz: Oh, absolutely.

D. Bumgarner: No. Not at the time I was running, I didn't appreciate it.

Rev. X. Lutz: During the games, yeah.

D. Bumgarner: You could see it.

Rev. X. Lutz: You could tell a difference.

Hamp Davis: Especially when you're playing both ways.

D. Thompson: Tommy Yearby. Charles Thompson. Curtis Cunningham and myself. They put... The bus put you out. You were going to be the last one come by, so we just take our time. So we start cutting up, just sitting on the bridge down there, throwing rocks and going on. "Where Yearby at?" "You better seen Yearby" Said, "Man, we better make it on up here to the store." So when we made it up to the store, the bus was gone. I said, "Oh, lord."

I went in and I got my uncle on the phone. I said, "Hey, come pick me up." "Where you at?" I told him. So he give us a ride up, where used to be the burger house. They fixed up the burger house. They got that water in the grass. And we jumped in the water, out there in the sprinkler, getting wet, because it wasn't but, what, two, three blocks to the school from the burger house?

And we went down there and got on the field and Jap (Coach Davis) said, "you all have a good time?" Said, "Yes, sir." "Go get your clothes and get in line, come out here and practice." Come out there to practice, I think he run about three or four plays and then he went back in. Told us to stay out there on the field. We stayed there on the field, he'd run us around the field with a car behind us at night. And then that next day, boy, it broke loose. He said to those who played hooky yesterday, come up front. We got up there in front and he opened their legs up, pow. Pow. Every coach and every player got a chance, you remember that?

D. Bumgarner: You had to go through the line.

D. Thompson: Had to go through the line.

Interviewer: Man, that's tough.

D. Bumgarner: It's worse than that. You go through that line. And if you slack up, you got to go through again. It sounds like abuse, but it wasn't. I don't think.

Rev. X. Lutz: But those five miles made a difference, though. That training, from the beginning of the season, it made a difference during the course of the season. We were well-conditioned. We were known as a second-half team. Known to be very strong in the second half. No matter what happened during the first half, we always knew and felt that we were going to be better than our opponent in the second half. Conditioning attributed to that. We knew we always had what it takes to come back if necessary.

Interviewer: Okay, last question. Where did the confidence come from?

Hamp Davis: I almost think it came from tradition. You think about all the teams, Ridgeview on down through the years. We were little kids, man. We couldn't wait to play football. Recess. We played football all the time.

Rev. X. Lutz: We were Ridgeview, so that was the confidence right there. And it had been passed down through the years. The uniqueness of who we are and what we were accomplishing. We just had that confidence. We were special. We knew it. We felt it. We knew it and we tried to prove it.

Interviewer: Did you play about every day?

D. Bumgarner: If possible.

Rev. X. Lutz: Yeah. Sometimes.

Hamp Davis: All the time.

D. Thompson: Come home from school, throw your books down and go in there and get the football and go at it.

D. Bumgarner: I have come home from practice at Ridgeview and got to East Hickory and they had a game going in on East Hickory's playground. And I'd run in and play with them for a little while. It couldn't have been too long though, because sometimes we get home, it's kind of dark, but they'd be out there, throwing it around in the dark sometime. Younger guys, the ones who couldn't make the team or didn't make the team, they'd get up and play down there.

Rev. X. Lutz: I mentioned earlier that when we had those pick-up games, even guys that had played in high school, they would come and join us and even some guys who were home from college, they would get into things too. As Hamp said, that tradition, that gave us confidence that we were special and whatever it took to win, we could do it.

Interviewer: Can you say something about the band?
D. Bumgarner: Wow.
Rev. X. Lutz: The band leader that year, Alfonso Evans, he had some routines in there, man, that were fantastic.
D. Thompson: College routines.
Rev. X. Lutz: Yeah, college routines. Back then, you'd see Florida A&M on television and they had all those fast steps. They had all those fast steps and we copied off of those. We did some of those. My last year, we had a terrific drum major, Roosevelt Williams. My goodness. I mean, he's a drum major of drum majors. He could be a star on any band anywhere. We were gifted. In fact, several years we were gifted with great band leaders.

But Roosevelt Williams was probably one of the best.
D. Thompson: Butch was in there. Pretty good too. Him, Butch and who else? Butch's brother?
Rev. X. Lutz: Jackie, yeah.
D. Bumgarner: I think a lot of stuff that Al got. Al went to A&T in Greensboro. And they always had a good band and I think he got a lot of his stuff from A&T also.
Rev. X. Lutz: And I don't think they could do the split like Roosevelt could. So that gave him the edge. Plus, he could step quite high. He was tall and slender.
D. Bumgarner: And the band was one of the motivations for us behind the team. They really got you stirred up. They was playing some up-to-date music.
Rev. X. Lutz: In fact, the folks that didn't really know much about football, they knew they were going to get entertained by the band. The community was crazy about the band, just as they were about the football team. The band made a great contribution to the atmosphere.

Douglas Bumgarner

Right halfback Douglas Bumgarner led the team in scoring in 1964. He had a total of 21 touchdowns, while also grabbing some key interceptions during the year. Some refer to him as one of the fastest runners they had ever seen, although he credits his teammates in the backfield with equal abilities, Ed Cunningham and Allen Burch. For this project, Mr. Bumgarner has been interviewed numerous times, in groups of fellow players. This interview was conducted during the Ridgeview reunion in 2017.

Interviewer: What position did you play for the Panthers?
D. Bumgarner: I was a halfback and I played linebacker on defense.
Interviewer: When did you become a starter?
D. Bumgarner: I started my sophomore year with linebacker, first position, and then my junior year, I moved into the firstback on halfback.
Interviewer: And did you end up playing both ways most of the time?
D. Bumgarner: Oh, yes. Yes. That was, that was the pattern. First year I used to go both ways.
Interviewer: And how many players were on a team?
D. Bumgarner: I can't be for sure. It's about 20-something, I believe it was as far as I can remember. About 20-something.
Interviewer: So what part of Hickory did you grow up?
D. Bumgarner: I'm from East side. I came up in East Hickory. The location would be over by intersection of LR Boulevard and Tate. Over in that section.
Interviewer: What was it like living in East Hickory?
D. Bumgarner: Living in East Hickory, we had sort of a disadvantage in a way. We had to come from East Hickory, which is about five miles from here, I'm pretty sure, the distance. We had to walk over here sometimes in 5:00 in the morning and would get on this bus and go out to Brookford

to do the five mile run and come back to the school. And we had, I guess, about an hour, an hour and a half training, maybe two. And then we had to walk back to East Hickory and come back over here at 4:00. We had to walk back over here and do our training, and then we did some more running around the block, and then we'd go back to East Hickory. So that was conditioning, it seemed like all day long for us in East Hickory, but it's just the joy of playing ball. You enjoyed it. You was young.

Interviewer: So did you have a bus that took you from East Hickory down to Brookford, or did you walk?

D. Bumgarner: Yeah. We came over here at the school and we had a guy that had, it was a truck, something like what you haul furniture in. And we got on that and he took us out to Brookford and dropped us off. And then they drove up the road about five miles, and then we started our run. And you had a certain time to be there. If you weren't there, then the bus would leave and you'd have to get from Brookford back to Ridgeview. And then if you were late for practice, you had to stay and do laps. So it was a job.

Interviewer: How long did they give you to run five miles? Do you remember?

D. Bumgarner: No. I'm not quite sure on that. Maybe 45 minutes. About 45, 30, something like that. Some guys would get off and they'd do it in time with time to spare and there were some that didn't quite do it. It was up and down hills and curves, and it took a toll on you, especially the first part of the season.

Interviewer: Was East Hickory a really different world from what you hear them describing about Ridgeview?

D. Bumgarner: I don't think so. It was basically about the same. We were all sort of in the same income bracket. I wouldn't say poor, but you're not rich and everybody's sort of in that same area. So you really don't know the difference and everybody basically dresses the same and got the same type of lifestyle, but we were pretty well taken care of. Nobody went hungry.

Interviewer: Did you play hot grease?

D. Bumgarner: Oh yeah. I think that was pretty much all over. We played that and when I started school, it was an East Hickory Elementary School, which was on Tate Boulevard. There's a little school house. We went to the eighth grade and we played down there, Hot grease, that was all over. And when we got older, we used to walk over to Ridgeview a lot and did a lot of communicating together and stuff. So I think the thing just picked up. Everybody had their own little hot grease. That was mostly at recess time.

Interviewer: Did you guys play football all year round?

D. Bumgarner: Oh yeah. Even in the winter time, if it wasn't too cold, even if it was cold sometimes, we'd be out there in jackets. If somebody had a football, we was ready the play.

Interviewer: Even summer? Even spring?

D. Bumgarner: Oh yeah, yeah. We played year round.

Interviewer: What was wrong with basketball?

D. Bumgarner: Well, for me, I couldn't dribble and I never liked basketball. I just didn't like basketball. I didn't like wearing shorts.

Interviewer: And baseball?

D. Bumgarner: No. Then baseball was too slow for me. I didn't like that. I just focused on football. That's all I was interested in.

Interviewer: So everybody around here played football, then?

D. Bumgarner: Oh, mostly. Yeah. Yeah. There was a couple of guys that just played basketball, but most of it's football. Some of them, basketball and football.

Interviewer: It sounds like you all had a lot of interaction with Ridgeview.

D. Bumgarner: Yeah. And only thing is we used to come over on this side of town for was the community center here. They had dances and stuff and at the school, stuff like that. In East Hickory, all we had down there was mostly stores and the school, churches. That was it basically. So it wasn't anything like we had a dance or anything. No.

Interviewer: Did you know much about Coach Davis in advance? Did he have a reputation?

D. Bumgarner: I only got to know Coach Davis when I came over here to high school in the ninth grade. He was a good coach and he was a disciplinary coach. He had this motto, 'kill a gnat with a sledgehammer', which meant when you're on that field, you don't have no pity on nobody as far as hitting. I don't care if you're 260 and the guy's 80 pounds, you hit him, but he was a real nice guy. He kept us going with jokes and stuff too.

Interviewer: Do you remember taking trips to go play other teams? What was it like? Did you guys have an old bus or?

D. Bumgarner: Yeah, we had a bus. Then they call it the Rig. The Rig. And we would take that to the games and we would be singing songs on the bus and picking at each other, talking, going on, just keeping the thing going. And after the game on the way back home, if we had a tough game, we'd be kind of quiet, but there's always one guy on there that's wanting to talk the whole time and everybody else want to just rest. But we had good times on trips. We came together as a family and then during practice, we'd be beating each other up like families do everywhere you go. But come Friday night, we came together and we took care of each other.

Interviewer: Did you guys ever stop for a meal on the way to a game or on the way back at a restaurant?

D. Bumgarner: I think we did one time stopped at a service station or something, but I'd probably just go in to get some orange aid, some potato chips or something like that. But most times we went to the schools to play a little distance away, they would give you some food and stuff. Most of it was close to in area where you didn't need to stop.

We went to Newton, which wasn't really that far, but if we went way off, like we went to Lexington one time, they fed us down there and stuff. So we had no reason to stop, so we'd just come on back. But I was talking about those plays, that one play that Alan (Pope) was talking about what the lineman is lined up here and the other one slipped down that side in the third bar, well, that's a good play and it works, but it can only be run one time. You can't run it nowhere else.

The only disadvantage in it. So you usually try to pull that out when you get into a tight spot and you want to get the fire going. So that was only a one-time shot, but when you do it, you got to make it work. If you don't, you just wasted a down. But if it works, it'll bring you out of a lot of holes. But we just love football. Everybody loved football and we played the year round.

Interviewer: What about Coach Scales?

D. Bumgarner: Coach Scales, he was pretty good mostly at the times when we were sort of down and not really playing to our potential. He would get us in the locker room at halftime or something like that, or on the field. He would call us off to the side for a while. And he'd tell you,

"You all can beat these guys. Now if they lose the game, it's because you gave it to them. It's not because they beat you, because you're a better team. And if you do what you are capable of doing, you can bring it out." And he made you feel like he was, I guess, Superman or something. You know? I mean you felt it when he spoke to you and you could see the concern in his face and the confidence that he had in you.

And when a coach tell you, you can do something, I believe you can do it. I know you can. Then it seems like that gives you a little more energy and spike. So I think that picked us up a lot of times. It helped us out because a lot of times you go out there and sometimes you have some bad nights, you're tired, your game is off, and just sort of all you want to do is just get it over with and go home. Then when you get that pep talk and you go back out there, it helps you. It helped me a lot.

Interviewer: Were you guys celebrities at school?

D. Bumgarner: I wouldn't say that. There was a couple of us that would say, "You're going to get me a touchdown tonight?" or something like that, or "That's the Untouchables," but I don't think they really just fell down and kneeled to us. No. No. We got the same treatment.

Interviewer: Even from the girls?

D. Bumgarner: The same thing. They didn't throw their cell phone, at least not to me. I don't know if maybe other guys got something better, but they respected you and they appreciate it, but I don't think it was too much overboard.

Interviewer: At least to us it sounds like just an incredible unique experience that very few people in this life remember having. So it sounds remarkable.

D. Bumgarner: Well, I always say that this season that we had, I would say it was a gift from God. That's what I look at it is because I don't think there's any coach or any players that can come up with some kind of a training program or a strategy to go unbeaten, unscored on. It just don't happen. So I see that's a blessing from God and he gave it to us. That's why it means so much to me.

Interviewer: How do you look back on this as far as the important things you have done in your life?

D. Bumgarner: I wouldn't say the most important. It's one of them though. And even now I seem to get more recognition now than we did back then, and I didn't really look at it as all that exciting back then, because Ridgeview has a reputation of getting championships, but it's nothing like that year. It was special. No, but I'm appreciative of it, and I get more recognition now than I did back then, and I didn't really think of it as being all that special because I was just thinking of it as we won the state championship and then later on it ring the bell, but you weren't scored on. That's different. A lot of people win championships, but you weren't scored on. So then on it started to have a little place in my heart, and I liked it.

I just loved to run the ball really. I just wanted to run. And a lot of times I would get in trouble with that because I was asked to come out a couple of times and I wasn't ready to come out and I'd get upset over that. And I'd say, "Look, somebody else want to play too," but I don't know. I just loved the sport.

Interviewer: How was it when you were heading down the field? If you got past the line, you knew you had it? Is that how it was or was it different?

D. Bumgarner: Yeah. Pretty much you get past the line and you pass the linebacker, you pretty much got it going, unless you run out of gas or something. I don't know. The team, somebody there might be a little faster than you, and I wasn't the fastest thing in the world, but I had the speed, but sometimes you could get caught. It depends on how you were running and performing that day. You might get a little tired, a little slack, but most of the time, once you get past the line and the linebacker, you're pretty much home free.

Interviewer: When did it occur to you in the season that we might go unscored upon the whole thing?

D. Bumgarner: I think that was the game before the championship. I figured after we got that far, if we can get this team right here, we got it made. And that was the most tense game I've ever played in because everybody was banking on that. No score. We've gone the whole season, nobody's scored. There's no reason why these guys should have to score. We're going to stop them. And every time they got the ball or we fumbled or something like that, you'd go, "Oh guys, keep it going." And you'd get down close to the goal line and stuff like this, "Oh man, please." The guy would get the ball and start running. "Get him! Get him! Get him!" You're just running all across the field trying to be in on every tackle because you was trying to defend that record that we had going on so long. So everybody was backing each other up. If the ball would go that way, we would shift going that way.

Once he crossed that line, we was all over there. There was no sitting over here, "That's on your side." No. We was all trying to cover each other's tails. So that brought us through. Plus, we'd been conditioned, but in a game like that, you don't really feel tired because to me, it was like the adrenaline was just going. I was up, so I didn't get tired. I was just running like I was on some kind of speed or something, I guess, but when you're in a game like that, some of that adrenaline takes a hold of you and you don't feel tired.

Interviewer: How would you characterize your classes at Ridgeview?

D. Bumgarner: I think they were very good classes and challenging. I don't think it'd be any different for anybody else. Based on the material that we had, that's what we had. And we had some good teachers too. I remember one teacher, as a matter of fact, when I was going to school in East Hickory, I was in the sixth grade and our teacher was telling us about how important education was. His name was Mr. James Calvin Killian. He was telling us how important the education was. He said, "You guys need to study hard and get this way. Once you get this up here (pointing to his head), can't nobody take it from you. That's how important education is. Once you get here, they can't take it from you. And you get here, you can go to other places. I know a lot of you all probably feel like, well, my parents can't send me to college, so I don't have to make the grades."

He said, "It's best to have the grades and not the money than to have the money and not the grades, because if you got the grades, there's always going to be somebody out here or maybe somebody in here who's been looking at you, he may even pay your way to college." And then he told us about his experience when he was growing up. His parents didn't have money and his last year in high school, the coach asked him to come out for football. And he went out for football, he made the team, he played in and he got a full scholarship to Federal State. He went to Federal State and played ball and came out and he became the principal. He was the principal down there at East Hickory Elementary School and then I think he was the principal over at, I think it was the school at Highland.

So he excelled, but if he'd been like some of the students that "My parents ain't got money to send me to school, I don't have to make these grades. I'm just going to go to the factory and work," that's where he'd have been. But he had the grades and he was able to do it. That stuck out in my mind. I always tell kids that now. "Don't worry about the money. Just get the grades. Somebody will look out for you if you want to go to school?"

Interviewer: Do you have children and grandchildren?

D. Bumgarner: Yes. I have three children. I have two sons, a daughter, and I got five grandkids.

Interviewer: How does their life look different to you than the life you grew up living here?

D. Bumgarner: A whole lot. They're blessed compared to my life. My life wasn't all that bad. I didn't have the things that they have. I had to share my bedrooms with my brother, but they'd get similar style clothes. I didn't buy all name brand clothes, but they were decent clothes. They had a nice home. Nicer than mine. They didn't have to walk to school. They had a bus, but it's a lot of times I would take them up to the bus stop and if it's raining, I'd let them sit in my car until the bus come, whereas when we was going to school, we had to walk to East Hickory when we was going to school back and forth. We didn't have no bus. And they got a lot of opportunities. They can get to play in sports and things. They don't have to worry about well, where am I going to get the money from my shoes? Where am I going to get money for this or that? So that's some of the things, and they know they're going to be taken care of.

Interviewer: Do your grandchildren know about the Untouchables team?

D. Bumgarner: Oh, yeah. The whole family knows about that.

Interviewer: What do they think about Grandad with 21 touchdowns for his team?

D. Bumgarner: Well, they don't brag too much about it. They're kind of young right now, so they don't think much about it. My sons, they went to Hickory High, and sometimes we get to talking about school and stuff like that, and they say, "Yeah, but Ridgeview is torn down." I say, "No, Ridgeview isn't torn down." I say, "The building's torn down. Ridgeview is right here in the heart." But they both played at Hickory High, and Chad, my oldest son, he played a wide receiver, played an excellent job.

And Lee, my youngest son, he was a halfback and he did well. And they both ran track. My daughter, she ran track. So they were all athletes.

Interviewer: What do you think about the reunions? This is quite a phenomenon of 50 years.

D. Bumgarner: I think the reunion is great, and I appreciate the people that started it, and I just hope they can keep it going because it's good to keep in touch with people and just to see what's going on in their life since playing on the football team. A lot of those guys are gone. So it's good to see people come back every two years to have a good time and enjoy each other while we're here on earth. I enjoy it. I hope it keeps going.

Interviewer: Did you stay in touch with any of the players from the other teams from other cities, or did you ever keep any contact with them?

D. Bumgarner: Well, we run in touch with most of the guys that's close around, like Newton. We pretty much stay pretty close to him, but the guys we played in Shelby, no. As far as I know, I have not. No. Every now and then you'll run across some of them. I've done it with Joe for about a year before I went in the service. And we've ran into some guys that came from the North and we'd all get together and talk. "I know you" and da, da, da, da, and we'd talk about the games and stuff like that. It's good. It's good to see those guys.

Interviewer: Do you give those Newton guys a hard time because I understand some of them married Ridgeview girls?

D. Bumgarner: I don't. No, I don't. I don't. We joke about it, but it's all in fun, but I don't say too much about it because I try not to get into that stage where people think you're bragging and all that stuff. So I'm sort of humble on that, but they take it in stride. We get along just fine.

Dr. Veronica McComb

As as an Assistant Professor and Program Coordinator of History at Lenoir-Rhyne University, Dr. Veronica McComb provides insight and context to understanding the world of 1964, the year of the Untouchables season. Also a board member of the Historical Association of Catawba County, Dr. McComb's "broader research and teaching interests include race, ethnicity and immigration, media studies, African diaspora studies; and digital storytelling." (L-R website)

Interviewer: Could we talk a little bit about what Civil Rights looked like in the summer of '64?

Dr. V. McComb: I think that '64 is such an interesting time in American history that a lot of people forget that while the Civil Rights Movement was occurring, this is also the same time as the Cold War. And I think there's an interesting dynamic that is related in a lot of ways. You have nationally a push toward spreading democracy throughout the world in the face of communism, and at the same time, have such tumultuous activity, while we're trying to make good on those democratic promises at home. And I think that's also why the Civil Rights Movement gained such momentum because you had this sort of national and international push for democracy with kind of this hypocrisy that was occurring on the home front.

I also think that '64 is an interesting time in terms of media. Right? So a lot of historians and a lot of literature will credit the rise of television with really making strides for improvements for African-Americans because a lot of the injustices that were occurring in the South were now very visible and very broadly cast, not just in newspapers and magazines, but also on television networks. And seeing young people being sprayed by firehoses or people burned and bombings and things of that sort. That is spread throughout the nation and really sort of tugs at the heartstrings of a lot of people, not realizing the actual visible violence that's occurring in some of these communities.

So I think '64 itself was a very tumultuous time. It was a time where you had a lot of unrest in terms of, how do we create a more free and equal and just society in all of these communities throughout the United States, particularly in the South. But you also had a period in which we're holding our breath in a lot of ways, both because of the Cold War. Are we going to go in an active war against Russia and the Soviet Union? Or are we going to break out into all out war because of the racial tensions that exist as we're trying to integrate a lot of communities in schools and businesses, et cetera, in the wake of Brown v. Board from the '54, '55 decision.

Interviewer: So where does that put '64 on the arc? Is it right there at the top? There's still a lot of things that haven't been decided by that point.

Dr. V. McComb: I think it's right there at the top because you have a series of legislative decisions that happened both in terms of the Voting Rights Act, the Civil Rights Act. The Hart–Celler Act was an immigration law act that all happened in rapid succession, '64 through '68. So I think it's right at the pinnacle at the time where real legislative change happens as a result of the decade prior, the decision from Brown v. Board.

Interviewer: On a local level, how much would a busy summer of racially charged events affect a community like Ridgeview?

Dr. V. McComb: I think that you had black communities taking very serious notice. It just depends upon the relationships they have with their white communities, how active and their reactions are. So many communities in which African-Americans may not have felt safe, their reactions may have been very private. Smaller conversations in their churches and their local community centers, et cetera. Other communities where they felt a little bit more empowered and maybe had a little more resources, they might have been marching. They may have been protesting. There may have been more outward displays of the kind of hurt and injustices that seem to be happening in these other areas. But local communities were certainly reacting. It's just how public those reactions were varied from community to community and were dependent on the relationship with white communities as well.

Interviewer: How would you characterize Ridgeview as a community?

Dr. V. McComb: I'm from Massachusetts. So I'm a transplant to Hickory. And what I found incredibly remarkable to learn about Ridgeview is just how vibrant and thriving of a community it was in '64 and it continued to be during the time of what we consider the sort of desegregation period. You had barbershops and theaters and schools and libraries and all of these things, a really tight-knit community that was really thriving economically, socially, et cetera. So to me, it's kind of a lost part of our national understanding of black communities at that time. I think the association with integration or desegregation, however you want to term it, is that all African-American communities during that time were somehow impoverished or struggling in some kind of way. And here you have Ridgeview that is just this kind of hotbed of amazing activity and accomplishments like the '64 team that are just really, really doing well overall.

Interviewer: What would the school represent to the community?

Dr. V. McComb: The African-American community, particularly considering the context in which folks were living at that time would have been a tremendous source of pride. I understand that the marching band was held in high regard. The cheerleaders were held in high regard. People really rallying around the high school itself. I mean, there was incredible educators at the school. I think that Ridgeview had something to be proud of and something that a lot of communities were kind of a little bit jealous of in a lot of ways because you did not see that in very many places in the United States, particularly in the South during that time.

Interviewer: What about the wider community of Hickory? What do you think the relationship would have been between the larger white community of Hickory and then Ridgeview within it?

Dr. V. McComb: What I find so remarkable about listening to the stories from some of the players from that '64 team is that they can walk from their communities that were on the other side of town to Ridgeview High School through white communities and actually receive accolades and praise and just encouragement from their white neighbors or white residents in ways that you don't really hear about in the historical record. That even though there was a separate but equal... I think it was something that was very real in the Hickory community and that when somebody deserves credit and deserves accolades, race didn't matter in that moment. People were really in awe of these players, of these people.

And I think that that is definitely unique and it's not something that you would see in very many places.

Interviewer: Does that make race relations in Hickory noteworthy?

Dr. V. McComb: I think according to the historical record, even what we've seen in publications, newspapers, et cetera, it would still be unique. I think it's because so much of these stories like the one that you're telling have been untold so far. We don't know exactly how unique this particular story actually is in terms of what is available in the historical record. It's incredibly unique for sure.

Interviewer: Is there anything else that should be noted about the Untouchables story?

Dr. V. McComb: I think that what I find kind of not so much heartbreaking, but you really wish that this was there. That you could actually have footage of these live moments in action because I think it would be really inspiring as a nation to see at that moment in time where we assume that there is so much distrust and violence and hatred and just disappointment in the nation that there's this real moment of triumph not just for the team, but for the surrounding community, black and white alike. I just really wish there were more visuals attached to that. But as we know, the nature of media at the time, this particular team, as much as it was getting press in the printed version, the video, because it was an African-American community, wasn't exactly high on the list of video footage coverage during that time. And admittedly in that time, it was very limited. So television stations and whatnot had to pick and choose which stories they were going to cover. And unfortunately, in terms of the video footage, we don't have that footage quite yet, but I hope it's out there. I really hope it's out there.

Interviewer: Coach Davis, and I think one of the players revealed this, had a philosophy that said you "kill a gnat with a sledgehammer."

Dr. V. McComb: I love that.

Interviewer: And my question is, did Coach Davis get that more from a competitive spirit? Or did you think he got it from growing up as an African-American man in the segregated South, even if we're talking about the upper south?

Dr. V. McComb: I very much believe that it is the latter. I think that when I read things like Isabel Wilkerson's *The Warmth of Other Suns* and the ways in which African-American children are raised, particularly if they're going to grow up and achieve anything, it's that old adage in the African-American community that you have to be twice as good to be half as well-respected. And I think the 'kill a gnat with a sledgehammer' is an extension of that. Right? You have to go above and beyond and go big in order to really get the job done and be noticed because to be subtle about it isn't going to cut it.

Interviewer: The players getting the recognition now so long delayed. Do you think that this story now has something to say about where we are currently as a society?

Dr. V. McComb: Absolutely. I mean, there's a whole line of historical scholarship that says a lot of what we produce in our present moment in terms of scholarship, a lot of what we're interested in has more to do with what's happening now than what happened then. And I think that now is the perfect time to tell the Ridgeview high story in terms of this team largely because as a nation, we're at a moment of just complete, I would say, crestfallen kind of ideas about the future of racial equality. And to know that there were such hope for racial equality and promoting African-American greatness honestly, even in '64, I think that gives a lot of people hope and that hope is much needed now.

Interviewer: Could you also comment on the fact of the educational credentials of Ridgeview? Because from what I've researched, it suggested that Ridgeview had a higher level of educational credentials for its high school staff than any school, black or white in the county. Does that speak to that same issue of you got to be twice as good?

Dr. V. McComb: I think it does in ways. I think in part, it speaks to the notion that you have highly credentialed people who quite frankly probably would struggle getting jobs in other school systems because of the race issue. But at the same time, that leaves a lot of really highly qualified folks who can enrich the local African-American community even further. And I think that that ethos, those highly trained folks that are passing on that ethos to their students of being twice as good, they just fueled generations upon generations of highly educated, highly talented people coming through the Ridgeview community.

Interviewer: On this campus at Lenoir-Rhyne, in 1964, African-American students weren't allowed and yet they play their championship game here. And it would be another three years, I think it is, before an African-American student is enrolled on this campus. Does the winning of the games, does the playing of the games here help to change that, do you think, in any way?

Dr. V. McComb: Absolutely. I think that there's real value in championships no matter what team you're on. And I think that for someone not to pick up on that and not to capitalize on that, it would be a poor business move on the part of the university. But I think that winning championships time after time after time has a lot to do with that.

Frank L. Sudderth

Mr. Sudderth played as a Ridgeview Panther ten years before the Untouchables. He was part of the group that established the tradition that the 1964 team built upon. He was interviewed in 2015 at the Brown-Penn Center (former Ridgeview High gymnasium).

Interviewer: Tell me about what it was like to play for Ridgeview High.

Frank L. Sudderth: We loved to play on the road because everybody had grass but us. Only thing we had was that red clay out there and little rocks that would stick in you and you had to wait 15 minutes for the dust to clear to spot the ball. So we loved to go to Charlotte, Morganton, even. Wilkesboro, Gastonia to play because everybody had grass.

We were very disciplined, not only on the field, but off the field. We were kind of mischievous, but we were all good guys, ex-Boy Scouts and things. We got a good education. We goofed off a lot. Being jocks, we goofed off a lot, but the ones that went to college that made it, they really made it because of the discipline.

One thing I like about the community, the church was the focal point of the community. You had to go to church and the coaches had it easy with us because like I said, we were disciplined from home. Be disciplined and pay attention, and that made us winners. We had that old Ridgeview spirit. We hated to lose though. We never did lose with grace. I don't believe in the good loser.

I appreciate being able to go to school here. I appreciate the community and being raised and born in Western North Carolina, because we had some good athletes come out of here and some good students. In proportion to what we had, the small group, we did pretty good. When I joined the Navy, like I said, I was already disciplined.

I was able to go around the world three times. One thing I learned at Ridgeview, be inquisitive, try to learn something from every place you go. I spent three months on the Island of Crete. That's where Apostle Paul was at for a while. I learned the language, a little bit of Greek. Sicily, I spent six months in Sicily, learned a little Italian. I spent six months in Spain, I spent time in Portugal. I went all through the Mediterranean and the Middle East.

In my last four years, I was in and out of Vietnam on the squadron on the USS America. Was able to go to Hong Kong, Japan, the Philippines, Singapore, and Australia and Rio de Janeiro. But you could tell the guys were from this area. We were nosy and inquisitive and tried to learn something.

I'm almost 80 years old now and I appreciate, like I say, I'm blessed to have come from this area and learn the games here. It made me a better person.

Down every two years for the reunion, the ones that are left. On the way down, my friend, my classmate, and my school mate and teammate's wife, she's from Texas. She's amazed at how we all stick together all of these years. We could still remember details about things. Like I say, I'm blessed to have been born and raised here.

Interviewer: Can you describe what Ridgeview was like in those days?

Frank Sudderth: Well, a lot of us didn't have new books. I remember I used to keep getting this girl's books from high school, a "Patsy Cline." The teacher would say "turn to chapter" so-and-so and so-and-so. I said, "Well, I don't have chapter so-and-so, it's missing." But it's no excuse for not learning.

You had to dress properly and they made you learn. It made it interesting, but they made you learn. I've never owned a bicycle, but because of here, I've owned four Mercedes Benz. Because of here, I dress decent. I didn't have a lot of things coming up, clothes, but we were clean.

I appreciate our teachers. They were interested in you learning. From Professor Broom down all the way down to the janitor. Because if the janitor saw you skipping school, he would make you go back onto the campus. It was just a well knit community. Like I said, we were at a disadvantage a lot of times, but I don't dwell on that. I dwell on this great city in this great community that I came from.

I remember sometimes I didn't have lunch money. I would go in the cafeteria and wash the pots and pans for the home ec(onomics) teacher to get a free lunch. We did that quite a bit. It was just a wonderful place to learn and it helped me with my values. I love nice things. I don't let it be my maker, but I like taking care of nice things. It all started right here on this hill right here, Ridgeview and in this community.

Interviewer: When you played, did you play for Coach Davis?

Frank Sudderth: I played for Coach Davis and Coach Brown, and Davis was a disciplinarian too. Brown was statistician. He kept count of everything. Everything that you did, he can tell you if you lost a yard or gained a yard. Davis, he was the man that he pushed. He pushed and pushed.

We had one guy that played in the National Football League, Ozzie Clay. He played after me. He went to Iowa State from here, and he did real well. He's passed on now, but he had a good business sense. He died a millionaire in the Washington, DC, area. I can go on and on and tell you about people that are success stories that played sports here.

My friend, Mr. Cade, he's retired Naval Air Force, like I am, and he's a retired chief petty officer. I remember one time I went by his squadron at Oceana Naval Air Station in Oceana. He was lecturing on indebtedness. I was very proud of him, the way he was lecturing, he had about 75 guys in this charge. He said, "Everybody here raise your hand that are in debt."

Everybody raised their hand but two guys. He said, "Why aren't you in debt?" He said, "I'm not in debt." Chief Cade said, "Well, you don't have anything then." How society dictates credit. I'm very proud of him. After he retired from the Navy, worked for the sheriff department, became the sheriff in Virginia Beach. He stayed there about 18 years and he retired.

Now when we go some place and people speed by, I said, "Why aren't you giving him a-" He said, "We're retired. We're not in a hurry." He's a wonderful guy. He got two wonderful boys and he's got a wonderful wife. She's a retired educator. She went to Old Dominion University. Then she was working on a doctorate there too. But we've been blessed.

Interviewer: Now did your friendship come from going here?

Frank Sudderth: From here, on up. On up. We've been together that long, right here.

We have Mr. Witherspoon, he's a retired educator here. My brother, he's still tried to work. He's an educator. So many here that have done well, considering the obstacles, but you don't look at the negative things. You look at the positive things because we got a wonderful country here.

Interviewer: Is that the secret to it? Is the attitude of people?

Frank Sudderth: Yeah. I can't think of anybody I played ball with that had a defeatist attitude. Jesse (Walker), very positive. If you noticed, she always talked about improving. Her family's the same way.

My grandmother, she came from Maggie Valley, up close to the reservation and you had to speak well. You couldn't mess with those verbs or do all this up yonder and all that stuff. You had to speak well, because she would correct you. She taught you voice. She played the piano and I can sing a little bit today. I wish I'd played an instrument and I've been better off today, but no, really. It's a well-rounded situation and everything. Like I said, I'm so happy because I'm back home.

Interviewer: What was going to school here like?

Frank Sudderth: It was happy times. But when that bell rang, you went down that hallway to your class and it was a serious time. You learned. I can go back to, I used to love Greek mythology. Zeus and all these people, and Athena, because it made it interesting. Mathematics was my worst subject, thanks to Jessie because she let me copy off of her. She would slide the paper over to me, but it was nice.

We have some brains come through here. I can think of the Carters, Jessie, Rosemary, Pat Chambers, Ralph Charles, and his brother. We've had some real marvelous students come through here. I wasn't one of them, but it was my fault. I was a jock, it was my fault.

Fannie Gaston Johansson. She married a Swede. She's the head person at John Hopkins in Baltimore, but started right here. She wrote a book on pain that's the best seller in the medical field and she'll be here. She told me she's coming.

She has a brother that's a multimillionaire that played ball with me. He lives in California. He said he's going to try and make it, started right here. In this place here, this ground that you stand on now, it's a lot of pride, like I told you. It's nothing to be ashamed of because look at the positive things, very positive things. I'm just as happy now. I'm speechless just being home, being in here.

Interviewer: Do you think the atmosphere of the school spilled over into the athletic programs? Or did it go the other way?

Frank Sudderth: I think it spilled over into the athletic programs. Everybody has played sports, but we had some happy people with the spirit and you played with that spirit. We were supported, a community, and our cheerleading section and our student body. It was great. It was really great.

Interviewer: What was it like to play in those games where you had all those people supporting you?

Frank Sudderth: You were so focused on doing well, I never could hear the band or the cheers. Only thing I could hear was the instructions coming from the bench and what the quarterback was saying. In basketball, trying to get the ball in the hoop or getting the ball down low.

I talked to other athletes. They're the same way, our mind was on the business at hand, but we had some great crowds and everything. But I couldn't tell you who cheered, I didn't hear that. I was focused. You had to be focused with Jap (Coach Davis) and Mr. Brown. The coach before that, I was one of the trainers and he's still living. He lives in Memphis, Mr. Johnson. He retired from Lamar and Orange University there in Memphis, and he was a great coach.

I learned a lot from him as a trainer about the system and the system is still here when Jap came, and Jap continued the system, Mr. Davis, Mr. Brown. We were just blessed to have these people. Mr. Fornay, Mr. Broom, Mr. Penn. Mr Penn, he didn't play in his science class of chemistry. When you went in there, you paid attention.

Miss Posting in the third grade, she was really serious about you learning. Miss Fuller in the seventh grade, I can remember all these people, and they would help you. They would really, really help you. Your parents, we had the type of parents that would take time out for you and focus on you. I'm blessed. I'm just blessed. Started right here, right here.

Interviewer: Anything else you want to say about being an alumni of Ridgeview High?

Frank Sudderth: It's the best high school in America. It's the best one in America. Now that it's no longer here, I guess Hickory is the best high school. Most of the guys that played at Hickory High School, we played with them out here in the community.

Like Bobby LeFevers. I'll never forget him. They lived right down the street. Used to be an old dump and his dad used to drive the tractor, putting all the trash at the side. He went on to play quarterback at

Hickory High School. What's the other ones down there? Was another family down there. Bowmath, I think they were in, and they played with us all the time. This was a nice close knit community. Very close.

I'll never forget Joe Buff, went over from Hickory High. He played in Lenoir–Rhyne. I think Joe Buff now lives in California. He played in Lenoir–Rhyne about 1954, 55. He was a good athlete along with, he played long with Jerry and Gene Robinson. These guys were good athletes over at Lenoir–Rhyne.

Stasavich, (head coach at Lenoir-Rhyne College; he led the team to the 1960 national championship) he'd come over here and give us equipment to use. He was instrumental in getting the first lights for this stadium. Statravich gave us his lights from over there. They got new lights. Some of our jerseys that we practice in were Lenoir–Rhyne's jerseys, and some of our helmets. So everybody chipped in, in the whole area, and we were successful.

Interviewer: So what was the era of segregation like?

Frank Sudderth: Well, one thing about Western Carolina, especially around here, the Shufords, KC Menzies, and the Geitners, they were the big money people and nobody messed with their coloreds. Really, they took care of us. The signs were up that you couldn't go here and go there, but I never did ride on the back of the bus.

My other grandmother lived in West Hickory. I used to ride in the bus with everybody else going up to West Hickory, nobody enforced it. I remember one time they built Sears Roebuck. My brother went to drink out of the white water fountain and some old dude said, "Boy, you shouldn't be drinking out of that. You drink out of the colored." My brother said, "I don't want no Kool-Aid today."

The little comical things, but they really didn't push you. They really didn't. I've talked to guys when I was in the Navy from other areas like even Charlotte and Rock Hill, South Carolina, Savannah, Georgia, different places. They couldn't even walk on the sidewalks with a white person. That wasn't the case here. You can walk anywhere you want to downtown.

At McClellan's five and dime, talking about their lunch counters, I always walked up to the lunch counter and got my stuff. It was no big thing in Hickory. The signs were up, but I didn't experience some of the things that other people experienced in further south, I didn't. Western

Carolina, we were so close knitted. I was always around, like down here on South Center Street, we had Caucasian neighbors down there. In East Hickory, we had neighbors down here.

I'm trying to think. I can't remember down here, down behind the ballpark, were white neighbors, we all played together. The laws didn't bring you together, but we did as the community came together. I don't knock America because, like I said, I've been around this world three times, this is the best place going for anybody.

We are the only country that's got to build a fence to keep people out, remember that. I hate to hear somebody knock us. I spent 20 years of my life in the Naval Air Force protecting our freedoms. I think Cade will tell you, we did a pretty good job. I got accommodations. It all started right here.

Interviewer: So Hickory was ahead of its time.

Frank Sudderth: To me, yeah. We didn't experience a lot of that. Like I said, good people, Caucasian people that were very devoted at keeping you with a decent living.

My father died when I was three. We never did go on welfare. My mother worked, my grandmother worked. She worked, my mother worked for Mr. Aiken, Paul Aiken, he's passed on now. My aunt worked for Miss Jane Lewis. These people looked out for you at Christmas time, birthdays. They remembered you. There was a closeness there, and these people were millionaires. They didn't have to look out for you, but they did.

James Kimball

Interviewed during the Ridgeview Reunion of 2019, James Kimball was a senior member of the Panthers football team that won the state championship in 1962, when the Untouchable seniors were sophomores.

James Kimball: My name is James Kimball, and I'm representing the football teams from 1959 through 1962. In 1959, the football teams were conference and district champions. In 1958, 1960, '61 and '62, we were conference district contenders of champions and state playoffs, went to the state playoffs. In 1962, we were the first team that won the state championship in 30-some years. We had great teams. During the course of games, we could hear the cheerleaders cheering, the band playing music and everything was mighty fine. But those young guys (the Untouchables), idolized the guys prior to them. Because they taught them something, especially about the love of school, have dignity with themselves and play ball. Many of those guys played on a championship team as freshmen and sophomores. Because they loved sports and they loved the team that they were playing with.

And they were just so fortunate to be part of two state champions, that being the football team in 1962, and of course, the football team in 1964. So many of them were in the choir with me, in the band. We had a small school and when we had a smaller school, in order to have a competitive football, basketball, and baseball teams, and band and choir, we shared different activities, such as football, basketball, baseball. It's fortunate that I was on the football team, a state champion football team. I was on the state playoff basketball team for three seasons. I was in marching band for five years, and I was in choir for four years. But Ridgeview High School was a great school and we honor them as much as we possibly can. And that class the Untouchables, need to be noted for what they have done.

Interviewer: Tell me about that '62 team. What was that like?

James Kimball: The '62 team was a great team. We had the classes up under us, we all were friends. Our junior year, we made a club called the ballers. And they were a group of athletes starting with football and basketball players. And during that time that we have a great respect and honor for each other, like a clan together. So we played football and basketball together. And we did social activities and stuff too. But there's guys that we played with who've played both ways, offense and defense, and we loved playing ball. It was known to me that we were having a class reunion. And a couple of guys said that they love Ridgeview, but they loved the football team best because of the kinship that we had with each other. Like I stated before, the basketball team was very tenacious, also.

The choir was the best choir in the state. We got the best marks in that. The marching band, as we marched down the downtown area down there, everybody was on the sidelines. Most of the white folks on Saturday night waiting for Ridgeview High School to come by to see the high stepping majorettes and the band members play.

But the team itself, we had some great guys prior to our time that need to be recognized also, that contributed to the whole spectrum of athlete athletics and academic areas there too. We had, of course, boys who played professional ball, Ozzie Clay, and a few others went through that team. A lot of them got football scholarships going different areas also. The team in 1962 had honor and love for the guys prior to them, because they taught them a lot. And it was a very disciplined team, both the upperclassmen disciplined you, plus the great coaches that we had. So you had to be on the money. And if you weren't on the money, then you're going to be ostracized in various ways.

And so you had to be focused at all times. And stay before the classes. The state championship Untouchables, they knew what they had to do to accomplish it. I'd like to recognize my classmates who were Leonard Clay who went to college and played football, Stuart Broom, who was the quarterback during that time. Everett Clarkson who was an end. Thomas Childs, who was a guard, and Richard Davis, who was a guard on the state championship team (1962). Donald Williams who played halfback and defense. And Donald Bumgarner, who was a center, and Clay Anthony, who was the center also. But we very much so enjoyed what we did and how we did it.

Interviewer 2: What was it like to go to Ridgeview High?
James Kimball: What was it like go to Ridgeview High? It was a challenge. My first year of going to high school, there was a group of guys in a stairwell. And would they recognize you and look at you and see how you would dress. "Look at Kimball, he got on a red socks. He must be bleeding at the ankles. Come up here, boy." And you didn't know what you were going to get into during that time. But after we knew each other, it was fine. And we enjoyed it, going to school and being with teachers who cared so very much for us. And like I stated before, if you didn't do well in school, in the classroom, your other classmates let you know. So they'd be one of your largest critics also. So you had to concentrate. And we had a great percentage of graduates who went to college. It's phenomenal. But that was the nature of the school itself, at least going to college, and to become a productive citizen in one way or another.

Jessie Walker

Interviewed during the Ridgeview Reunion of 2015, Ms. Walker was not only a student at Ridgeview, she came back after her college career to teach there. For many years she has been president of the Ridgeview Alumni Association where she has seen a rise in attendance at the reunions, held every other year at Labor Day.

Interviewer: Tell me about what those games (Ridgeview football) were like?

Jessie Walker: Now, I probably went to quite a few, but I'm pretty sure I went to the homecoming parade and the halftime activities. And they were spectacular. They had flowers for the Ridgeview High (homecoming queen and king), and then they had it for runners up. And then the band was very good. The band director at first was William Penn. And then one of the graduates from Ridgeview High School came back later. His name was Alfonzo Evans. We really called him Amos, but his official name was a Alfonzo Evans. So he took over the band at that time, but the activities were very good. On football night, just about everybody in Hickory turned out to see the games. The streets were deserted. Hickory wasn't very large anyway, so everybody went to all the games. That was it. That was the big event, football at the Ridgeview dirt field on Friday nights.

Interviewer: And can you describe what what that field was like?

Jessie Walker: They called it the dust bowl because it was just just dirt. I was there in '64 until '66. And I think they did get grass afterwards, but I'm not sure, but I know they used to... Mr. Davis and Roger Scales, they were the coaches of the team and they themselves would have to come out and run the markers, marking the lines. They had to do that. And so I'm thinking that they did have grass at that time, but for a long time, they didn't.

Interviewer: And you were teaching here?
Jessie Walker: I taught at Ridgeview from... I came in '63, '64, until they closed the school, I was here. They closed it in '66. That was the last year they had it.
Interviewer: And what did you teach?
Jessie Walker: I taught a history, and I also taught sociology.
Interviewer: What were they like, your students?
Jessie Walker: They were very quiet, but very good students. Very quiet, nothing like the students of today. They didn't talk. I could go out of the room, and when I came back in, everyone would still be in the care of Ridgeview cemeteries right over there.

Big rivalries (between schools). Everybody was equal as a rival, but Morganton and Newton, especially, Lenoir, everybody hated Hickory. Everybody hated Ridgeview High School. Those were the good days.
Interviewer: How'd you feel when they shut down Ridgeview?
Jessie Walker: Very bad because I was the teacher. They took me over to Grandview. That's where they transferred me to, from the high school to the middle school. And I could teach middle school, but I was a high school teacher. So it was very, very sad when they shut the schools down. Very sad.
Interviewer: From what you were able to see, how did the students react to that? Was it a good thing or a bad thing?
Jessie Walker: No, it was a bad thing because when they went over there, they were treated differently. It was supposed to be integration, but they sent all the blacks together and then they had the whites together, and it was absolutely different. And of course I was a teacher; I taught at Grandview Middle School. There was a certain amount of hostility seen by the teachers, not the students so much that I taught, but the teachers because they really liked me. But in that time, we could paddle. They instituted a law that said if we paddled a student, we had to have another teacher out there to see us paddle a student. So it was a certain amount of hostility among the teachers. I really got along pretty good with the students, black and white, but you could see a difference. There was a difference.
Interviewer: Anything else you'd like to say about Ridgeview High or the team from '64?
Jessie Walker: At Ridgeview High School, I went to Ridgeview High

School, I played basketball at Ridgeview High School. I was on the track team at Ridgeview High School. I was a cheerleader at one time. I was also in the band. So Ridgeview High School to me was everything. This is why now that I am the president, I've been the president of the Ridgeview Alumni Association since I think 1999, and this is why I continue to try to be the president, try to keep the legacy of Ridgeview High School alive, because to me, Ridgeview High School was some of the best days of my life. And so this is why we keep it going. This is why we have so many people that come back every two years to celebrate the legacy of Ridgeview High. And now I have found out that there are kids who were in the class of '80, '85, but they were little kids, down in the grades.

But because we keep talking about the legacy of Ridgeview High, we have had more and more coming back to celebrate Ridgeview High every two years. This year we have 200 people. That's the biggest number we've ever had. We usually have 100, 20 to 50, and stuff like that. But now it's up to 200. And I think one reason is because they have learned about the legacy of Ridgeview High. Their parents have told them about the things of Ridgeview High, we have told them about Ridgeview High. And so consequently, we get more people coming back. Ridgeview High was a great school to me. We didn't have many books or anything like that. We had one moving projector and that was it. But we still managed to do well. They still managed to do well. So that's what Ridgeview High means to me.

Interviewer: Because you were still more or less in the era of separate but equal until '66, '67, do you think that that hurt the spirit of the school, only having one projector?

Jessie Walker: No, it really didn't. Even when they got the books, we knew they were secondhand because they had the names of the kids in there, you know how you have to put your names in the textbook. And even at that, they had to wrap the books because they had to pay a damage fee if the books were damaged in any way. So it was bad, but even in spite of all of that, the kids didn't care. I guess maybe they foresaw what was going to happen, because basically they were pushed to the back, and whites were pushed to the front. So we didn't want it. We wanted separate but equal, equal pay, equal jobs, equal everything. But if we could've stayed separate, we would have been happy.

Interviewer: Why did you come back here to teach?

Jessie Walker: Actually, I taught here five years. After that, I moved to Florida and I've been in Florida ever since.

Interviewer: But why did you want to come back to Ridgeview and teach?

Jessie Walker: Why did I want to come back to Ridgeview? Well, this is what happened. well actually, Mr. Broom, who was the principal, played a very significant part in that. And also, I went to all girls school, and after I left Bennett, I taught in High Point, North Carolina, for six months. And then when I came home for the summer, because I had never been to the Eastern part of the state, so I wanted to see the Eastern part of the state. But Mr. Broom came to my house, talked with me, sat down with me and convinced me to come to Ridgeview. (He) said that Ridgeview needed good teachers, and I'm from Hickory, and I went to Ridgeview and I could make a difference. So that's how I got back to Ridgeview. And I never regretted it. Hate it that it closed.

John Thompson

As a sophomore, John Thompson played on the Untouchables team. He went on to play at Hickory High, when the schools integrated in 1966. From there, Mr. Thompson played college football at the University of Minnesota and for a time with the NFL's Houston Oilers. The interview was conducted in 2015 during the Ridgeview Reunion.

J. Thompson: Thinking back on it, rather than when it was occurring, I'm in awe as what we accomplished, that today is being recognized and the magnitude at which it is. Not only for the community, how it's applicable, but more so for those students who played and went to Ridgeview at the time. To see what a difference it made, not only those who came before us and what we pretty much, trailing in their footsteps, climbing on those shoulders, but to see what we were able to accomplish in that process.

At the time, it was a football game to me. I was out playing ball. What I was taught, trained to do by the coaches and pushed on by my brothers and uncles who played before me. It was like a legacy type of thing. The torch was passed on. Each game was special. Each game was another challenge. Each game was another victory. And as they progressed in victories, to realize that we were still winning and nobody was scoring on us, which pretty much happened the previous years. There was only a few times that teams had scored on us or the teams that preceded us. So it wasn't unusual to me.

Interviewer: Because you played both for Hickory and Ridgeview, you were there for the end of Ridgeview High and the integration of Hickory. What was that like?

J. Thompson: Honestly scary. It wasn't welcomed. You were leaving behind when you, as a high school student, always waited for that moment where you became the senior. You were the top, cliched top dog of your high school. All the underclassmen looked up to you and what you did and you tease them, harass them pretty much jokingly, nothing seriously. That was removed. Now you moved on to an area where you didn't know anyone other than those who went with you. And some, a few went before us, who went over the year before.

But once we got there, we were welcomed by the coaching staff, the instructors. Many of the students, some of the students not as much, that eventually warmed up. And I think that came about because of the winning of the season, the football season. It became more of a camaraderie now. More of a celebration, celebratory type of process. But there were times when you were ready to pack up your bags and go back home. It got that hairy at times. There were more good times than bad times in my experience. But I wouldn't trade it because it was another step in our development, our challenge, our education, future. And then for those behind us to proceed and follow.

When we played at Hickory High, to my knowledge best I can recollect now. I think it was like 10 years since they'd won a championship. We together were able to accomplish that. We won a championship. The recognition for the school was very significant. It brought more eyes to it and its programs, to its coaching staff, the players. I feel that in the legacy of what we had from Ridgeview to bring that forward, I eventually gelled really nicely.

There was some shortcomings to it that, I felt. I like to dwell more on the positive than the negative, but I must speak of when I felt the negative. Our coaching staff didn't get a fair shake there, which in my opinion should have transitioned to some degree. That did not occur. Coaches, staff, the head, they did do a good job. Very good. I felt that we didn't have that crutch to fall back on. The students from Ridgeview, with the coaching staff we had grown up with, but we were able to circumvent that and everything was fine. Yeah.

Interviewer: When you were at Ridgeview, can you describe what the games were like?

J. Thompson: Very exciting. When I was on the field, I didn't see anybody else other than the players on the team. I didn't see the crowds. We never really heard the bands because when they're playing or even out on their, during their marching, I was zoned in on the game, per se. Until you were on the sidelines, somebody's slapping you in the back of the shoulder, which was a neighbor person in the community saying, "Great job, way to go, keep going, guys. You're doing a great job out on the field." A lot of camaraderie as far as community support. And it's generational. It was the families before us who had children who played. Then we were playing, now our children who played in another setting since then. But it was just a carry over and carry on, very warm, cuddly feeling.

Interviewer: What position were you playing?

J. Thompson: I played offensive tackle and defensive tackle.

Interviewer: So you played both sides?

J. Thompson: Both sides. Yeah, pretty much every play, everyone played both ways.

Interviewer: That's got to be a long 60 minutes.

J. Thompson: It's long, but as was mentioned earlier, we were conditioned. Really conditioned to endure a game. We'd run about the five miles every morning, getting the training, the regimen through and through. And I personally think it was superior to what we did as I went on to college. What we did, there was nothing like what we did in high school. High school superseded anything we did as far as physical training in college. I was fortunate enough to get drafted. I didn't play as long as I would have hoped to, but even the conditions there professionally with Houston Oilers was nothing like what we had in high school. High school would have made those guys like girls out there on the field, practicing. It was that condition that we endured the games as we did and did as well, I think, as we did. The mental and physical.

Interviewer: So do you think that's one of the keys to why you guys were so successful?

J. Thompson: I think so. Yeah. We were very conditioned and well coached to endure a game. Because you playing literally both sides of the ball. There wasn't literally time off to you go back and rest. The defense goes on and you go back and rest the offense. You just changed positions as the whistle blew. Yes.

J. Thompson: You were in a rather unique position. Since you played both for Ridgeview and Hickory. Was integration of schools a good thing? What's your opinion?

Interviewer: I think it was a good thing. But again, being selfish as a potential senior now, to have removed that mentality, I am now the 'King of the Hill' at my high school. And now go to another where you now are not in such a position. That was a little takeaway for me, but we overcame that. Everyone blended in together. We had a great time. I share a couple of moments with you that I thought was really special in my life.

One of the coaches, I was really fond of math, and we had an algebra class, which he was the instructor. He let me teach his class a couple of times. I had a French instructor who thought I was goofing up a little bit more in school than I should have been. She took me down to the principal's office to have a conversation that I was wasting my energy and time. If I wanted to go further in my future, these are the things I needed to do and accomplish that. And those two things kind of really set me on the continued path of going forward. And I still treasure those moments.

Interviewer: Because those were the instructors that really cared.

J. Thompson: They did care. They did care. Yes. Yes.

Interviewer: Can you talk a little bit about your career after?

J. Thompson: Well, I was fortunate enough. Now you tend to see you have someone really close to you in school, as we all were. His name was Anthony Parks. He and I grew up and of course my cousin, Doug. We were like brothers. And if any of us had an opportunity to go to a college, Anthony and I, at the time we got offers to other different colleges in the area. But none of them were offering full scholarships or partial scholarships. So we visit Lenoir-Rhyne. We visited Appalachian. We started to get offers. And then all of a sudden my offers were starting to branch separately, that I got offered to Duke, but the coach was recruiting me from their department. And I didn't know what had happened when he ended up in Minnesota whereby he continued to process at that point of trying to get me there.

I signed with Cincinnati University, but I didn't like the water. The water was bad. Because of it, I didn't want to go there. So he allowed me to break that agreement. And I signed with the University of Minnesota, is how I ended up there. After about the first winter. It's darn cold up there and still is. I cried. I was coming back to North Carolina and a few guys were on the team there. Well-names who've played professional since then, Kevin Boss, Mat Darren, recently deceased Charlie Sanders with Detroit Lions. They were from North Carolina and they convinced me that it will get warmer. They didn't say it would take six months, but it did get warmer. And I stayed, but it was a great transition. I loved it. Love it. Yeah.

Interviewer: And then after college?

J. Thompson: While in college it was said that only maybe three of us would get drafted. It was very expected that I was, I was drafted by the Houston Oilers 12th round. And to my surprise, and there were six of us that got drafted and went on to explore that opportunity, went down for training camp and whatnot. And as I said, their regimen was nothing compared to what we experienced at Ridgeview. And it was just a smooth transition. But I didn't make it, which was fine. And after I left there, my agent tried to get me to go to a couple of different teams, but I couldn't within the continental US because of my contract. So then he tried to get me on with Canada, and some of the world league teams that were playing back then at the time. But at that point, I don't want to play anymore. Anyway. I lost the love, I guess, at that point for the sport.

Interviewer: Playing for Ridgeview, and for Hickory, but mainly playing for Ridgeview. What was special about that?

J. Thompson: It was wearing those colors. That orange and blue is beautiful. And when you were a kid to be able to wear that at home and wear it to a game, and then you had your jersey, you walk through your community back. I used to lived on the other side of town, which is called East Hickory. So you had about, I don't know, I always joke with my grandkids and tell them it was like a 10 mile walk. I honestly don't know how far that was, but it was long. But to wear that through your neighborhoods, that jersey was really special. And you were proud of that, that you wore the orange and blue. And it was just something to behold. Never ended up with one, wish I did, but no, that was very special.

Interviewer: Okay. Is there anything else you wish to say about the experience?

J. Thompson: I would say this weekend (that year's reunion weekend) is evidence of what the community is about, what those teams are about, what the people are about. The camaraderie, the getting together, the support still, the reminiscing back on. And you see the little kids who are also here seeing people they've heard of, maybe. Their parents talk about it, their grandparents, talking about. To them, those living legends here, to see that and experience that. I thought that was really a great combination, great combination to the community. So that being said, that's it.

Larry Williams

As a junior in 1964, Larry Williams was a part of the Untouchables team. Raised in Little Berlin, a neighborhood adjacent to East Hickory, he grew up playing football and was told that one day he would be a Ridgeview Panther. A strong supporter of the Untouchables project, Mr. Williams gave his time and input as part of the public art committee that established the Ridgeview Arch. His interview was held at CVCC in 2018.

Interviewer: How did you start your football career at Ridgeview?

L. Williams: There was a guy on the team. I used to wash his uniform and take care of his equipment. And I went to practice with him one day and one of the more famous guys at the school named Leonard Clay, he looked at me and he said, "You going to play football?" And I said, "Yeah," and he said, "If you don't, we going to beat the daylights out of you every day you come to school." That's what they tell you, and so I said, "Yeah, I'm going to play." And so in the ninth grade year, I had a leg injury and Coach Davis called me in, and there was another guy coming back that was already on the team, had made the team the previous year, Coach Davis gave me a playbook and he said, "I want you to learn every play in this book, every position in this book, and come back next year," and that's what I did.

Interviewer: Do you remember how you physically prepared for that year?

L. Williams: Coach Davis used to take us over to Bakers Mountain and he would put us out and we had to run I think it was five miles and he came back out the 127 and, if you wasn't there when the group came back, you got left.

Interviewer: How long did he give you to run five miles?

L. Williams: All of us had to come back in basically together. I don't remember how long we had, but we basically come back in as a group. We never left anybody over there, but we all got back in time.

Interviewer: Nobody ever got left?

L. Williams: No.

Interviewer: Tell us about practice.

L. Williams: The seniors always told us that, "We going to be gone next year and you better be ready," and they played like that and you got roughed up, beat up, and everything else, but the thing was, when you get to the top, you get to beat the other guys coming up. That's what we did.

Interviewer: They were as rough on you as they were on opponents.

L. Williams: Yes. One incident: I was playing in front of a senior named Nelson Brockenborough, a real heavy guy, and he hit me in the jaw, and I just stood there. My jaw was froze. I couldn't talk, and, for about five minutes, I couldn't even move my jaw, he hit me so hard, and that's what we did. That's the way we played.

Interviewer: Did you get in fights for all this or did everybody get along, it was just part of the deal?

L. Williams: It was just part of the deal. You didn't want to get in a fight with nobody, especially the older guys. You didn't want to do that, and we didn't have much fighting on the team.

Interviewer: Okay. Did most of the seniors play both ways or did you end up having a separate defense and offense?

L. Williams: Some of them played two ways and some of them didn't. Actually, the center of the team, which I was a center too, the center only played offense, and I played offense. I played wherever I could get in the game until my senior year. The people wanted to get in the game so bad you didn't care where they put you as long as you got in.

Interviewer: But I guess Coach Davis had you memorizing the playbook because he wanted you to play center and you're starting every play as center?

L. Williams: No, no. When he gave me the playbook, he told me to learn every play, every position, where every man's supposed to be on every play. And how I got to be center is, one day, the center didn't show up and Coach Davis says, "Anybody know how to snap the ball?" and I said, "I do," and that's how I got into being a center.

Interviewer: How tall were you and how much did you weigh?

L. Williams: My senior year, I was six foot and I weighed about 165.

Interviewer: That's pretty small for a center. Were you taking on nose guards and tackles that were about the same weight and height?

L. Williams: No, we very seldom had a nose guard.

Interviewer: You had another linebacker?

L. Willaims: Yeah, they would come in the hole, but they had to stay back and protect what was behind them. If the linebacker came up in the hole, the quarterback just threw the ball behind him and that gets him out of the hole. Now the only way I had somebody over me if they went to a five-man line, so I had a guy right on top of me.

Interviewer 2: How would Coach Davis motivate you?

L. Williams: He gave us a speech every year, but it was unnecessary because we wanted to play football and it was a tradition and it was a family thing too. If you didn't play football at Ridgeview, you wasn't nothing. That's the way it was.

Interviewer: Can you say more about that? What do you mean that you were nothing if you didn't play? There are a lot of guys that weren't playing.

L. Williams: Yeah. See, the guys that played football, we were respected all through the community and the school and everything, and all the girls wanted the football players and stuff like that. If you wasn't playing football or basketball, you wasn't important.

Interviewer: Do you think it had anything to do with discrimination and segregation?

L. Williams: Well, one year, Coach Barger at Hickory High was supposed to have brought his team over to scrimmage Ridgeview, and Barger pulled up at the gate and went to unload his guys and he looked out there on the field and our team was out there fighting each other, so he loaded his guys back up and took them back to Hickory High. We never had a scrimmage with them. Some kind of fight happened on the field before the coach got there and they was fighting. I don't remember what happened, but they would never let us play Hickory High, never.

Interviewer: There were pick-up games you played in East Hickory before you joined the team. When you guys played pick-up games, did East Hickory play Ridgeview or did you just choose up? How did that work?

L. Williams: We just played the guys in East Hickory and what was there, the older guys, when I was 12 years old before I started playing for Ridgeview, I was playing football with guys that was 35 and 40 years old. They would have a game going on and they would come out and all of us young guys would be sitting there and so they would pick a guy to get on their team and you had to be able to play real good to get picked. You wanted to get picked, so you played at your top game, and sometimes you'd get run over by a guy that's ... I'd get run over by a guy that's 40 years old.

Interviewer: Did that toughen you up?

L. Williams: Oh, that's what it was all about. They said, "You guys is going to be playing for Ridgeview and we want you ready," and that's what they did. Ridgeview did the same thing. The people that lived around the school in East Hickory was the same thing, it was a pride thing that, if you was a large guy, you better play football or you're going to have trouble.

Interviewer: When it comes to the season, you was talking about the equipment and that sort of stuff, what were your pads like?

L. Williams: Probably like two slices of bread. It wasn't much of nothing. The equipment was old. I got a plastic helmet cracked off of my head. And there was a guy in Hickory, I'm thinking he was connected with sporting goods, I'm not sure, but that guy, he made sure that we had whatever we needed. And I remember what would happen after a game, after a Friday night game, Coach would go up on the square in Hickory and, this guy, he would come by and ask Coach, said, "You need anything?" And the Coach'd say, "Well, we need a couple helmets and this," and this is on a Saturday morning. Monday morning, it was there at the school. The school board didn't do nothing for us, nothing.

Interviewer: Did people around town know that you played football, in the white community?

L. Williams: Yes. There was a group of football players that they would come and watch us play at Ridgeview when they didn't have a game and we would go watch those guys play. We knew each other. They just wouldn't let us play each other.

Interviewer: Ever play them on a pick-up game or anything like that?

L. Williams: No. No.

Interviewer: They kept you apart.

L. Williams: Yes.

Interviewer: Okay. Did you have a part-time job or anything when you were in high school?

L. Williams: Yeah, the cornfield. We had a little farm, a little farm thing going on. I had a part-time job at the Inntowner Hotel in Hickory, right there where Flowers Auto Parts and all that is, right across the street. I worked there for a little bit when I was in high school. Didn't work very much.

Interviewer: Where was the farm?

L. Williams: It was in East Hickory. We used to sharecrop with a man named Mr. Winfield and he was right there as you come where all those restaurants down there on Lenoir-Rhyne Boulevard, That used to be a huge farm. We used to sharecrop with him. He had a huge farm and all his children had moved out and gone and we had five boys in the family and my father, so we went down there and worked the land with him and shared the take.

Interviewer: When you started the season, what kind of coach was Coach Scales?

L. Williams: Coach Scales was a real smart coach and he did a lot of strategizing and stuff and, probably, I would say that, without Coach Scales, we wouldn't have been as good as we were. That's just the way it was.

Interviewer: What about Coach Davis? What was your impression of him?

L. Williams: Coach Davis was a good coach, but head coaches don't have to do much when you got good people behind you. They stand out front and get all the glory from having good guys around them. And Mr. Brown, Mr. Brown, he was there for a while. Well, we had good coaches. Yeah.

Interviewer: And it sounds like you had older players bringing you along.

L. Williams: Definitely. Yeah. Yeah, definitely. You go to Ridgeview and a guy come out there and tell you, "You going to play football," you better be playing some football or you're going to have to run home every day.

Interviewer: You think they were rougher on you to toughen you up?

L. Williams: Yeah, I'm glad they were because, what they did to me, I did it to somebody else. It was my turn. That's the way Ridgeview went.

They'd look at you and, if they think you suitable to play football, they tell you that you're going to play football and, if you don't, you're going to have all kind of problems. But everybody wanted to play.

Interviewer: How did it feel going into those games, because you guys were so dominant that you probably scared the life out of some of these other teams, don't you think?

L. Williams: Yeah. There's one team, every time we'd play them, we'd beat them 40 to nothing and they'd invite Ridgeview guys to come to their school reunion each year. I don't see why. We beat the death out of them, but they invite a bunch of us down. I haven't went yet, but they invite a lot of guys to come down from my class that played football and the only thing we talk about is how we beat them, and I never understood why they want to hear that.

Interviewer: What school is this?

L. Williams: Lawndale.

Interviewer: And North Shelby?

L. Williams: Yes. We played Shelby too. We played Newton. Newton was our biggest competition. At the end of the year, whoever won that game went on into the finals.

Interviewer: Because that '64 year, they were undefeated too, but people had scored on them, not like y'all. What was that game like?

L. Williams: It was fun because, at that time, Coach Brown had went to Newton to coach, head coach down there, and the football game, it was so rough that half the first string was thrown out of the game and so I went in to play center and, while I was in the game, another fight broke out. And I was standing behind one of the other players back to back and we were fighting like crazy. One game, we played Morganton.

Interviewer: Can you tell the whole story from the beginning and how that happened?

L. Williams: Morganton? Oh, that was a rough game. Let me see. I had a friend played on the Morganton team and he got his leg broke and, when that happened, it went crazy and, after that, just like every other play, there was a fight on the field and they was throwing people out left and right. And so what they did, the police came and they stopped the game and they escorted us back to the school and told us to get out of town and the score was about 32 to nothing and the game stopped in the third quarter. They told us to get out of town.

And they backed the bus up and they had two police officers standing on the side and they marched us through there onto the bus and then we had a police escort back to the school to get dressed. And we dressed at the school and came over to the field, it was a different field, and they would not let us change our uniform. They said, "Go and get your clothes and get out." We rode all the way back to Hickory in our uniforms and changed after we got back home. 32 to nothing and the game was in to about five minutes into the third quarter and they stopped the game, told everybody to go home.

Interviewer: When did y'all know that y'all were dominant? Did you know from the first game or did it creep up on you?

L. Williams: Well, actually, we always knew that. We played the game with that mindset that we was better than anybody else and, even when we lost, we still thought that, and that's a good way to have it. You think you're the best and you play like the best and the competition between us guys made us all good. I wanted to play just as much as the other guy did, but they had so much talent, you had to wait your turn.

Interviewer: And in terms of these games, I take it you've got two battles going on. Number one, you're fighting for a position on the team, like a starter, and then you got the other team. Which is tougher?

L. Williams: Well, there's actually three. The first one is to get in practice at the game. When we was practicing, first thing you want to do was get in the practice because sometimes that was even hard. But getting on up to the game, the competition just made everybody strong. When you got up there, your turn, you know you was going to be starting and you had to play at that level and keep it because somebody might bump you off.

Interviewer: It was pretty brutal on the line then, right?

L. Williams: Yes, it was always brutal. After I got out of high school, they started doing it, it was a block called a crab crawl, and we standing like this and the defensive man would come in and he would cut my leg here and then another guy would come in from this side and hit me and, most of the time, if you got it right, you'll break somebody's leg.

Interviewer: Chop block, it's what they call a chop block now, right?

L. Williams: I think it was the same, but we called it a crab crawl, but they made that thing illegal because, if they get you right, you'll break your leg.

Interviewer: What's the trash-talking like on the line?

L. Williams: A lot of it, a lot of it. I did some trash-talking one time. What a lot of the schools did my senior year, it was so tough ... Newton started this. We got in a game with Newton and our coaches had us prepare for everything and we got in a game with Newton and, all of a sudden, Newton sent a flanker out. We had never played a team where a guy went in motion out of the backfield and we had never seen that, but we was ready for it. And, all of a sudden, this guy goes in motion and the cornerback has to go in motion with the guy and there's nobody on the corner. They didn't think we was going to catch it.

When they did that, I was the middle linebacker, this one guy named Aggie, I run up into the line, I told him, I said, "Back out and play linebacker," and I shot down on the corner, and then that other guy took the guy down the field and they isolated me one on one with a guy that's my cousin that played for Newton, and I wore him out. He juked and faked and all that stuff, and Coach Davis taught us that, when a guy's shaking and baking, you look at his belt buckle and keep your eyes on that because that's where the body going to go. And he's shaking and baking, I hit him in such a way I picked him up and slammed him down headfirst to the ground and I said, "Hey, Mr. Brown, how you doing?" because we're right there in front of their bench.

Interviewer: That's pretty quick thinking to pull a lineman back to backer and then you take the corner there.

L. Williams: Well, that was something that just happened. When you in the game, you know what you were supposed to do. And we had never seen that. That was the first team that ever did that on us and it forced us to go to a five-man line and everything that anybody ever threw at us, we adapted to it. We knew what to do, good coaching.

Interviewer: What does trash-talking in 1964 sound like?

L. Williams: Well, what I used to do, I'd go up in the hole and I'd tell the guy I was with his mama last night. And do you know what happened? I did that and was way back in the secondary, when that ball was snapped, he forgot about the game, he came straight to me, he came straight to me and tried to throw a cross-body block on me, and they taught us how to deal with that. When he tried to throw a cross-body block on me, I caught him and then dropped him.

And then, on the second play, he came back again and he threw another cross-body block at me, but I let him come up to my knees just before he hit me and, when I went down, I took my knee and jabbed it between the shoulder and the helmet. And the referee was standing behind me, I got a 15-yard penalty at the wrong time of the game. But that guy, he put his mind on me and forgot about what he was supposed to been doing, I had him so upset. I didn't even know his mama, I didn't even know him, but it worked.

Interviewer: Now I understand when you guys came on the field, you had this chant that you did, "Let's go down and get this thing over with." Where did that come from?

L. Williams: I don't know. All I know, when I got there, that was always the fight song, "Let's go down and get it over with," says [singing]. That's what we used to sing.

Interviewer: And you know that had to hit a nerve.

L. Williams: Well, when we played at home, we came out of the gym all the way down to the field singing that song til we got on the field, and that was the song. That's what they'd be hearing. And when we went out and played other teams, they heard it there too.

Interviewer: When did it dawn on you guys that, "Nobody's going to score on us the whole season?" How far in the season are you before you start thinking, "We could do this?"

L. Williams: I never thought about it. I was too busy trying to get in the line-up. It had never occurred to me. I never thought about it, and it happened, but I never even thought about it. I don't know if anybody else was thinking about it. The coaches probably was, but I guess, a lot of the guys, we were just playing ball like we normally do. We weren't thinking about that, let the coaches worry about all that stuff.

Interviewer: When you came back for the '65 season, was it different?

L. Williams: What, my senior year?

Interviewer: Yes.

L. Williams: Yeah, because all the guys, all the Untouchables, the senior guys from that team was gone, and, see, we were juniors on that team and now we're seniors and so we wanted to be like all the rest of the teams and make our mark, and so that was on my mind and the guys' too. And so we was trying to keep the tradition going.

Interviewer: Do you remember the Shelby game, where it got rained out and they postponed it, and then y'all played them the last game of the season?

L. Williams: Yeah, I remember one game did. Yeah, I remember that game. But we beat them so bad they should've stayed on home.

Interviewer: How does it feel in the fourth quarter when they're tired, you guys are still in good shape, and you know you got it and they ain't even going to score?

L. Williams: Well, for one thing about it, you'll go back to the times that Coach Davis and the coaching staff had us over in Mountain View running up all those hills out there and the conditioning. We stayed in good condition, and so we'd actually wear the other teams down and then, when the first-stringers come out and the second-stringers, they fighting to get in all the way down to the third string. Everybody wanted to play and so you had to play hard to get into all that line-up. It made us better.

Interviewer: Was there ever a concern that the second string or third string might let somebody score late in the game?

L. Williams: I don't think so because we were so far ahead.

Interviewer: Y'all averaged winning by 37 points [crosstalk].

L. Williams: We didn't worry about that. We just played football.

Interviewer: And so would you guys just keep scoring all the way to the end? Y'all never called off the dogs.

L. Williams: No mercy. It was no mercy because, if you was on the third string and you got your chance to get in there, you want to impress the coach, so everybody from the top to the bottom, it was always competition.

Interviewer: And was the second string able to score?

L. Williams: Yeah. We go all the way down to the third string because they got in there behind the big line and they were scoring too, everybody. You got your chance to score, you was going to score and our thing was to get you in the end zone and that's what we did, everybody. There were some third-stringers scored a lot of times.

Interviewer: How complicated was the playbook? Do you remember how many plays there were? We've heard about Coach Scales being an offensive genius, where he had all these different schemes and formations and plays. Can you give us an idea of what that was like?

L. Williams: The most famous one was the Faggart play. What they would do, you would go back into the huddle and everybody would break the huddle at the same time, but on this play, the guard, the center, everybody would start out and they would holler check, which means you're going to call another play, so everybody would go back to the huddle. And so the center and the guard, it was three people went to the line of scrimmage and everybody else went back to the huddle.

When they saw everybody going back to the huddle, the defense would stand there and start talking. It was the center, a guard, and one halfback stayed out, we didn't go back to the huddle, and so the defense would start talking to each other. They'd think we're still in the huddle, and the center would snap the ball to the halfback, then everybody would turn around and the team didn't even see you going and, by the time they look around, we strutting down the sideline. Every time we called the play, it was always a touchdown, sometime it was 30, 40 yards because we caught them off guard. But you could only play that once in the conference and you could only do it about three times a year because people catch on to it.

Interviewer: Were you more of a running team or you wore people down and you burned up the clock or was it you were more of a passing offense?

L. Williams: I think we were more of a running team. We'd run you to death. I think the quarterback, Allen Pope, he threw, I think it was two touchdowns and ran for three, and Doug Bumgarner, had, I think Doug had something like 20-some touchdowns. And so we did a lot of running. We'd wear you down because all that running out there in Bakers Mountain that Coach Davis made us do that and Coach Scales, and we was all in good shape and everybody wanted to play.

Interviewer: Let me ask you about something different here. Okay, so '64, people are talking about the civil rights movement, they're talking about segregation, desegregation, all that stuff, and I don't know how aware y'all were of all that stuff in the background because in '65, if I remember correctly, you got some Ridgeview students going over to Hickory High, there, and then you've got full integration starting with the '66 season? How did it affect your spirit about the place?

L. Williams: It was a sad thing, but what happened, there was a group of Hickory High football players came over to Ridgeview and they was trying to get us to leave Ridgeview. I could've went to Hickory High and graduated over there as a senior. And a guy named Fletcher Eckerd, he went over. I think he might've been a sophomore, he was the first Black to play football at Hickory High, Fletcher Eckerd. And then there was six girls out of our class, they left and went to Hickory High, and they talked to me about coming over there and I told them no.

And the reason, because there was a guy named Bill Bovender, he played center for Hickory High. We was real good friends, and Bovender was third string because Barger had his two sons in front of him. Bovender was a better player, and so I was talking to the principal at Hickory High, Miss Ann Stalnaker, and she asked me how come I didn't come over there and I told her. She said, "Well, if the coach had his two sons playing center and Bovender was playing, that would've made you a fourth string." I said, "Yeah, that's the reason I didn't go." And that's how that went down. They wanted us to come over and then, the following year, it was total integration and so everybody had to go.

Interviewer: When we hear about segregation, we think about white people here and black people over here and they're kept separate, but we have heard so much about white and black people interacting. What were relationships like between white and black people during this period?

L. Williams: Well, the football players was different. Some of the stars at Hickory High, we'd never get to talk to them. But the only thing we wanted is to have the same books and stuff that they did. We didn't want to play football with them. We didn't care. We didn't care one way or the other. We just wanted the same opportunity and be treated the same way and that's what happened.

Interviewer: Did you ever have any negative experiences being around white people during that period, even growing up or attending Ridgeview? I just want to get a sense of the tone and the atmosphere.

L. Williams: Right there where Tate Boulevard, when you get into where the neighborhood is there and you go on down that hill, the old school's just sitting down there, well, I used to live over there and that place was called Berlin, Little Berlin, they called it. That's what the police called it. It was called Berlin, and, over there, it was black and white and it was in the county. If you would come over there to see somebody, if it was a white man standing in the middle of the road or a black man and they asked you who you going to see, you better have a name or you better run.

You couldn't come over there and visit unless you knew somebody. If you have a name, fine, you'll get in, but if you don't, you better run. Black and white, we protected each other. If you did not live in that neighborhood, black or white, you'd better not go over there.

Interviewer: That was an integrated neighborhood, right?

L. Williams: I grew up there.

Interviewer: What I'm saying is y'all were integrated?

L. Williams: Yes, we was integrated way before ... I was born over there. I didn't go to the hospital. I grew up in that neighborhood.

Interviewer: What did it mean for that neighborhood to be integrated? Did you have white families and Black families? Did you have people who were in relationships together?

L. Williams: Yeah, yeah, there was some of that going on.

Interviewer: Was it normal? In other words, was it something unusual for that to happen?

L. Williams: No, if you had the mentality to get you a white woman or get you a black woman, that's what you did, didn't nobody care.

Interviewer: Why were y'all so protective within that neighborhood?

L. Williams: That, I don't know. I was just born there. That's all I know. I was born in a house there in 1947, and that's the way we grew up. Well, we protected everybody in the neighborhood, didn't make no difference if you black or white. We didn't want nobody coming over there messing with us. And, see, actually, there were three Black neighborhoods. There was Berlin and then there was East Hickory and then there was Ridgeview, and so I was in what they call Berlin because we didn't have to worry about the police.

Interviewer: Did the police ever bother y'all there or were the police trying to protect y'all? Be direct.

L. Williams: Now one part, where the county line comes through, my aunt had a house and my uncle used to stand with his back to the wall like this and the police right there (pointing) and he would cuss them and they couldn't mess with him because they was in the city and he was in the county. And so then on the other side, where I lived at, when there was trouble, the sheriff came over, and when big-time trouble happened over there, and everybody was cool about it, and the sheriff came in and it was a white family and a Black family at odds with each other. And the sheriff came in and said, "This is what we're going to do," he solved the problem and everything went back to normal, and it was bad. It was a rape. And so the sheriff came in and settled it, nobody went to court, nobody was shot, everybody went back to bed friends, once they found out the particulars of what happened.

Interviewer: What were your views on integration? Did you want to see it? Did it matter? How did you feel about that?

L. Williams: I didn't care because it happened on my senior year and I was not about to go to Hickory High, but the guys that did go (next year), Hickory High run the table that year with guys that I played with. And I really didn't care. I would never have left Ridgeview anyway because I knew, if I'd have went to Hickory High and played football, I wouldn't have played because that's what they did.

Interviewer: Was it heartbreaking for the guys that went over there, do you think?

L. Williams: No, the guys that went over there, they just played like they did at Ridgeview, but it really didn't matter because you played in a position where you was not a star. They put you in the line on offense, put you in the line on defense, and put you on the kick-off team, but running that ball wasn't happening.

Interviewer: You played a position where you weren't a starter or a star? What do you mean?

L. Williams: Well, okay, the skill positions is like running back so the guys that went over there from Ridgeview that was real good, they played the offensive line or the defensive line. You didn't get to see that ball. You didn't get to run it much. And then, after a while, it came to a point that they couldn't stop it, and being quarterback, they didn't think we were smart enough, but we were.

Interviewer: You're saying that the guys from Ridgeview played out of position?

L. Williams: They didn't actually play out of it. The guys that played on the offensive line and the defensive line, yeah, they would go right in there to get in and be playing a lot, but the skill positions, they didn't. It took a while for that to happen.

Interviewer: Even the defensive backfield too?

L. Williams: Yeah. The first couple years they went to Hickory High, I know the first year and the second year, most of those guys was started in the defense and the offense and defensive line because all those other guys had been there for years, they were still there. It finally broke out.

Interviewer: But it took them a while?

L. Williams: Yes. Well, that's natural. You're going in to something new and the players really didn't care. It was the coaching staff that was the problem. But it came to a point that Hickory High wanted to win and the black guys was helping them do it, so they fit them right in.

Interviewer: What was school like at Ridgeview, the classes that you took?

L. Williams: We didn't have books. We didn't have new books and, if you had a book, it had some white guy's name in there from Hickory High. We got the hand-me-down books. We never got new books. And, a lot of times, we didn't have books. You shared books with somebody else.

Interviewer: What were your teachers like?

L. Williams: The teachers, they was real good people and they wanted you to learn and they did everything to help you and, if you needed some help, you'd tell them what's wrong and they would help you. We had good teachers. They tried their best to do, within the system, do whatever they could.

Interviewer: Guys from Ridgeview talk about the fact that they couldn't get in trouble because everybody in the neighborhood knew what was going on and they'd tell your parents and that kind of thing before you got back home. Was it like that in Little Berlin?

L. Williams: Yeah. Yeah, yeah. Like I told you, we used to work on the farm thing down there and we had a cow and we would take the cow out grazing, and this one man, he seen somebody beating the cow and he thought it was us and he told our father and he come home and we got a whupping and we told him, we say, "Hey, that wasn't us." And he said, "Well, you probably did something somewhere and I owed you one." We couldn't get away with nothing. They were pretty strict on us. And the whole neighborhood was like that. You couldn't go down the street four or five blocks away and get in trouble because they'd come back and tell on you. What they would do, they'd whup you and then take you home and you'd get another whupping. It's a good neighborhood thing.

Interviewer: That kept you out of trouble.

L. Williams: Yeah, because you couldn't go somewhere and get in trouble and try to sneak back home because, if somebody see you, they're going to tell your parents or going to whup you on the spot and then you're going to get another whupping when you get home, so you just didn't do nothing like that.

Lewis Collins

Lewis Collins was a junior the year of the Untouchables. He played quarterback. Before he made the team, he was a member of the Ridgeview High band. Since, he has become a renowned musician. He has entertained at reunion events. He was interviewed at Brown-Penn, the old Ridgeview High gymnasium in 2015.

Interviewer: What do you remember about the games?
Lewis Collins: Exciting. I was proud to be on the team. I went out as a freshman. I didn't make the team, but I was in the band and I played in the band. And then when I became a sophomore, I went out again for the team and I made the team. Of course, I didn't get a chance to play until my junior and senior year, but every game we won, we didn't lose no games. The only game that we lost was the championship games (sophomore year, 1963), but the regular season, we won every game. And so we were a terrific team. They feared the Ridgeview Panthers there, every high school, they hated to play us because, we played at the dust bowl. We didn't have any grass, but it was exciting. And I enjoyed playing.
Interviewer: What years did you play?
Lewis Collins: Well, my best years were junior and senior, and we were the last class of 1966; that's when we integrated. I played my last year as a senior. And of course, we lost that last championship game at Lenoir-Rhyne college. I got injured and unfortunately my cousin, he was a halfback, and I believe we could have won that game. I think I threw a pass the wrong way (during the 1965 season), and he couldn't catch it. He couldn't catch the ball. And that kind of stuck in my mind ever since I did that. And I took the blame for it, but I believe if he had caught that pass, he could have run all the way, and we would have won that game.
Interviewer: What were the crowds like who came to see these games?
Lewis Collins: They loved when we played, we pretty much sold out.

When we went to Lenoir-Rhyne. They was really, really crowded. Those are the championship games when we played the last game of the season. And then we, if we win that game, we go undefeated. But, that's the year of 1964. We were called the Untouchables, no team scored on us. We won every game and my cousin, he was a reporter and he wrote up the Untouchables and you know, we had newspaper articles on that for our team for that year. And that was exciting, you know, and that's something that we can say no other team in this area have ever went unscored on and won every game.

Interviewer: Is that where the name comes from? His reporting.

Lewis Collins: Yes.

Interviewer: How hard was practice?

Lewis Collins: I mean, that's one of the reasons why we could do what we did. They would, early in the morning, we would get on a bus and our coach would take us out in the country. And we had to run from like 4:30 or five o'clock in the morning. And our coach would take us out to an area where we can run and we you know, stay in shape. So we did that for every season. We couldn't drink, we could only drink orange juice, no sodas. And especially when we had a game that night- we played at night, and we couldn't drink anything that may bother our playing, you know, because we had some liquid in our system, but we had the exercise, you know, every day, every practice we're exercising before we ended that practice, we had to run around the field. And so we were in shape.

Interviewer: What do you remember as being like your best and worst moments of that season?

Lewis Collins: Well, in my worst moment, when I threw that pass to my cousin and he was looking one way and I threw it the other way and it didn't work. So that was my worst, worst episode. When I played my best? When I scored a touchdown, I mean, one game, it seemed like I couldn't do anything wrong. The passes were there and I was handing off the ball. And I remember, I recall like this play, 44 crossback. And I handed it to my, my cousin and he, he ran about 50-, 60-yard touchdown. And so that was the best game I ever played. And I remember that.

Interviewer: What was the Ridgeview community like back in those days?

Lewis Collins: We were a "2A" school and, you know, but that was the exciting part of our school system. You know, we had football and basketball. Now baseball was good too, but it didn't draw that crowd like football and basketball. And I played basketball as well. And that was, that was exciting. I think I did a little bit better with the basketball than I did football, but again, those two sports, I enjoy playing.

Interviewer: And how was the school, the center of the community? How does that work?

Interviewer 2: Well, of course during that time, we were not integrated. So predominantly black school and, and that doesn't bother us. We came to school, we did what we had to do, and we took our sports seriously, because that was something that kept us busy. You know, we didn't have the time to hang around and be idle. We come to rehearsal after school is out. We go to rehearsal, we put on our football outfits and go out on the field and get ready to tackle and, you know, to practice. And fortunately, well, unfortunately, I got my ankle (injured) and that put me out for a long time. I had put a cast on it, and I was kind of disappointed about that. That's one thing you don't want to happen, get injured, because then you can't play, so you have to sit on the bench. So that's something that you don't like to happen.

Robert "Mac" Rowland

Mac Rowland was the quarterback of the 1963 team. When the Untouchable juniors were underclassmen, he guided the team through an undefeated regular season, but did not win the championship. He was interviewed at the Ridgeview Recreation Center during reunion activities in 2015.

Interviewer: What was it like when you were at Ridgeview?

Mac Roland: I started Ridgeview in 1960. That would have been my freshman year, and I graduated in 1964. So, all of the time coming from East Hickory Elementary, the whole thing for a young kid like me was to make it, Ridgeview football team as a freshman.

But in my case, it didn't happen. That's the whole community outlook. Once you go through first through the eighth grade, your main thing was to be good enough to make Ridgeview's football team. That's the way our community was. And I grew up on the east side of town in East Hickory, where what we considered all the faster runners were. And then, on this side of town where the school was, we always thought them as the bigger linemen, the more physical guys.

But going to Ridgeview, it was good for me as far as the education. But East Hickory gave me the basic fundamentals to make it through anywhere. You know, as far as education is concerned. So, Ridgeview was sort of like, I don't say a piece of cake, because those instructors over there at the time were intense on training children at the time.

I made it through and everything. I was excited being at Ridgeview, because the loyalty in the whole town was, make it through Ridgeview. Because at the time, it was the only black school in the neighborhood besides the elementary school in East Hickory.

I enjoyed my time at Ridgeview. I thought the instructors over there had good minds to train youngsters to be better than what they were. So during that four year tenure at Ridgeview, it was a blessing and an eye opener for me, because it enlightened me on what is going on in the world, just as much as in the community. So it was a good thing for me to go to Ridgeview.

Interviewer: When you made the team, what position did you play?

Mac Roland: My freshman year they didn't let me play. Said I was too little. My sophomore year, he let me play a little bit. I won one game from them in Newton, which yeah, I did good my sophomore year. See, but my main thing is that I didn't get along too good with the staff at the time, because I always thought my skills were better than what they were letting me do.

So, I guess I was sort of rebellious to a certain extent. My senior year, that staff left, and I made the team as starting quarterback. Broke all the records for a senior, one year. And that's when I thought I was off and running, and I decided I was going to go off and go to college and all of that stuff.

But I was involved for those four years, but I only really made that team one year. And I was the quarterback then. And I was a quarterback with the same team that they say 'The Untouchables' were the next year. They changed my position and the two lineman's position. That was the only difference in the team in the Untouchables and our year.

And you know, one thing I want to say, see, Ridgeview had a legacy where they won the (conference) championship, maybe 10 years every year, '58, '59, '60, '61, '62. But the only one that succeeded the way The Untouchables in '65 (graduation year), that was that team. But we won the championship every year.

If you went to Ridgeview and didn't win the championship, you were either a long time ago, because there wasn't nothing too much after us, because the whole school changed in '66. But that's just the way it was at Ridgeview. It was a, this was a sports town at the time, you know what I mean?

And then another thing, here's what we got to realize during that time. And then, I'm talking positive, not negative. See, that was during the time when the Martin Luther King's and the Muhammed Ali's, and they were sort of protesting. So that kind of put a picture on you, being from "a black school." See, just like I say, the school didn't integrate until 1966.

But I didn't have to worry about that transition, because I left in '64. And then, I graduated from college in California and played sports out there. They let me play. And but, the thing is, having all of the Ridgeview training and what went on then, it made me be successful there. But Ridgeview, it was a good school to go to.

And the only thing bad about Ridgeview, because when I say bad, it has the same name, and I spent 25 years in Atlanta, and the detox center down there's named Ridgeview. So when I first moved there and put in applications, and I always put Ridgeview, I was declined because they related that to the Ridgeview there. And so, finally I start getting smart and say, "I went to Hickory High." But I never went to Hickory High. But I just got that off my resume, you know what I mean? And soon as I took it off, I got a job working with probation and retired.

Interviewer: In the season you were quarterback, how did you guys do?

Mac Roland: We won our championship. We lost in, I think it was Lexington, beat us in the playoffs that year. We missed winning and everything by two games. Two games. Matter of fact, I might have dropped the touchdown pass that could have tied the score that night. But I wasn't a receiver, I was just trying that.

But we had two games before we'd win the championship in (the class of) '64. And then we left, and left it to the class of '65, and they took care of business, yeah.

Interviewer: Did you follow what the team did after you left?

Mac Roland: I was off in college at the time when the class of '65 did that "Untouchable." But see, we had guys like, and I'm going to mention some of the names that was on the team. Ed Rogers, he went to A&T, Nelson Bockenborough, he went to A&T. I had the same backfield, Doug Bumgarner, Allen Burch, Edward Cunningham. And then, I had two ends, Herbert Morrison and Dwight Thompson. And that was our team. You know what I'm saying?

And just like the guys talking in the interview said, we just moved on the other side of the ball. And see, the guys in my year, we was dedicated on being number one in football, because that's just the way they grew us up. It's almost like from college to the pros, you're primed for that. And we follow guys. I remember guys like Billy Fingers, Bobby Rowe, Ernie Warlick, Ozzie Clay, these guys went on to do (good). And that's what the inspiration was for the younger guys to make it and go off to the pros, let's say.

Here's another thing about Ridgeview and our community. See, we didn't go too far outside of our land. We played the same schools every year. Might have been one or two different on certain years. Like, we went to Central, we went to Olive Hill, we went to Lenoir, you know, and then we start stretching out. We go down to Lexington, Shelby, you know. And we played against some guys that got into the hall of fame, like Bobby Bell, those guys from Shelby.

But it still was like a camaraderie thing where you were an athlete at Ridgeview, you were like, "a little superior." I mean, we didn't say that. But it was just a mystique in the air about where you're from and that kind of thing. But I enjoyed Ridgeview, and I wish I could just go get all of my papers and just explain to you everything went on. See, because another thing we had at Ridgeview, we never changed our system.

We never changed the system. You know how you come into some schools, and they got new plays? These plays might have been back from 1940, I don't know. But we used the same system over and over. And those guys learned the system, got acclimated to the system, and they know what to do. And when it got tough, they knew what to do, because they knew the system. And that's the one thing I like about our coaching staff. They taught you the X's and O's and ABC's before they taught you how to be strong and physical. And that's what I liked about Ridgeview going at that time, yeah.

Yeah, and basically, I could talk about it forever. But I just wanted to get my other two cent worked in, because the Untouchables was my team. That was my team. It just so happened I graduated the year before. Yeah, it sure was.

Interviewer: What did you think when you read about what they were doing?

Mac Roland: Well, it was almost not unbelievable, but the unbelievable part, and it's still kind of unbelievable, that nobody got a score period, the whole year. Now, I mean, I ain't never heard of that before. When they said, "Well, they're doing good." And nobody got a score. That's the part, even today, kind of like, nobody couldn't even get three points? Nobody scored on them, and I think it's amazing. That class, The Untouchables, if you got them privately, they'd give me the accolades of that was my team. But I don't want to take their glory, because I wasn't there. You know.

I was off thinking I was getting ready to go to the pros. I took off and went to Vorhees College, which was a junior college at the time. And I did well there. And you know, now I'm thinking I'm better than what I am, so I wanted to go to California and explore my skills. And then I got out there, and I graduated from college, and did good. They didn't let me play quarterback. I played split end.

See, that's the kind of skills I had. Now, my skills at the time when I grew up, like I say, they taught me how to play baseball, basketball, football, which was the three main. And I had a touch of pros in all of them except basketball. But I did start on the college basketball team.

But I tried out for the San Francisco Giants. I tried out for the Los Angeles Rams. And later on in life, got on the PGA because I was a sports enthusiast. Some people say sports “nut,” but I was a sports enthusiast. And I learned all the little things, except with me, a little bit that helped me because of my size. I probably, during that time in the '60's, I probably didn't weight but 160 pounds. And they weren't taking guys like that in, you know.

And I only got fat and big after I got old and didn't play no more. And that's the truth. Yeah, and basically, that's what it was. But I'm in love with Ridgeview and love everything that went on. And just like you say, our main thing is when we got to play at Lenoir-Rhyne College and on them fields, it was like going to the pros. It was something we weren't used to, because of the facilities we had at the time. Which at the time, they were all right. So that's where I am.

Interviewer: The crowds when you went were enthusiastic.

Mac Roland: Oh, they enjoyed it too. You could see the enjoyment in them too. That everybody that was visiting, because our name as a football team was a big name. And when I say "big," not necessarily way out, but in the community. And we had just as many followers on that side of town as we had on this side of town. You see, that's how big the name was. See, because that let us know that the Hickory area is a sports town. And that's why they followed us. If we were doing good, then they would follow us. We never lost championships. We always won the championship.

Now, we might not always won the state, but we were close, you know. And to me, for us to lose, I might have cried for a whole year, because we had a tradition of winning, winning, win and win. And I'm not talking about one or two years before me. I'm talking about 10 years down the line. I know some of them old football players, when I say to know them, to have looked up to them and heard about them and that kind of thing.

And you know, even when you talk about the pros, I watched the ones that went to the pros. And I wanted to be like that too, because I went to Ridgeview too. But it just didn't pan out that way. But I got enough education where I could make it, so I'm satisfied with it, and give credit to coming through the Ridgeview area. You know what I'm saying?

And when I say the Ridgeview area, yeah, over here. But I hung out around Lenoir-Rhyne College and Hickory High. Because at that time in the mid '60's, things were starting to expand from your community. And then you know about what happened later on in the '60's and that kind of thing. So that's basically when I went to California, thought I could see better. But I had the same eyesight.

Milton Johnson

Playing for the cross-county rivals, the Newton Central Hornets, Milton Johnson faced the Untouchables head on. Later he married a Ridgeview Alumni and willingly discusses playing the Untouchables. He was interviewed in 2015 at the Ridgeview reunion.

M. Johnson: They will meet on that field (indicating the Dust Bowl). That night (1964 game) they put out three of our players, the same guy. Reverend Lutz, Johnny Hodge, them boys was terrible. They were terrible. And they had another big attack over there. Craig Wilfong. He was quiet. All he did was maul you. He just ran over you.

I'm telling you it was just something to see. If Newton was playing Hickory, you had to get earlier. Wherever they was playing you had to get there early because there is no standing room. Some reason out of four years of high school, we lost four games. I was on a team that lost four times. One game, a year; Ridgeview.

That was something. Just playing against them was a... Now God gave us this honor to come back and laugh and joke about it and talk about it. But that's something that we can share. It's also, cause we did play them and we were supposed to have beaten them, but that game was never close. 36 - 0. Ridgeview was a team that you really didn't want to fool with. You had to prepare and I mean, we trained, you had to run three and four miles, come back, run around the field, practice till it gets dark.

Ridgeview, they had a community center, but they had clubs all kinds of stuff like that. You didn't hear all this stuff about killing each other, right? They loved each other. They were more together by playing together, growing up together. And that came all the way up until they finished school. It was just a group of guys that loved each other. They was tough.

Interviewer 2: But y'all had a good team too, didn't you?

Interviewer: We had a good team. We were scoring more points than they were. We had been scoring them until we got to Hickory. Ridgeview, they're "Untouchable." Scored enough, for three other team's schools. They came at you hard. When you bond together, you remain together. So that's what they were; they were tough.

Never want to play them again. And matter of fact, I won't. And so after I had quite a bit of scholarships my senior year, that was '66. We had them beat my senior year and I won't call this guy named for Hickory. That boy that was our worst nightmare, Hickory. That team. I tell you, I can't say they had that much to choose from, but there were guys, you know, just like if you're in a ring boxing, you come to Hickory, you better prepare.

Pete Oglesby

One of the players that preceded the Untouchables, George Edward Oglesby was known in the community as Pete. One of the oldest members of a Ridgeview football squad to be interviewed, he can recall helping to convert a vacant field into what is now the Samuel William Davis, Jr. Multipurpose Field, known as the Dust Bowl.

Interviewer: Tell me about when you went to Ridgeview.
Pete Oglesby: I started Ridgeview when I went to the first grade on through. And I went back in the '50s. I'm class of '57.
Interviewer: And you played football?
Pete Oglesby: I played football for Ridgeview, and that was the best time. That was back in the '50s. I went for football when I was in seventh grade. You have to weigh 105 pounds. If you didn't weigh 105 pounds you had to be twice as fast. If you couldn't run fast, you'd know to hang it up. Now that was the fact. And then for Ridgeview said the field, football field, we cleaned our field off and made it ourselves. The students and the shop, and recreation, and the community.

Mr. Bumgarner, he had a grading outfit. So he graded the field out for us. Eulie Bumgarner. And Irving Finger. Here in Hickory. They lived in East Hickory. They had a construction business. Wasn't nothing out there but pine trees. Activity time we would go and cut those pine trees out, bulldoze them over and fill in everything. We built the bleachers, cut into the bank. And the school gave us the lumber. And then the nursery out there by the airport gave us trees to grow, so couldn't anyone watch the games (outside the fence), so they had to come in. So that's why I played football. I played basketball, and I ran track. There was always activity at Ridgeview to keep you motivated, to keep you going, and the teachers and everything, you just couldn't do without them. And they make you feel important. That we had a football team, and had basketball and girl's basketball. Couldn't beat the girls back in them days. They were good. Championships, but nobody talked nothing about it.

But they was recognized. And our team, well they said "untouchables" and all that. They was good. But no one never mentioned in '52, when I was playing, we won the championship, but they wouldn't give it to us. We didn't have enough players. No substitutes. We didn't have but 13 players.

Interviewer: And you all did the same thing with 13 players?

Pete Oglesby: The thing about it is, see, back then your transportation didn't hardly exist. We had only one bus, our own swimming pool, our own gymnasium. And we played less games, but we played them twice. Played twice. Yeah. "We going to play you this time, you come play us this time. Homecoming this time, homecoming next time." See, we all communicate together. They would play 11 or 12 games or something, 13, something. Okay, so they'd break it down so that we played eight games, which we did. We played more than that, we played a team twice. And we won. And back during the time I was a fullback. And I would play all them positions. Quarterback would have to call the plays. And I was good for two, three touchdowns per game. And I weighed 150 pounds.

I took my thoughts after Jim Thorpe. Now you see it, and now you don't. The knees hit you in the chest, nobody can get to them. Keep your head forward and that's what I did. To start first, Coach Johnson, Jerry Johnson, and then Sammy Davis (coach of the Untouchables), and Brown the assistant coach. And I ran different from anybody else because I studied it. And I'd run five miles home every day. And my classmates, we all stuck together. Ridgeview was togetherness.

Interviewer: Why do you think that was that Ridgeview was tight as a community?

Pete Oglesby: Because everybody looked after everybody's child. You do something wrong here you get punished over there. Because if you're going to do something wrong, you come home and tell it, you get another beating. That's how tight.

Interviewer: Anything else you want to say about the Ridgeview community?

Pete Oglesby: Well, it really has improved a lot. When I was coming on this was all cotton fields. You ain't going to believe that, but it was a cotton field right here. But the improvement of a lot of activities and things for kids, for growing up, for education. A lot of them have left here and came back. A lot of them left and didn't come back, but for the education and the activities and the knowledge to help kids learn and everything. And this facility here is a good thing. Keep them busy and occupied. And that makes a difference.

Interviewer: What do you think about the education you received at Ridgeview High?

Pete Oglesby: Well, I received a pretty good education. I didn't go off to college or anything or nothing like that, but I went to work and I took a little training and I wound up to be a mechanic, and a furniture installation supervisor, and I retired from it after 43 years. And I can't complain. I'm still here. And that's it.

Interviewer: Anything else you want to say about Ridgeview?

Pete Oglesby: Well, it's a little community and we all stick together. We do the best we can, and reunion, that's the biggest thing that ever happened.

Interviewer: Why do you think so many people come back to the reunions?

Pete Oglesby: Memories. They don't realize what they had until you leave here. Surprised that people come back. See, want to enjoy their self.

Rev. Xenophone Lutz

A leader of the team both in their high school era and again in the 21st century, Reverend Xenophone Lutz has been vital to the Untouchables project. Always willing to recall the stories of the team, Rev. Lutz has been interviewed, either alone or within a group of players, no less than six times. His insights are key to understanding the dynamic of the group and the brotherhood that has kept them strong since 1964.

Interviewer: How far did you live from Ridgeview High School?
Rev. X. Lutz: Approximately a mile.
Interviewer: Did the other players and the other kids live fairly close, all within a few blocks? Were you out on the edge or were other people spread out too?
Rev. X. Lutz: As a whole, we were, I say, basically spread out. Some stayed in this area that I lived. Some were in a place called East Hickory. Then some were in a place called Washington Forest, which is around Longview.
Interviewer: Where was your house with regard to the school?
Rev. X. Lutz: Two blocks down. Well, a landmark may be the block down from where Ridgeview Library has been established and dedicated. The one that has been preserved.
Interviewer: What did football represent for you when you got out there and played? I mean, was it an escape? Was it pressure? Was it just fun?
Rev. X. Lutz: I think it was a combination. It was an escape in the sense from the pressures of, say, society. But then on the other hand, it was fun. And it was, I would say, a privilege really to be a part of such a rich tradition. So it was a combination of things.

Interviewer: Did you guys play neighborhood football growing up, or played at Ridgeview, like in junior high or something, the first opportunity?

Rev. X. Lutz: I'm glad you asked that. We all, I would say, got our initiation from what we called "hot grease." Hot grease. It was practically every day, a few times a week, guys would gather and surround the football and throw it in the ring, so to speak. And whoever was brave enough to pick the ball up, everybody ganged up on them and tackled them. We called that hot grease. So that was initiation. And then throughout the years before we became eligible for high school football, we would constantly have games in the fields and here and there. But yeah, it was always usually a football game going on somewhere in the neighborhood.

During my time, we only played organized football when you reached the ninth grade. There were no little leagues or community football teams or anything like that.

Interviewer: Would kids at that time have had a lot of free time, or would you have had so many chores that your parents kept you busy from the second you got home from school?

Rev. X. Lutz: We had chores that we were supposed to do before we went out and played. Yeah. Yeah. We had chores. Cleaning the house, cleaning the yard and such. Homework. We had different chores to do before we went to play.

Interviewer: But you organized whatever happened yourselves. I mean, y'all didn't have adults managing you. Y'all got games together. You got hot grease together.

Rev. X. Lutz: Oh, absolutely. Now, there were usually some older guys who say, "Yeah, let's get a game going." Then everybody would join in. We'd pick what we call a couple of captains and they would choose the people they wanted on their side. And that was usually main process, the method that we did.

Interviewer: What was tougher? Getting tackled in hot grease, or getting tackled in high school football? And did hot grease prepare you for what you were going to get when you were in high school?

Rev. X. Lutz: In a sense, hot grease prepared us. But hot grease was not as tough as when we went to high school, organized football. People would pile on you and things like that. But I can not remember any injuries, anything like that, from hot grease. I would say we looked after each other. We did not try to put anybody out of the game, so to speak.

Interviewer: How many of the people who ended up playing for Ridgeview came out of the hot grease crowd? Did y'all have a group and they all ended up coming up together in Ridgeview?

Rev. X. Lutz: I would say everybody. I would say probably 100 ... well, close to 100%. There may have been some Ridgeview players who came from out of town, but for the most part, we all came up basically the same way. Playing hot grease and playing games in the fields, wherever we could get a game going.

Interviewer: Does that even include the Longview kids and East Hickory kids or more just the Ridgeview kids?

Rev. X. Lutz: Yeah. Well, in particular, we had a special rivalry, I would say, with the East Hickory kids. Every now and then, we'd go and get a game with them and see who was the best. East Hickory or Ridgeview. We've had many of those contests.

Interviewer: East Hickory and Ridgeview would combine eventually with Ridgeview High School.

Rev. X. Lutz: Eventually, we began to play together at the high school. High school was ninth grade on up, yeah. So again, we did not have what we call a junior high. So when you made the football team, you were on the varsity.

Interviewer: Ridgeview's head coach was Samuel Davis. I understand he had a nickname of "Jap." Any idea why?

Rev. X. Lutz: I think he said he was a good basketball player. And during that time, I think he had a deadly shot. And of course I think around that time, there was war going on between the States in Japan. We called them Japs because they were a good opponent. Put it that way.

Interviewer: Like a deadly enemy?

Rev. X. Lutz: Yeah, absolutely.

Interviewer: So did he have a reputation before y'all ever started playing for him? Do you know when he came to the school? Do you have any idea how long he'd been at Ridgeview when you got there?

Rev. X. Lutz: I think he came when we were in elementary (school). He came in the early '50s.

Interviewer: Did he have a reputation that y'all heard what it'd be like to play ... Was he a hard nose coach?

Rev. X. Lutz: Yes. I would say for the most part, he was tough. He demanded discipline. His thing was making sure that we were well trained, well conditioned. So he, in a sense, he demanded that we be in shape.

Interviewer: Did he talk much about you being black young men and the community and how you reflected on the community? Or was it more discipline and structure and it was up to your parents to more keep y'all in line in terms of outside of football?

Rev. X. Lutz: I think that was more or less left up to our parents. But as a coach and as a teacher, he reminded us of the way society is and that we needed to be disciplined and learn as much as we can, so we can take our rightful place one day in society.

Interviewer: Did you experience many slights or racist situations when you were growing up? Did you interact with white people a lot? And can you talk about what that experience was like?

Rev. X. Lutz: I interacted a lot with whites. Some positive, some negative. There were a large number of whites that came to the community to play basketball in particular. And we got to know a lot of them in the gymnasium at the center. But I say, as far as racism there'd be times when we would have to ... Say if we were out late at night, we'd have to be careful of cars coming down the street, throwing things at us, stuff like that. Then you might hear somebody holler out a name or so. Of course, when you go to some of the stores or some of the establishments, you might experience disrespect. But overall, it was a mixture. There were many who befriended us and helped us a great deal.

Interviewer: There are stories about how there were white people who were involved in the black community who helped send people to college, helped people get businesses started. So it must've been a range of people who were supportive and encouraging, and then other people who sadly wanted y'all to stay in your place.

Rev. X. Lutz: We had a great support. At a football game, there were a lot of white people who came and supported us on a regular basis. Knew a lot of us by name, and we got to know them. They supported us in that sense. And when you went to some of the stores, sporting goods stores in particular, we knew them well and got along. And some of the other stores, they knew our parents. So they treated us fine. For the most part though, I think it was pretty good. Back then I realized that there were good people, there were bad people. And that was something that I think our parents and people in the community instilled in us. It's more positive than negative, I would say.

Interviewer: Were there particular people in the community or the school who were leaders who really shaped you? Told you about what you could achieve or shaped your thinking about yourself?

Rev. X. Lutz: First, I would say my grandparents. They taught us to always be the best we could be. Shoot for excellence. We had teachers who I think saw a lot of potential in us and encouraged us. Teachers like Mrs. Thompson, Ms. Jean Thompson. Our principal, Taft Broome. teachers, Mrs. Posten, Mr. Marcellus Miller. They just tried to encourage us to always do the best that we could at whatever job or occupation we sought to do.

Interviewer: Coach Davis, what kind of routine did he have you go through in terms of practice, lifestyle? Did he have a a strict set of things he wanted you to follow like being in bed, what you ate, what you did? Or was it more, you belonged to him during practice and the game and that was it?

Rev. X. Lutz: He demanded conditioning. We ran five miles before the season, getting prepared for the season. The first two weeks, we ran five miles.

Interviewer: Every day?

Rev. X. Lutz: Every morning. Yes.

Interviewer: At what time?

Rev. X. Lutz: 5:00 in the morning. And then after that, we'd come back for practice. Then they had a practice in the afternoon. As far as Coach Davis trying to mold us, he encouraged us. One of his favorite sayings was "Eat football, sleep football, live football." And we really bought into that. He did much to help shape us. One of the things that I think was the main contributor, perhaps, was we were fundamentally sound in what we did. We believed in ourselves. As mentioned earlier, some of the guys, we'd known each other since the early grades. Yes. So we knew each other, respected each other, had the utmost confidence in each other.

Interviewer: When did you become a starter on the team?

Rev. X. Lutz: I started my sophomore year on defense. And then of course, my junior and senior years, played both ways. Offense and defense.

Interviewer: Did just about everybody play both ways?

Rev. X. Lutz: For the most part, I'd say the seniors for the most part, there were several seniors who played both ways. Offense and defense.
Interviewer: What football conference did the team play in?
Rev. X. Lutz: During our time, The Northwestern Athletic Association, I believe that's what it was called. And I think earlier, they may have called it a Negro League. But it wasn't labeled that. There was no racial label during, that I can remember, during when we played. It was just, again, the Northwestern Athletic Association.
Interviewer: In your four years as a Panther, how did the team evolve?
Rev. X. Lutz: Yes. First year '61 to '62, we won the conference. Very few teams scored on us, but we lost in the state championship to, I believe, Chapel Hill. Of course that was my first year and the first loss that I experienced. My sophomore year, I started on defense and that year we beat everybody, and won the state championship. And that was an invaluable, I would say, experience, learning how to win and learning how to go all the way. My junior year we were undefeated and went into the playoffs and lost against Lexington. And that was, well, my first defeat as a starter and it really hurt. It really hurt.

And so I said to myself, and a lot of us said to ourselves, "This'll never happen again." It was a game that, even some of our opponents, the opposing coach said, "We had no business beating you guys." So that stayed in my mind and the mind of many of us, and our senior year, we started the season, with Lexington on Our mind. Get Lexington, get Lexington. Again, we played our hearts out every game. Again, we dominated about halfway through the season, some of us realized that we were unscored on at this point.

And the coaches would say "Just focus on winning, just focus on winning." And as it got close to the last few games, someone said, "Well, let's go unscored on. Let's not let anybody cross our goal line." But again, the coaches cautioned us, just make sure you win the game, win the game. But again, all that... really in the back of our minds was, we're waiting on Lexington. And we realized, then we found out that Lexington had moved up in class. So there was no Lexington. But again, and the goal was, to win the state championship again. Going unscored on was really secondary. Just winning was the main thing.
Interviewer: What was the closest call you had with the possibility of someone scoring on you that season?

Rev. X. Lutz: It was the state championship, last game of the season for us, last game we were going to play at Ridgeview for the seniors. The score was zero-zero at halftime and Hamlet was the opponent. They were at the two yard line with a first down. And I'm the one that said "You guys, not going anywhere." I kept pointing out, "You're not going anywhere." And John Hodge, who was our captain said, "Man, shut up and play some ball." I remember that well, "Shut up and play some ball." So they came at us four times and we turned them back each time. In fact, when it ended, they were back further than when they started. We rose to the occasion, we had the utmost confidence that they were not going to score.

Interviewer: Where was that championship game played?

Rev. X. Lutz: At Lenoir-Rhyne College.

Interviewer: Do you remember crowd reaction? Do you remember anything else that was going on around you while that drive was pushing them back?

Rev. X. Lutz: Only thing I remember is a reaction afterward. People standing behind us and clapping for us. And then at that moment we knew we had it then. We were known as a second half team. We were usually better in the second half than the first. So we, no pressure, anything. We knew that we were going to defeat this team in the second half.

Interviewer: Is that conditioning that you guys were so much in better shape than the rest of the teams you played that you were still good before the quarter [crosstalk] ?

Rev. X. Lutz: I think so. I think we can attribute that again to conditioning. Conditioning and confidence. We seemed to always be stronger in the second half than we were in the first. We had the ability to reach down and do what was necessary to win that game. Yeah.

Interviewer: Could you see that sucking the wind in your opponents in that final quarter, could you see it when you lined up, could you see it in their face that they were done?

Rev. X. Lutz: Absolutely. Well, when you have an opponent in the position we had them, you could see the eyes and you can tell by their actions, the response, that you've got them now. Yeah. You've got them now.

Interviewer: When you play, you play both sides, right?

Rev. X. Lutz: Yes sir.

Interviewer: What position specifically, offense and defense.

Rev. X. Lutz: Guard. Guard, mostly.

Interviewer: And you forced more than a couple of fumbles and/or recovered them, right?

Rev. X. Lutz: Oh, absolutely. Yeah. Yeah. I had my share of recovered fumbles and forced fumbles. Yeah. But again, that was typical to a lot of linemen, so we all had our moments, what we call "Shaking that ball loose."

Interviewer: How much did you guys weigh on average?

Rev. X. Lutz: On the average, our senior year, we were probably averaged 190, 195. I was around 195, two or three others were around the same.

Interviewer: You guys were typical size for the teams you played? In terms of weight?

Rev. X. Lutz: Often teams were bigger, larger than we were. Yeah. Yeah. I remember a team from Monroe in particular that were guys average, perhaps 230, 240 on the line. But it didn't matter. We moved them around like anybody else.

Interviewer: You guys seem like you were pros. Like men playing the boys.

Rev. X. Lutz: Yeah. Well, at times it felt that way. Most of us had been together a long time and most of us were what you call athletic, we were athletes. And again, strong for our size. We had the utmost confidence that it doesn't matter who we are facing, large or small, we were going to win, we're going to dominate.

Interviewer: Any idea where the name Untouchables came from? When did you first hear that? Where did that come from?

Rev. X. Lutz: The term came from Ellis Johnson, our announcer. After we had accomplished what we did, during that time, there was a program called Eliot Ness and *The Untouchables* on television and so Ellis somchow applied that to the Ridgeview Panthers and called us the Untouchables, and it caught on.

Interviewer: Did he use that term during the games when he was announcing?

Rev. X. Lutz: Well, it was really applied after we'd accomplished everything. We weren't really "Untouchables" after we had really gone through the whole season. So at that last game, best I can remember, that last game, that's when he revealed it and announced it. And soon it was in the papers.

Interviewer: Is he the same guy that wrote the articles?

Rev. X. Lutz: Yes. Sports announcer and the sports editor for the *Hickory Daily Record.*

Interviewer: And you guys got really good press from the paper.

Rev. X. Lutz: Oh, absolutely. Yes.

Interviewer: How did you feel seeing the headline up on the press like that?

Rev. X. Lutz: Oh yeah. It was a great feeling. Great feeling.

Interviewer: You get off the field and I'm just imagining life was very hard.

Rev. X. Lutz: For the most part, yeah. But it was a way of life, most of us get a little job here and there and help with our own needs and things like that. But again, that was what we knew. I had plenty of love, adequate clothing, plenty of food, many friendships. And I would say the outside pressures of the world took a back seat at that particular time. So we did not feel the full brunt of it.

Interviewer: Did you go off to college or did you start working after high school?

Rev. X. Lutz: Went to college one year at Winston-Salem State on a scholarship. And after that I got married and then worked at General Electric for years.

Interviewer: And the whole era of integration hit, with the high schools and everything, in the mid to late 60s. Were you integrated at that point?

Rev. X. Lutz: Yes.

Interviewer: What do you remember about the community and how it affected the community all of a sudden for things to be integrating and, whether it was Ridgeview High School, whether it was people in the community, do you remember how people responded to the idea of suddenly being integrated?

Rev. X. Lutz: There were many who did not like it and wished that Ridgeview could have been preserved. And I think if that had happened, it would have benefited us as a community overall.

Interviewer: You're saying "Keep the high school in place"?

Rev. X. Lutz: Yes. Yes. But, then again, on the flip side of the coin, you knew that integration would give you basically the same opportunities as anyone else. So it was just at a time, and so you had to accept that and that this was the best thing to do at this particular time.

Interviewer: Where did Coach Davis, after integration, move?

Rev. X. Lutz: I think our coach went to one of the junior high schools, I think College Park.

Interviewer: Could you talk a little bit about playing the dust bowl?

Rev. X. Lutz: The dust bowl is the ball field down below the school. It was the football field and, for the most part, it was red dirt. So at halftime in particular, it was so dusty you could see the dust where it had raised up to the lights. You look at the lights, all you see is deep red, pink, whatever. And that's when we started calling it the Dust Bowl. Yeah. Again, it was a time when we practiced, it's something you didn't really look forward to, falling on that ground. We had what we called strawberries and skinned elbows and knees from the dust bowl.

Interviewer: Was it grass at the start of the season or was it just red dirt on top?

Rev. X. Lutz: They would try to, at times, replant but it never did have time to really take, I don't believe, because once it got going good, it never did really get established because of the practices that we had in the games. In fact, when we went to play somewhere else and they had grass, all we did was look down at the ground, "Look at this grass, man, this a nice field." So things like that.

Interviewer: What was your equipment like, the helmet and all that? Could you talk a little bit and describe what that is?

Rev. X. Lutz: For the most part, we had what they call the old Notre Dame leather helmets. They were, again, most of them were leather with very little cushion on the inside. And we did have several that were more modern, put it that way. But personally, I love what they call the old Notre Dame leather helmet. They just felt, to me, better. I don't know if because it's what I was used to or what.

Interviewer: What about your shoulder pads and hip pads and knee pads and all that? Was it leather, was it foam, what kind of stuff was it made of?

Rev. X. Lutz: Well, foam and plastic. We had a fairly good pads. Most of them were from years down. Some of them were, I think, given, donated to us from Hickory High, LR, and then every now and then, somebody had a new set of pads.

Interviewer: What about your jerseys? Did somebody make a special Ridgeview jersey?

Rev. X. Lutz: Our jerseys, yeah. They were special. We had orange and blue. Some of them were dark. And then we had one that was mostly orange that we received mostly my sophomore year. Yeah. My sophomore year we received new jerseys and new outfits.

Interviewer: Was that supposed to last you three years?

Rev. X. Lutz: Yes. In fact, they lasted until integration came.

Interviewer: What happened if one got torn?

Rev. X. Lutz: Well, they tear them or they rip them back, tear them or sew them back or whatever. Yeah.

Interviewer: And then they managed to wash them without destroying them? All those years?

Rev. X. Lutz: Yeah. We cared for our own uniforms basically. Yeah.

Interviewer: So you're wearing a washed shirt and you had to keep yours clean for three years?

Rev. X. Lutz: Yeah. We took them to the laundromat ourselves. We took care of our own jerseys and pants. Yeah. We cleaned those ourselves.

Interviewer: What did you feel like your options were after your education was complete?

Rev. X. Lutz: I knew that the opportunities would be limited. As I mentioned earlier, some of our parents and some of our teachers prepared us, for what was going to happen after we got out of high school and got into the workforce. So therefore whenever we took a job or whatever, we were told that we needed to excel, do those extra things, go far and beyond what we were required to do, because that would be necessary to gain employment and perhaps a sense of security. And show that we were just as good.

Interviewer: So you were prepared to live in a world without equal opportunity?

Rev. X. Lutz: Absolutely. Yeah. We were prepared and conditioned for that. We knew what people were going to do and were going to say, so we knew we had to overlook some things and overcome some things.

Interviewer: And how was it for you leaving the Ridgeview community for your work and dealing with that? Was it a struggle for you or was it, "This is going to happen. I'm prepared for it. I got it." This is a little bit like playing football. You got to be disciplined.

Rev. X. Lutz: Yeah. And I think, again, football helped in that sense. We were successful in football and from that we knew we were tough, we knew we were smart, and that, applied the right way, we could accomplish our goals. Yeah.

Interviewer: How important has the success you had in football been to the way you perceived yourself or the way you viewed yourself, the rest of your life? How has it affected everything afterwards?

Rev. X. Lutz: I think it was very positive. Again, discipline, just discipline yourselves, have the utmost confidence in yourself and in God, and there was nothing that can prevent you from being successful. Yeah. And you got to remember there are more than one level or one idea of what success means. There are many types of successes, I believe. For some, just graduating from high school, that's a success. Not going to jail is a success. Getting a job and raising a family, that's a success. It doesn't always mean being at the top of everything you do.

Interviewer: How does it feel for you to look at Ridgeview now?

Rev. X. Lutz: Overall, I would say I'm very thankful for the memories, but I do wish that there were something more tangible from the school that still exists. Something more that we can put our hands on and go, other than the center and the fields. Yeah.

Interviewer: You know, one of the reasons why we're interested in this story is there are people outside who have never heard of the Untouchables. So one of the things we want to do is spread that story, let people know how amazing that team, and you guys were. Was that something that followed you throughout your life when you were 25, 35, 45, 55, do people say "There goes one of the Untouchables"?

Rev. X. Lutz: For the most part, yes. Yeah. You go into the barbershop, people still remember and people will still bring it up. Yeah. You even meet some of the children of those who played back then, they pass that information on and you meet some of the children, they say, "Oh yeah. Okay. Yeah. My parents told me about you and told me about what you all accomplished." So yes, it's something that's, I would say, still alive. And it will probably be in our memories long as most of us still around.

Interviewer: Has the world changed a lot in terms of racial relations when you look at it now versus the 60s, in terms of your personal experience, maybe in this community?

Rev. X. Lutz: Well, absolutely. Yeah. Things, I would say, are better, more positive, but yet there are a few situations and things that will pop up every now and then that will cause people to lose focus on the progress that we have made. But overall, we're headed in the right direction. Yeah. We're not there yet.

Interviewer: Could you talk about the intense rivalry with Newton? Because they were the ones, right? They were your biggest rival.

Rev. X. Lutz: They were our main rival. I believe during my freshman year, Newton had us on the ropes at halftime, and we come back and beat them. I believe my sophomore year we demolished them. I think our junior year, they had us on the ropes, we come back and beat them. And my senior year, we demolished them. Of course, that was the year nobody scored on us. But Newton has always been our number one opponent, particularly when coach Bobby Rowe went to Newton; he's a former Ridgeview player. And they really seemed like they had our playbook at times, but they were our number one competition.

Interviewer: And that year, they were undefeated going into the game with you guys.

Rev. X. Lutz: Yes. Yeah. My last year they were undefeated and we were undefeated. And let me point out that they were scoring high numbers too. They were scoring high numbers too, but we shut them out. Beat them soundly.

Interviewer: You've got two undefeated teams playing at the same time? What was the noise like? What was the sound like?

Rev. X. Lutz: Oh, it was incredible. Yeah. When Newton and Hickory got together, that was like the Super Bowl, that's what everybody looked forward to. Again, we were neighbors, knew each other, worked with each other and all that kind of stuff. So it was a big, big rivalry. And, for the most part, friendly.

Interviewer: Would people drive up from Newton-Conover to Ridgeview, to watch or was it mainly played in front of a home crowd?

Rev. X. Lutz: Yeah. Newton would come to Hickory and Hickory would go to Newton. Yeah. So at their own stadiums, during our games. Yeah. But again, it was great.

Interviewer: Could you talk about some of your teammates on that '64 team?

Rev. X. Lutz: First I'm going to talk about our captain, John Hodge, Johnny Hodge. He was the jokester, but yet he was our leader. And again, he was, I would say, the backbone of our team. Allen Pope, our quarterback, our leader, very able and very well-respected as a leader. Douglas Bumgarner. The fastest and what somebody called us prettiest running back, you ever seen. Edward Cunningham, who had a wonderful gallop, or stride, as he ran. Allen Burch. One of the fastest ever at Ridgeview. Could stop on a dime, had so many moves, what we would say, "He could fake you out of your shoes." Danny Carter, great end and player.

Craig Wilfong. One of the strongest individuals anywhere. Dwight Thompson. Changed positions in his last year from end to tackle, did an amazing job. Hubbard Morrison. End, fast. James Thompson. Can not forget about James Thompson, one of the most gifted punters and kickers at that time, anywhere. Mitchell Anthony, our center. Mitchell was comical, a jokester, very talented, athletic. At times, he would come out of the whole huddle, turn a flip, then be right at the ball, ready to snap it. That was the kind of gimmicks he pulled at times. And I know I'm missing a lot of folks, but those are the ones that stand out. And that's, again, that was one of the signs of our greatness. Talented people like those I've mentioned, guys that could play anywhere really.

Interviewer: Did you all stay in touch over the years?

Rev. X. Lutz: Some of us, yeah. Some of us. Yeah. I think most of us have. Of course, probably more than half of those that I've mentioned are gone now, but we still stay in contact. We still look forward to being with each other whenever we can. Yeah.

Tillis Rendleman

One of the seniors in that storied year of 1964, Tillis Rendleman was unsure if he would play for the team that season. With an injury he thought would not allow him to do his best, Coach Davis coaxed him to join the team after the first game. He played in various lineman positions and remembered the experience as formative for his future career in both the Army and Air Force. He was interviewed on the campus of CVCC in 2017.

Interviewer: When did you play for the Ridgeview Panthers?
Tillis Rendleman: I made the team four times, from '61 to '64.
Interviewer: So you would've played in 1961, '62, '63, '64?
Interviewer: Yeah. We won the state championship in '62 and '64. The '64 we did with class and style.
Richard: What's the difference between those two years?
Tillis Rendleman: Well, we lost. My junior year in high school we lost the state championship and that left a sour note in our mouths and made us feel really bad. And I remember after school, after our junior year, we got together and we said, "Man, this really stinks. To get this close to the state championship and lose."

And so we decided amongst ourselves that the future seniors coming up that we were going to do something special. We were going to get in shape. We were going to stay in shape. And our coach was big on running. And I mean he said, "Run." You ran.

And we ran and ran. And it was just amazing. I think one of his goals and objectives was be able to put a team on the field that could last the whole game and then some. And I think we met that challenge big time.
Interviewer: Are there good examples or illustrations of what your running involved? Did he drop you off in the country? Or did he say, "Give me five times around town, or something?

Tillis Rendleman: All of the above. He got a truck, a long bed truck and took us out to the golf course, the one off of 70 down by Home Depot, that golf course out that way. He took us out there and said, "Run back to Ridgeview." And you know where is Ridgeview is downtown. And that was a long haul.

But we decided amongst ourselves that we needed to do better to achieve the goals and objectives that we had, we had to be stronger, faster, smarter. So the day after school was out after our junior, coming into our senior year, we started running.

I think I got up the first time it was 4 o'clock in the morning. And we met, it used to be a little store beside my grandmother's house that my grandmother used to live right across the street from the Ridgeview Library, the present Ridgeview Library is there now. But the old Ridgeview Library was there.

So my grandmother lived directly across the street from that location. And right beside it was the Spot Grocery. So a bunch of us met right there and we started running. And we ran all around the community a couple of times. And then we took a break and then came back after lunch and ran some more and we did that for weeks.

Because Coach Davis, his conditioning program was tough. I mean, it was tough. I was in the Army and the Air Force and it was comparable. That training was comparable to the military training. Because when I got to the Army, they said we got to run. The only difference is they gave us a 50-pound pack and we had to run with that.

But we ran. We didn't have sophisticated weights and all that kind of stuff. So we invented things like we found some iron poles and cinder blocks and we made weights and we used those. And there was a hill out at the old Ridgeview football field behind the bleachers.

And we would run up that hill and run back that hill about 20 times. And it was hot. It was very hot. But I enjoyed every second of the training because I got a chance to spend time with my buddies.

We started playing ball together by the time we were six or seven years old. And we, I mean, from the time we got up until the time it got dark and my parents and grandparents call me into the house, we played ball. So by the time we got to our senior year, we were ready. We were ready and determined.

We weren't like a lot of high schools. We went to some high schools that were, oh, they were seriously funded. They had some serious equipment, serious fields. The locker room was a place like, man, it was better than some people's homes. It was just beautiful.

We played the championship, a state championship at Lenoir-Rhyne and we thought we had died and gone to heaven. It was just fantastic. If you've been to Ridgeview, the old Ridgeview football field. It didn't have any grass. It has mostly dirt and a few spots of grass. But we get to Lenoir-Rhyne for the state championship and it is beautiful. It's got grass everywhere. The locker room is just like heaven. It was beautiful. Just beautiful.

Interviewer: What were you used to in terms of your locker room facilities?

Tillis Rendleman: The locker room at Ridgeview was in the basement of the gym. And it was spare, sparse, very limited, didn't have much. The trainers did all our taping in the locker room and we had old lockers, old racks for our equipment. And when we went to some of these other schools, I realized that they had different things other than what we had and I thought that was interesting.

If they had grass on the field, that was nicer than what we had. And the bleacher systems were bigger. And you got to remember at that time, in Ridgeview's history, we were pulling fans from everywhere in Catawba County.

I mean, they were Ridgeview orange and blue up and down. They backed us everywhere we went. But the schools, our school is small. I think our school was a 2A playing in a 3A world. And we played some teams like Chapel Hill, oh, places like that. Those guys were huge. We thought they were semipro. I mean, they were just unbelievable.

But our coach emphasized the fact, "Yeah, they big. They strong, hard. Play football tough." We didn't play any pushovers. And there's no participation awards for coming in third or fourth, so we went for the first place all the time.

Interviewer: So y'all had this conditioning. You had running. Were there other things he did to condition you?

Tillis Rendleman: Wind sprints, running, calisthenics for an hour. Nowadays in 2018, these schools would not push their athletes to that point. But we wanted to. We volunteered to. That loss our junior year at state championship level, that was devastating. I don't know. I'm not a crying type person but, boy, I cried.

I know a lot of team members cried. We were upset because we were better than them. And the coach emphasized, "Hey, it's okay. We know who was the better team. It just wasn't your day." So we vowed, we going to make it our day.

Interviewer: What about the year you won the state championship, 1962?

Interviewer: Edenton. The players were small. The lineman was small and after the initial kickoff we got lined up. I think they got the ball because we kicked to them. They got the ball and so I played, well, I played defense and occasionally offense.

And they got the ball and we lined up against their offense. And this little guy in front of me says, he called my number he says, I think in those days I think I wore number 60. He said, "I got your number, dude. I know who you are. I know where you come from. I know your plan style."

And I thought who is this guy? I mean, they had film on us. And I was like, whoa. That's what the pros do. High school teams in our area hadn't been taking film that I know of. But he says, "Well, I've seen the film on you." And I thought, uh oh. We better change it up a little bit."

Interviewer: So they had come and filmed your games.

Tillis Rendleman: Somehow or another, yeah. And I thought we were blown away like, "What? What? He's got film on us? So let's do something different here." So we did some different things. Now they'd call them now in today's football stunts and different rushing patterns. But we won.

Interviewer: What about next year? What happened in '63?

Tillis Rendleman: Well, we lost. And I don't really know what happened other than, I don't think we ran out of strategies. Of course, everybody was upset. And this was our junior year. And we believed that we were going to win that game. We should've won that game because we were the better team, but we didn't.

And I think it was a combination of a lot of small things that we did not do. Plays weren't exactly right. I feel positioning wasn't exactly right. We didn't defend our end zone, and we lost. It was devastating.

It was the next day, Saturday morning. I would work at Winn-Dixie after football season, and I was sick on the stomach. I couldn't eat.

And for me, at that time, I ate like 20 times a day. It was just devastating that we lost. Yeah.

Whenever I started playing football for Ridgeview, before you could walk on the field, you had to walk through a crowd of alumni that had played for Ridgeview before. And they like, "Hey, boy. You going to go out there and play, you better be playing or go home to your momma."

So it was tough. And after... They were there every practice, every game cheering us on. "Hey, man. You did good today. We appreciate it. Keep going. But next time get lower than your opponent. Knock him down."

Interviewer: What positions did you play?

Tillis Rendleman: I played, well, we only had like 34 people in the whole team so you had to play both sides. I was an offensive guard, defensive guard, tackle if they need it, linebacker, and I worked on special teams on the kickoff. That's why it was necessary to be in shape all the time.

You had to be in condition to do that. Some of those guys, some of my friends they stayed on the field the whole game. They played offense and then the defense. The only time they got off is at the half break.

And they're like, "Oh, wow. That was unbelievable." And took a drink of water and 15 minutes later, back on the field. And that was, I think, why our conditioning program was so important is that we had to last longer than other teams.

Interviewer: Were there any games you played besides football that toughened you up to play organized football?

Tillis Rendleman: We played, oh what is it? Two players get on the ground and they're facing up and the coach comes up and drops the ball on one of them. And the other one becomes the defender and whoever gets the ball is the runner.

You have to get off the ground from your back position with the ball, if you got the ball. And then you've got to make a move on the defensive player and that's tough sometimes. Because they'll nail you as soon as you come up off the ground. Bam! And then you're like, ooh.

And he'd say, "Hey. You did good. But let's do it again." And then you'd do it again, and again, and again. And I just loved it. Yeah. I was into sports even though I only played football, but I was a good runner. I liked baseball. I didn't like basketball.

I think I disagreed with the coach of the basketball team. I liked his daughter, and he didn't like me liking his daughter. I think that football was the thing for me because I loved hitting people, and my friends all played, so that was a way to just keep playing with them.

Interviewer: When y'all were at practice, much trash talking going on?

Tillis Rendleman: All the time.

Interviewer: What would that sound like? I mean, what's 1964 trash talking sound like?

Tillis Rendleman: "Hey, boy. Hey. What are you doing out here? Your momma's calling you home. Why don't you go on? You don't know what you doing. Oh, you didn't have breakfast this morning? Well, good. Nobody had breakfast this morning. You better get on the ground. There's some worms down there. Eat them. Do something, but just don't stand there looking stupid."

And some of the old football players be standing around. They be cracking up. They be like, "Uh-huh. Hey, boy. You ain't low enough. You need to get down on the ground if you going to beat this man." That's when the position of the tackles and the guards on the line, defensive players need to be lower than offensive players so that we win that moment. And if you don't, they just run all over you.

And considering, I was small in them days. God, I maybe weighed 190, maybe 200. Something like that. I mean, look at these guys now. They got kids in high schools 6'7", 300 pounds, can fly. I mean, unbelievable.

Interviewer: How tall were you when you played?

Tillis Rendleman: 6'1", yeah.

Interviewer: Coach Scales, what kind of guy was he?

Tillis Rendleman: Oh. He was really, really a scholastic-type coach. He believed in systems of plays. He's the statistician for the team. He designed all these really cool plays. He designed a play that we used in, I can't remember which year it was.

Where the center and the quarterback line up on one side of the field. The rest of the team is in the middle of the field and they hike the ball. We throw it down to the rest of the team and they run right down the field.

The pros did that. I think the Panthers did that. Was it last season or the season before last? It was unbelievable. He was great. He designed a lot of the plays and positions that we had and he was a quiet man.

Coach Davis, he was huge. He was I guess what? 6'3", 6'5" somewhere up there. He's bigger than me. And he yelled. He didn't talk softly to you, "Hey, man. You going to do so-and-so." He wanted you to know that you're important. You're important to the program. You're important to the school, community and the county and the state. And you need to act like it. Don't act like no idiot.

Football players now, I mean, they protest this. They protest that. They don't like this. They don't like that. If you played for Ridgeview you played for Ridgeview and the community, and the city and the state.

You just weren't an individual just running around acting like an idiot. And they stressed that. Coach Scales was, he was the quiet genius of the two, I believe. And then my senior year they brought in Coach Witherspoon. He helped us with strength. And boy, he was an ex-Marine.

Gosh. That guy. Pushups, sit-ups, squats. We crawled around on the ground like earthworms for weeks. It was unbelievable. But once we got through that, I never felt, physically, I've never felt that good ever.

I went onto college for a year-and-a-half. Didn't like it and I quit so I joined the Army. And their training was comparable to Ridgeview's training, in fact. I mean, first thing in the morning we'd run five miles.

Ridgeview did the same thing. He prepared us for later on down the road and I thought, I told him during the Black History celebration, I told him, "I really appreciate you because you prepared me for a three-year journey in the Army. And I also spent 10 years in the Air Force, too." And I said, "I was ready. I was ready."

Interviewer: How special was it to make the team?

Tillis Rendleman: A lot of kids came out for the team, but everybody didn't make it. I was blessed and pleased I made it for four years. But some kids didn't make it.

Interviewer: Did you have try outs every year?

Tillis Rendleman: Well, you show up for conditioning. And then, of course, you try out for the team. And during that two, four weeks of whatever it is in there, the coaches were checking you out. Making sure you knew what you could do. You would follow their lead and follow their instructions.

Some kids just had attitudes. "I ain't going to do this. I ain't going to do that." Hit the road jack. If you going to play ball at The View... We call it The View. If you're going to play ball at The View, you have to do what the coaches say. He says, "You will not stay up longer than 9:00, 9:30. You not running around the streets drinking beer, smoking, carousing with whoever. No. You not going to do that."

Because somebody in that community will pick up the telephone and call him. I mean, you had 5,000 people reporting on you. "Oh, yeah. That boy, he didn't go to bed last night until midnight. He was out there on the front porch drinking Budweiser." No. That could not work. You would not play for Mr. Davis. Not going to happen.

He expected you to give it all because he wanted to give it all. And if you wanted to be a winner, good. He would support that. He would push you in every way he could to make that happen for you. But you had to participate. It's simple as that.

Interviewer: Did any players get outed trying to have it both ways? Try to have some fun and get found out and get kicked off the team?

Tillis Rendleman: No. Not that I know. We had a couple kids that were not allowed because of, I think, grades to play. And see I missed a game my senior year because I had got dinged on the knee my junior year and I had just, personally, I just had lost my confidence that I could play 100%. Maybe 75%, but 75% wasn't good enough.

You had to play everything and be everything and you had to play all night. It's not like, "Oh, yeah." Like these guys run out there and run a play and they come back and sit down for an hour. No. No. You played. Wherever he needed you, you played. And you didn't complain about it. Because you were blessed and lucky to be on the team.

Yeah, well, I got dinged and I said, "I don't know if I want to play this year." My senior year. "I don't know if I want to play." So I missed the conditioning part. And I was in conditioning anyway because I had been running with my friends ever since school was out, so I was already in condition. I'd been doing the same exercises and everything. And I still had a problem with this knee.

And he had me come talk to him and I talked to him about it. And Dr. Goodman was our team doctor. He checked it out and he said, "Well, yeah. I think without going to an orthopedist you'll be fine. You can do this." He fitted me with a brace. Boom. I think I missed a game, but I was back on the team playing just like everybody else.

Interviewer: What was the difference in the team between 63 and 64, say with your quarterbacks?

Tillis Rendleman: Well, Mack Roland was a little shorter. Allen Pope, his daddy was one of the police from Ridgeview area. He was very, very intimate about what he did, how he did it. He was just real precise. Boom, boom. I mean, he could throw the ball, I mean, flatfooted 50 yards each. Yeah.

And we had players like that, that were just outstanding. You could compare them to some of the players they have coming out now and you're like, wow. They would be, I mean, neck to neck on their abilities and skills.

But I liked all the quarterbacks. Pat Broome was the quarterback, I think, when I was a freshman and I can't remember the other one. But they were all really good, all really good. Allen Pope added a different dimension. He not only could pass but as a quarterback, he played one of the deep backs too. So he played offense and defense and he would hit you.

Interviewer: Did you play both sides of the ball all the time?

Tillis Rendleman: No. Sometimes I would play it mostly defensive and other times I'd play defensive and offensive. It just depends on what the coaches needed at that time. Coach Scales would look at the scheme, the guys that made up the team, and he'd say, "Oh, let's adjust this a little bit."

Like there were several guards that were small and Joe Lutz and I were guards and we were a little bit bigger than some of the junior guards like Aggie White and Pete Heard. They were smaller and they were quick.

Watching one of them line up and next thing you know, he's gone. He's past you. You can't even, I mean, where is he? Like he disappeared. And so different schemes when different situations came up, Coach Scales would change the scheme and change the players.

Plus the fact that we heard that a lot of teams were looking at us to knock us off. We'd been winning the conference championship every year since 1958. So they were looking to knock us off that crown. Just, "Nah, we going to take them out." They didn't do it.

Interviewer: So there was a bunch of trash talking on their part, too?

Tillis Rendleman: Always. Yeah. And back in the '60s anything went. "What's your momma doing? I had a date with your sister. She's so ugly." Things like that. You like, whoa.

Interviewer: What would happen when you guys would get way ahead because you would bury people in the first half?

Tillis Rendleman: Oh, yeah. Some of the teams they resented it. They'd say, "Oh, this guy's just piling on now." But see, that's the way we were trained. You go and play the game. You played the game. You don't pull up after you've made 20 or 30 points. No, no. We play the game from the beginning to the end. And at the end whoever wins it, wins it. That's it. And, I mean, we got ran out of Morganton.

I think it was—was it my junior or senior year?—we got run out of Morganton. We were killing them. I think we had them 80-something to nothing. And the fans just got mad, and they ran us off the field.

We were rolling. I mean, our team was, everybody was boom! Boom! The plays were, I mean—we were performing the plays just like they've been scripted. And the halfbacks were running. The defensive backs were not allowing Morganton to gain any yardage. And we just virtually took the ball from those guys and scored, and we continued to score.

And I remember we were getting ready to kick off to them. And we were lined up and Charles Redman, he's one of my cousins, he was assigned to me. He was a big tackle. Charles Redman. And then Dwight Thompson, he was a defensive end on the kickoff there.

And we were lined up on the right side and the fans were just raising sin. They were booing, booing, booing. And then my cousin, James Thompson, now that boy could kick. He kicked the ball and you hear boom. And you just start running.

And you look up, the ball is coming down. And I'm hauling. I'm flying down the field and I look over to see where Charles Redman and Dwight's at because the middle is covered by a different part of the team.

And we had to cover the right side and the left side was covered by another group and then the middle. And so we're concentrated and worried about the right side. And we were flying down the field. And look over and there's no Dwight. And I thought, "What in the Sam Hill is that?"

And Charles Redman zooms by me, he says, "Look out, look out." And I looked over and all the guys from the Morganton side was coming across the field. And I thought what in the world is this all about?

And then I looked on the other side and the Ridgeview side was coming across to meet them. And we got caught in the middle and the coaches were out there, "Get off the field. Get off the field. Get back to the bus."

So they got us all together and out and the police was there. Some of the Morganton staff were there to get us out of that area off the field and back to our buses. And they put us on our activity buses and brought us back to Hickory still in uniform. Unbelievable. And I don't know if they got censured for that or what, but that was unsportsmanlike big time. We were taught to play ball and play ball. Not play *at it* but play ball.

It was just chaos with all those people running across the field at each other and we got caught in the middle. And so their players, their coaches got their players off the field. Our coaches got us off the field and then, of course, the security people showed up. And the Hickory people, they got us out and put us on activity buses and got us out of there.

I just saw all the bodies all over the place. In some situations everything slows down. In this case it was just really fast. Like, what in the world is all these people out here for? That's not what a football game looks like. But I always wondered about that. Because I thought the school should've been held accountable for that. The team, the school, the coaches. I mean, that's nonsense.

Interviewer: Can you talk about Coach Davis' philosophy of play? How would you characterize that?

Tillis Rendleman: My senior year, the coach, we were playing some team. I can't remember what it was and I had played both sides and I was tired. And he pulled us all over to the sideline and I was standing there and blood was running out of my nose and I thought, God almighty. And he said, "Boys, I want you to remember this, kill a gnat with a sledgehammer." We're like, "What the Sam Hill is he talking about?" "Go ahead, do it. Play. Don't stop because you got 60 points or whatever it is. Keep playing. Finish it." And that's what we did.

And I've used that philosophy from then until now and it hasn't failed me yet. I don't halfway do anything. I'm never late. I don't have to apologize because I try my very best to do it right the first time.

Interviewer: What kind of crowds did you have when you were playing away games that followed you to where you were playing?

Tillis Rendleman: All of Catawba County. And you got to remember this is the height of the Civil Rights era too. And a lot of things were going on in the community and in surrounding communities mostly. I mean, I wasn't aware of any major racial problems in Catawba County or Ridgeview or anywhere in our area at all.

I didn't know about that until I went to school in Durham. Then it's all of a sudden wake up. I'm like, "What? What's going on." "You can't do this, you can't do that." I'm like, "Wait a minute. I'm from Hickory. I can, too." And you had that attitude if you went to The View.

Interviewer: Explain the difference.

Tillis Rendleman: Oh, like when I went to school in Durham, you go to places and they had bathrooms for black only, bathrooms for white only. I was like, "What?" I just went to the bathroom. I don't care. I mean, who cares? You got to go to the bathroom, you got to go to the bathroom.

But I never felt that in Hickory. I felt real supported. And at any game you could look around at the fans and you'd have a mixture of different colors of people from everywhere.

In the program. Look at all the people. The different companies that supported us. I mean, there were tons of them. And they all came to the ball games and away games too. I thought it was interesting.

Interviewer: You say you didn't experience any of that kind of segregation stuff in Hickory?

Tillis Rendleman: Not really. No, sir. I didn't feel pressure in that way until I got to college. And everything was just, it was a whole different world. It's like we were treated and guarded in a special way in Catawba County and then we got out into the cold world, boom, this is how it really is.

Interviewer: So is that because you spent most of your time in Ridgeview? Or when you went to Hickory, you didn't see any of that either?

Tillis Rendleman: I didn't see any of that at all. A kid asked me, he said, "Have you ever went downtown to Woolworth's and to their lunch counter?" "Yeah. Every Saturday." Whenever I was a kid, I'd go shopping with my grandmother. We'd go over to Woolworth's and get a burger and a soda. Sit down at the counter and eat. No problem. Ain't nobody said, "No, you can't do this. You have to go to the back."

No, we just ate, and that was it. Durham is a different environment altogether compared to Hickory. And I think that's one of the reasons I didn't want to continue going to school there. It was just too big for me. It's just huge.

The college campus was just huge. The dormitories like big as the whole complex. I mean, it was just huge. And compared to little old Hickory, I said I don't know if I want to continue there.

So I surprised my parents and said, "Hey, I'm quitting college and I'm going to join the army and volunteer for Vietnam." And they said, "You out of your mind. You are crazy." And I did. I needed a jolt.

Interviewer: So no real segregation in Hickory?

Tillis Rendleman: No. As kids, we ran all over Hickory and I'll say Catawba County. I mean, we run and run. I heard when I was in the Army, some of my friends say, "Oh, yeah, we was walking down the road and somebody came by and threw a bottle at us." I never experienced any of that.

Interviewer: Or did you have much social interaction with whites during that whole period?

Tillis Rendleman: I worked at Winn-Dixie as a kid. Let me back up. I drove the school bus. I was one of that set of teenagers in high school that had enough credentials and a clean record who could drive a school bus for the state. So I drove a school bus, and after football season, I worked at Winn-Dixie on Fridays and Saturdays. I never had a problem.

I enjoyed working with those guys at Winn-Dixie, and we'd see each other. I'd drive the school bus, and I'd see them driving their school bus, wave at them and keep going. But we never had any personal conflicts with anybody.

Interviewer: What about the coaches knowing what you're doing in the classroom? Did they have a finger on what was going on?

Tillis Rendleman: Yes, sir. I do believe they did. I know there were several players that were having problems. And the coaches talked to us as a whole that as players, we have to toe the line. We have to be better than just the average Joe. We have to really try. We just can't thumb our nose at assignments and reports and tests and things like that. We really have to go through the process as a student. If not, hey, you can't play. As simple as that.

Interviewer: So your grades really had to be good?

Tillis Rendleman: Yes, sir.

Interviewer: In order to be able to play. It sounds like you looked at playing as a privilege?

Tillis Rendleman: Oh, yeah. To play at The View was a privilege and a blessing. I mean, you look at this scrapbook here, you'll see, we had some serious players. The Charles Brothers, the Warlick Brothers, the Clay Brothers. Jesus, those guys. When I was a kid, I used to pick up a football game. I'd get to play on one of those teams. You'd have 20 people on this team and 20 people on this team.

And when we'd go out to the field and we'd be banging into each other. It wasn't no tag ball or rag ball. It was football and it was tackle. And that was early experiences. And I thought it was fantastic.

Interviewer: Now those pickup games, did you play with white kids that were playing, too?

Tillis Rendleman: No.

Interviewer: So was it mainly Ridgeview and East Hickory? Or was it just Ridgeview?

Tillis Rendleman: It was Ridgeview, East Hickory and sometimes kids from Newton come up.

Richard: What about that rivalry with Newton?

Tillis Rendleman: Yeah. It was tough. And you know we will run into some of those players now and they say, "Oh, yeah. You boys, yeah. Yeah, we made y'all what you turned out to be." I'm like, "Yeah, you did. You did."

Interviewer: How do you mean?

Tillis Rendleman: By playing so hard, they made us play even harder. Yeah. I can't recall us playing a team that was not qualified to play in our league. We played some big time schools too. But everybody we played on Friday night, sometimes we played on Thursday night, they were tough. They were tough. And on any given day or night, whenever the game is scheduled, you can win or you can lose. The best team wins and we wanted to be the best team. And when we hit the field, boom. We showed it.

Interviewer: Now, that game that you played in '64 against Newton, that's next to the last one, they were undefeated and you were undefeated. Do you remember any of that?

Tillis Rendleman: I know I got hit in that game and it hurt big time. Yeah. I got hit and it's like, boom. For me, everything used to go in slow motion. And it was like I was charging into the offense and the next thing you know, the ground just came up. I'm like, "Whoa. What happened?" And there I was. I'm like, "Oh, shucks. What's going on?"

And John Hodge, he was our middle linebacker and I remember him standing over me. He says, "Boy, you better get up from there. Your grandmother is going to arrive here on this field and snatch your stupid looking self up off this field and take you back over there on the sideline."

I says, "Where is she?" He said, "Uh-oh. She looks like she's coming on the field." I said, "I'm getting up. Get me to my feet." And they stood me up and everything was swirling. I thought, Lord, have mercy. Who hit me? A truck? And he said, "Get it together. Get it together."

And so Xenophone Lutz had me one side, John Hodge had me one side. They walked me over to the sideline. And my grandma looked around, she's about five foot tall, 90 pounds. But she was tough and she looked at me and I said, (indicating good). And she went on back to her seat and I said, "Oh, boy. That would be embarrassing. Your grandmother come on the football field and carry you off." Oh, that would be the end.

Interviewer: How long did you stay out? The rest of the game?

Tillis Rendleman: No. Ain't no rest of the game unless you dead.

Wright Cade, Jr.

One of the oldest living members of the Ridgeview Football Panthers at the time of this interview, Mr. Cade was an all around athlete during his playing days at Ridgeview. He remembered when his team was up and coming, during the time when Coach Davis first came to the program. His interview was conducted during the 2015 reunion at the Brown-Penn Center (old Ridgeview High School gym).

Interviewer: When did you play football for Ridgeview?

Wright Cade, Jr.: '52, '53, '54 and '55.

Interviewer: And what do you remember about playing?

Wright Cade, Jr.: I had a good time.

Interviewer: How hard did you have to work?

Wright Cade, Jr.: Oh, I had to work very hard. We had some mean coaches back then.

Interviewer: What did they make you do?

Wright Cade, Jr.: Regular calisthenics that you do in football. The up-down, jumping jacks, push-ups, and shuttles, and laps. Back then, I was in pretty good shape so it didn't bother me one bit. I loved to go to practice, but mainly, basketball was my game. The coach said if I didn't play football that I wasn't going to play basketball. Well, that talked me into coming. I was a defensive back on the team. That's all I played was defense and stuff like that on the team, so that was fairly easy. I did all the hitting the other teams. I didn't have to worry about getting hit.

Interviewer: Why did you have to play football so you could play basketball?

Wright Cade, Jr.: Well, I was tall. I was tall and I was fast, and he needed defensive backs to go back to watch them passes and stuff. And usually when somebody put one in the air, I got it.

Interviewer: So you picked off quite a few?

Wright Cade, Jr.: Yeah. I picked off a few passes.

Interviewer: What do you remember about those games?

Wright Cade, Jr.: We went undefeated. That's the best thing I liked about the whole thing. The team that we was playing, I wasn't an offensive player. I took a play in for him to run for the last play and I lined up at the end. I wasn't supposed to be involved in the play. I had them run a pattern and run down in the end.

I had good friends and good teachers, good coaches, and everybody helped everybody back then. You needed some help, everybody'd help you.

And Boy Scouts. Boy Scouts Camp. I loved all that stuff around here. It was a nice place. And right now, looks like we all falling fast. There ain't that many left of us.

The Last Interview

For various reasons within the documentary (sound quality, framing, etc.) I asked a group of players for one final interview. Reverend Xenophone Lutz, Tillis Rendleman and Douglas Bumgarner graciously came to the campus of Catawba Valley Community College for an interview in late 2019 to repeat a few stories but also to elaborate on things I had since discovered about the team. For example, what I labeled their theme song was not the only song team members sang.

Interviewer: Tell me that story again about how often you played hot grease, what it was like, that sort of thing?

Xenophone Lutz: Hot grease was a game that all the guys in the neighborhood, young and old, would gather, and hot grease was where they would throw a ball on the ground, and whoever was what we called brave enough to pick the ball up and try to run, and then the rest of the crowd would try and tackle and pile up on them, you know. That was one of the ways that you proved that you were what we call tough, you know. And so often, you find somebody who wouldn't do it, but the guys who really wanted to prove themselves, yeah, they'd grab that ball and run, and after everybody tackled them, they'd feel good about themselves.

They'd know that they were what you call accepted, you know. And so, again, that was hot grease. It was a mixture of young and old, guys that played years ago, and guys that didn't even play organized football, and just from young to old. Whoever felt like they would want to participate, did. I always say those games probably occurred probably a few times a week. Yeah. Usually always on the weekends. But again, that was hot grease. Again, that was more or less a stepping stone to making a name for yourself. Yeah.

Interviewer: Any of the rest of you remember playing hot grease?

Douglas Bumgarner: Yeah, I don't know exactly where it got started or when, but we used to play hot grease. I was on the east side of town, East Hickory, so we would have a circle type thing. And they would put the ball in the center, and somebody would go out and pick up the ball, and then naturally you'd try to tackle them and stuff like that. And you dropped it again, and somebody else would go in and get it. And it was just a game I think, a house thing that we just created. Just activities, because we played it at recess, and on the weekends also.

But it was, like I said, a gladiator game I guess. Whoever had the most guts to pick it up, and you know you're going to get hit, but it's just how long they're going to get to take you down. That was the challenge for us, to see how long you can stay up.

Interviewer: Mr. Rendleman, do you remember playing?

Tillis Rendleman: Yeah. Every time the afternoon came, it cooled down a little bit, a group of people would sit over there in front of the community center or library, and next thing you know, run down the street to the fields, and boom. It's on. And you have men and women playing ball. Yeah. I'd be snagging balls for Ozzie Clay. I think I did. Yeah. Caught balls for Ozzie Clay and Leonard, and one of the Warlicks. What was the other guy? Bobby?

Xenophone Lutz: Bobby.

Tillis Rendleman: They had a sister, Sally Warlick. She was tough too. We got a chance to play with a lot of those guys.

Interviewer: Now what did it mean to play football for Ridgeview High?

Tillis Rendleman: That's the best thing that ever happened to me. I mean, we had several coaches, they were interested in us as people, and they wanted us to be the very best. Not quit. Not make excuses, but be the best that we could be and never give up. Never. No matter what. That's why the phrase, kill a man with a sledgehammer came up with the big coach, Davis. Some of these new teams out, you'll see them fading in the second quarter. He wanted us to play the whole one hour with all the time outs, everything, straight through, not quit, no matter what. In fact, I would feel good after the game. I hated practice, but the game was the big enchilada.

You'd practice hard, but the game was so satisfying. The people everywhere cheering for you, patting you on the back. Half of them don't even know your name, but still. They appreciated it. The City of Hickory appreciated it. We were sponsored by a lot of people from downtown, so that's what made it special for me.

Xenophone Lutz: Yeah, you know also, talking about what made it special, every now and then, we'd gather, and people would tell stories about different players, you know. Some of the great players of the past, and so once you became Ridgeview, once you became a member of the football team, this is what you were joining. This is what you were becoming a part of. One day, perhaps they would tell stories about you too. But again, when you made the football team, you knew you were somebody special. When you go through the community, walk through the community, people know you, and everybody's interested in you, everybody's encouraging you, and supporting you. It's just a tremendous feeling.

You know you were part of something special.

Douglas Bumgarner: I think when you started the seventh and eighth grade, that's what one of your goals were, to become a member of the team at Ridgeview. That's what every young guy wanted to do, and it was just an exciting time for when you found out that you made the team. A lot of people came out. They couldn't make it through the training. It was tough. It was really hard, and I can understand. But if you really wanted that title of being a football player for Ridgeview, you would stick through it, and it was hard. But I think what really kept me in tune, driven, was the Friday night excitement.

I mean, people say, "Do you like football?" I try to think about, do I like football, or do I just like the excitement? Nobody likes to get beat up and pushed around, but that's what comes with the game. But on Friday night when you hear the cheer of the crowds, and when you do something good and you hear the roar of the crowd, it's just something that motivates you and keeps you going. So I think the Friday night glamor is worth all the training and stuff that you had to go through. But to get something good, you've got to go through something bad, so it all tied hand in hand. So I loved it.

Interviewer: Can you tell me the position you played and how you got to that position?

Douglas Bumgarner: Well, I played halfback on offense. At the time,

I was running left halfback, but you can run right or left if you're in the backfield. And I always wanted to be a halfback, because I would see people like in my time, Ozzy Clay. He was one of the famous players at the time at Ridgeview, David Slacks and Holloway, and Tommy Probst, some of the good backs at Ridgeview. And I just liked to run the ball more so than blocking. I knew at my size, I couldn't do very well at that, especially on the line. So my concentration was in on running the ball, being a halfback.

Interviewer: And you were also scoring on defense, too, because you were a defensive back, right?

Douglas Bumgarner: Yeah, there was a few opportunities on defense, mostly if you intercepted the ball and took it back, but basically recovered a fumble in the end zone or something like that. That's about the only time on the defense that I would have probably had an opportunity to score, because on defense, you were trying to stop the opponent from crossing over as you know. So unless you've got the ball, you can't score. So interception, there's a possibility, and there was a couple interceptions that I scored on.

Interviewer: That's got to feel good.

Douglas Bumgarner: Oh, it does. It does. And at the same time, like I've always said, I got to give credit to my linemen. I can't keep it to myself.

Interviewer: Well, let's talk about the line.

Tillis Rendleman: We were running. I was blocking for Bumgarner and we were running down the sideline, and he said, "Come on man. Speed up. Speed up." And I said, "I'm running as fast as I can." And then, here comes a player from the other side, and I'm like okay, that's it. And I fall down in front of him, and the paper said, fantastic block or something. I thought that was a hoot. I thought that was a hoot. It felt good to me.

Interviewer: And tell me the position and why you wanted to play it.

Tillis Rendleman: Well, when I started out, seven to eight, whatever age group, I played quarterback, played fullback, played end. And I just didn't like getting hit and popped all the time. I thought well, I'm going to be the popper instead of the pop-ee, and so I think I started playing center or guard, and when I got in high school, the coach said, "What position do you want to play?" And I said, "Guard," and that's where I wound up. But then, since we only had like what? 36 players. You had to take on a different role. You had to do a little bit of this, a little bit of that. And he said, "Hey, can you play that position?" "Yes sir. I'll get in there and try it." I played everything but center and end.

In the final days of Ridgeview, I think about it a lot. They're preparing me for life. They prepared me for life. Be ready to change, do anything, because I wound up in the Army as a medic, and then later on in the Air Force as a combat nurse. So it prepared me to make a quick break, change, do whatever I had to do to keep going. Beautiful thing.

Interviewer: So it prepared you for a whole lot more than just playing football.

Tillis Rendleman: Oh yes. Oh yes.

Interviewer: Tell me about your position and why you wanted to play it.

Xenophone Lutz: I'm going to tell you the truth. I always wanted to be a running back. Yeah, I wanted to be a running back and wear low cut shoes and all that stuff, because the linemen mostly wore high tops. But I was a little slow to be a running back, and plus I didn't have that skill. But I guess ever since I was seventh, eighth, ninth grade, I was pretty strong, and somebody one day said, "Man, you're going to be a good guard. You're built like a guard," so that stayed in my mind, and so that's what I accepted. That's the role I accepted, and then I grew to love it, being a lineman, being a guard.

And it's just a beautiful position. You know that a lineman was the heart of the team, so I always knew I was playing an important part of what I was doing, and so I always say, soon as I joined the football team, the older guys molded me into becoming the best guard I could be. The guys that played the position, there were a few. James Childs, Thomas Childs, Richard Davis, those guys were all conference players or so, and they would show me tricks, what we call tricks. You know, what are called tricks, and how to take care of yourself basically, and then how to get the other man, take advantage of the other man.

So I used to say to myself, well, I have 101 tricks. So things that I could do on the line that nobody else could do. If I ran into an opponent that gave me trouble, there was always some kind of adjustment I knew I could make. But again, my size, I was what I call five eleven and a half, junior year around 200 pounds, so I was a classic high school guard at that time.

Interviewer: And both sides of the ball, right?

Xenophone Lutz: Yeah. I played guard on both sides of the ball, and often linebacker on passing plays. But it was nothing like being a lineman. Every play, I get to tee off on somebody, and I really loved that. And that's what I looked forward to. I believe my brother said that he looked forward to the glamor, the lights and stuff, but I looked forward to hitting somebody. I looked forward to taking somebody out. So I just loved contact.

Interviewer: Offense or defense better? Which do you like better?

Xenophone Lutz: I actually loved playing offense. Yeah. Making a block, opening a hole. And again, I could make the contact I wanted, being an offensive lineman, because I knew exactly what I was going to do, and I didn't usually have to react. On defense, you've got to react mostly, but I think offensively, being offensive guard, that was the edge, because I loved making that contact and loved making a hole. Defense was great, but it was something special about that bang, bang, bang on offense. So I looked forward to that. Yes sir.

Interviewer: And I think in an earlier interview when we were talking, you said that after losing the state championship your junior year, that's when you decided it ain't going to be like that senior year.

Tillis Rendleman: That was one of the most hurtful times in my life that I can remember. I just, ooh. We worked so hard to get there, and then we lose the state championship? We were that close and lost. And we had to handle that. A lot of people say, "Oh, you boys did a great job right up until the last." Why would you tell somebody that? We knew we lost.

But determination. We said, "We're not losing again. We're going to take it all the way." We didn't know we were going to take it all the way, but we hoped we could and would. And that's what made me want to play ball, and then I had words with the coach, and I had words with the principal. I was a school bus driver, and so I said, "I'm not going to go out. After all of that training and conditioning," I said, "I'm not going to go." And so, I stayed home, drove the school bus, went to school, worked at Winn-Dixie, and one day, Dwight Thompson and John Hodge showed up at my house after I brought the bus back and parked it, and said, "The coach wants to see you."

And I said, "For what? I don't play ball with you guys no more."

I was just ooh, a little rebel. Whoa.

I got my jacket, and I ran down the street. I guess it's about a mile. My grandmother lives about a mile from the school, and the coach said, "Boy, do you want to play ball or what?" And I said, "Well, not really." He says, "We need you. This is going to be special," and I said, "Yeah?" And John Hodge gave me the look, and Dwight said (fist in hand). I said, "Okay." And so, the next day, I was out there in my practice gear. I didn't have real good shoes. My old shoes were tore up, and the next day after that, Mr. Scales brings me a brand new pair of high tops. I was like, "Man, I want some low cuts, but..." Yeah. Brings me some high tops, and boom, I was off and running.

Interviewer: Now, do you remember that loss? The state championship the previous year?

Douglas Bumgarner: Oh yeah. Yeah. I still remember it. It's something that just haunts you. It was a very devastating time, and everybody was hurt. We're not used to losing like that, and we shouldn't have lost then. Sometimes you have a good season, sometimes you get slack. You think you're sort of cocky like, you know? I don't know if that was the problem for us losing or not, but we lost, and it just stuck with us. I'm just thinking, if we could have won that game and did the same thing we did the time before, we'd have been scored on, it still would have been two championships back to back, and so it was real devastating. It hurt. And you just don't forget things like that.

Interviewer: Did you say, "I ain't going to let that happen again?"

Douglas Bumgarner: Oh yeah. Yeah, definitely. I think we all decided that, but I was sure I was going back out, because I just wanted to play ball, and loved ball, and so I knew I was going to go back out the next year, and it was just hoping that we're just going to play better, and take that defeat from last year, and sort of get us more motivated for this year. And it seemed like things worked out for us.

You know, football, playing football, to me, you've got to have things that's going to motivate you, make you better, make you stronger. Like I remember things, like my brother told me, "Every time you run the ball, run it like it's your last time."

So to me, that would give me incentive to run harder, faster. One person's not going to stop me or something like that. I'm just going to keep struggling until I can't go anymore, okay? And there was a time when they was getting on our backs about hitting the holes slow. They jumped all over me about that you're hitting the holes slow. But I was thinking, with my speed, by the time I get from here to there, in the T formation, you're not that far apart. I said, I've got to give the quarterback time to get the ball so he can give it to me. So I'm delaying then going, but not realizing that it's just like boom, boom, boom. That hole opens, and it closes just like that. You take somebody maybe 185 pound guard, trying to hold back a 210 pound defensive player, he can't do it but so long.

Now, he can get the jump on him, because he knows where to block and where the play is coming. So I decided, okay I'm going to show this, because the quarterback got all down my back about being slow, you're scared, and Coach Davis said, you're scared. Get in my back pocket, and all this stuff, and I'm like, "Oh wow. Okay, I'm going to show them, I'm going to be through the hole before the quarterback gets the ball," and then I'm going to say, "See? That's what I've been trying to tell you. I have to slow it down."

But when I did that, and I tried to beat the play, the ball was right there, the hole opened, I was gone. So then I realized all this time, I'm thinking you're all that fast, the quarterback ain't going to have time, the quarterback did have time because it's just like snap, snap. And I learned from that right there, and that's what makes a good running back I think. When you hit that hole as soon as they make contact, because I'm sure the lineman's going to tell you, they can't hold them holes open too long, especially if you're playing against somebody that's bigger than you are.

So I used that. And then, I used some crazy stuff just to make me mad. This guy, they'd be all saying this guy right here slapped my sister or something, anything to psyche me up. One of them Mike Tyson things. And so, that sort of helped me get my motivation going.

Interviewer: Was there any competition between you and the other guys in the backfield?

Douglas Bumgarner: No. I think we were pretty much equal. No there people would probably say, "Well, he was a better back than you." I say, "Okay, fine. That's your opinion. That's fine. You might like Jay Z, and I might like another rapper better. That's your preference." But to me myself, I thought we was all basically equal, you know? We had about the same speed. We could reach out and touch each other any time we raced, and wasn't that far apart. It wasn't like I'm on the 25 and he's on the 50.

Our moves were different. We had different move styles, but about the same height, same weight, a couple pounds difference. No, I don't think so.

Interviewer: Okay, you had 21 touchdowns and they didn't.

Douglas Bumgarner: Well, that was just blessing. Blessing. Just luck. I didn't do anything special. It just happened.

Interviewer: Can you talk about their different moves, how they were different from yours?

Douglas Bumgarner: Well, mine was more, I guess quick, and maybe lateral, back and forth. Burch was more of a shifty type, and he had a running style that was sort of unique. It looked like he was running sideways to me. It looked like he was running, but he was shifty and he was fast, stopped on a dime, and moved. Cunningham was more stride-ful, like an OJ Simpson type, I would say, with power and stuff like that. That's what I would see it.

But we all had the speed. It was just in different moves. Mine was short and quick. Cunningham's was fast and long, and Burch was just like, he was just hard to touch. He just kept moving, and that's a good thing. A sitting target is easy to hit. He just kept moving and shifting.

Interviewer: Talk about that loss and your resolve the next year.

Xenophone Lutz: Oh man. We played Lexington Dunbar, and the last half, we were coming back. We felt like we were going to come back and win the game, and we were coming back strong, but time ran out. And man, when time ran out, it seemed like that was the end of the world. I'm going to tell you. In that locker room, guys didn't have to shower. We were crying. Everybody was crying so heavily. I mean, tears were pouring from everybody. And so I said, "Yeah, I ain't going to feel like this again, man." I said, "I ain't going to never lose like this again. Man, we ain't going to lose again. I ain't going to never have this type of feeling again. This hurts."

And during the off season, during training, getting ready for the season, one of the things that I would say and the others would say, "Remember Lexington. Remember Lexington. Remember Lexington," and, "We want Lexington. We want Lexington." We wanted to make up. We wanted to make up. We want Lexington. And after the season got going, we discovered that Lexington had moved up in the class, and we wouldn't be able to play them anymore, but still we had that determination, that resolve that we are not going to lose anymore.

And we were really rolling, and so again, that's just a thought of losing. Of course, we put that on our back burner. We got to the point where we never really thought about losing anymore. It was just going out and executing. And again, we were confident that if we play our game, do what we're supposed to do, nobody would beat us, but again, just that loss man, it hurt. And after 50 some years, it still hurts. To tell the truth, we should have had three state titles, because that year we lost, it was potentially the best team we'd ever had, the biggest line, a lot of fine backs, the backfield, and we just had no business losing that game.

But for some reason, we lost. And so, after that, again, just take advantage of every situation. Just do what you're supposed to do, make sure you're going to win. Just give it all your best. Do what you have to do to wrap that win up.

Interviewer: If you read the newspapers, going into the season, the Untouchable season, Coach Davis says, "I don't know if we've got a good enough team. I mean, we're soft, we're weak this year." Is that just him saying that or is that the way he did? Or do you think he really believed that? Because you guys sound determined going into that.

Xenophone Lutz: Yeah. That's what he did, just for psychology purposes. Psych purposes. He didn't want us to be overconfident, and he didn't want to sound overconfident. But yeah, he knew that we had something special that year. They knew. The coaches knew we had something special, and we knew we had something special.

So again, he used those words, I think, as a caution. I look at it as a caution. Remember what happened to you last year, you know. So just downplay it, and of course, that didn't hurt. When he said that, we knew we had to always do our best. He was just downplaying the situation, making sure we don't become overconfident.

Tillis Rendleman: But it did make the other teams become overconfident.

It made the other teams overconfident, because they read the same newspapers that we read, and they said, "Oh, the coach at Ridgeview says these guys are not ready. They're too small, not fast enough. Hey, they lost too many seniors, dah dah dah dah dah." And they said, "Ah, we got you now."

Xenophone Lutz: Maybe this is our opportunity.

Tillis Rendleman: Bad choice. Yeah.

Interviewer: Do you think Newton read that?

Tillis Rendleman: Oh yeah. Newton's in Catawba County. They get the same paper. And Ellis Johnson, I think he did some great articles for Hickory, and I'm sure they got the message.

Interviewer: Did he work you any harder going into the season than he normally did? Or was that running something that the Ridgeview team did every year?

Xenophone Lutz: That was something we did every year.

Tillis Rendleman: Yeah.

Xenophone Lutz: Yeah. Yeah. Every year that we were a part of the team, we ran that five miles every morning in preparation for the season. Yeah. There was nothing unusual or different that I can remember that we did. Coach Scales was always introducing new plays and things like that, but no special exercises, no different drills or whatever. Just that mindset to just play football. Keep doing what you're doing.

Interviewer: Did you do anything different?

Xenophone Lutz: I don't think I did anything different, other than I think if anything, I made sure that whatever I was doing would contribute to winning. But never anything different. Make sure I was alert, and make sure I did my part. That's it.

And I always tried to encourage the other guys. Doug talked about hitting the line as a halfback, and one of the things that I think me, myself, John Hodge, Tillis, when we used to do like that. Everything is clockwork, you know? Clockwork. When the ball snap, boom, everything's clockwork. You've got to do what you're going to do, because Doug's coming. The backs are coming, so everything's clockwork. Do what you're going to do, and it's going to work. So that was... Yeah, I like when Doug brought that up, because again, it was clockwork.

If anything, we did anything different that year, it was probably just reminding ourselves, be on the spot. Do what you've got to do, because this is all about clockwork. So when that ball, the snap, boom, boom, boom, you know.

Interviewer: Did you all do anything different going into that season?

Douglas Bumgarner: Maybe just being more serious minded about it, but I don't think anything changed honestly. I think the reason is, the year before we just got relaxed in our playing, and not taking it too serious because we'd been used to winning. But no, I didn't do anything different. Just tried harder, and tried to keep from making mistakes, missing tackles, which is not too many of those. But sometimes you miss some of them. But no. It was about the same.

Xenophone Lutz: Yeah. I was just going to say, you know, we figured now that Doug's talking. That game we lost, that year before, I think we were just probably too relaxed.

Tillis Rendleman: Yeah.

Xenophone Lutz: And felt like we were coming back anyway. You know, we're going to win the game anyways. But then as time started to expire, and opportunities were no longer there, we started to realize we're going to lose, but I think even during that game, we felt like we were going to come back, because we were coming back, but again, we didn't have enough time.

Tillis Rendleman: Then there's the final whistle and the gun.

Xenophone Lutz: Yeah.

Tillis Rendleman: End of it.

Xenophone Lutz: That was the big hurt.

Tillis Rendleman: Yeah.

Xenophone Lutz: And again, that carried on off season, the summer, training, until the season started.

Tillis Rendleman: Yeah.

Xenophone Lutz: We hurt. I think everybody hurt until then, and then once we started playing, it took a back seat to what we had to do. We knew we could lose if we did not go out there and do what we had to do. We knew that nobody was going to lay down for us, and that the team would beat us if they could. And so, yeah, we were always on guard just to make sure that we did what we needed to do to win the game.

Interviewer: These teams were gunning for you. If they can knock off Ridgeview, then they're a good team.

Tillis Rendleman: Yeah. They're probably going to the state championship. And a lot of people don't understand that whenever we practiced, we were practicing against conference champs, state champions, and so every day is a challenge to put on the uniform and go out in the field, just to practice with these guys. And a lot of people didn't understand that.

We had a lot of responsibility on our back to the communities, to the city, the county, to play ball, and play good ball. And that's what always scared the crap out of me, is that I'm going to make a mistake, and disappoint these guys. And you would stand out. So I mean, it would be such a grave mistake, you'd be like, "Oh, god."

And of course, Mr. Scales would say, "You know, it's going to be all right," and then Coach Davis would be like, "What the crap?" So that's the two different levels of coaching. It's unbelievable. But I always appreciated Ridgeview ball, because we've known each other forever, for a lifetime in fact, and we played together.

And that final season, even though I played in different places during the game, you felt that togetherness with the other team. I mean, I didn't have to worry about Bumgarner was going to do. I knew he was going to do it. "Jobo" (Xenophone Lutz), hey, boom. He's going to take the player out. Boom, Bum was going to hit the hole and gone. God help you if you get in his way. He'd just run over you and keep going.

But it was special. It was special. Very special.

Xenophone Lutz: Yeah, and again, that was one of the keys. We knew everybody so well. Tillis, myself, John Hodge, and some of the other guys, ever since first grade we knew each other. And I knew Doug and some guys over there in the early grades, when they were in East Hickory. But again, we knew each other. We trusted each other. We could depend on each other. We believed in each other. We had our flaws, our faults, and everybody knew about them, and we'd get on each other every now and then, but we were such a great unit, and that togetherness, I think that was the key to our success, those 12 seniors in particular.

We were together. Everywhere. We did things together. And all that time, we just knew each other well, and you just couldn't measure that experience that we had with each other. It was just great, and like like Tillis mentioned, we knew each other. We knew what everybody was going to do, so...

Interviewer: Well, by that season, having known each other all your lives, you're ready, and especially with that loss, you're ready to have the kind of season you had. And then, you start going in and destroying teams, like 52 to nothing and 56 to nothing. That has to make you feel pretty good, right?

Xenophone Lutz: Yeah. Oh yeah. And talking about the way, how awesome we were, the reality was, teams were not going to beat us. They knew they weren't going to beat us, so if somebody could just score, that would be their victory. If a team could score, they would be satisfied. But they knew they weren't going to win. And we knew they weren't going to win, but again, after so long, just if they could just score, that would make their season.

But fortunately, we were so gifted, talented, that nobody scored. We just knew that on defense, we bought into the system. We were fundamentally solid, what you call. We depended on everybody to do what they were supposed to do. One important thing was, you did not necessarily have to make a tackle.

If you would just tie a guy up, slow him down, cut him off, somebody else was going to get him. That's the kind of pursuit we had. You didn't have to always make an individual tackle, because you knew that somebody was going to corner the guy and tackle him.

Interviewer: Now, could you tell that story about getting hit?

Tillis Rendleman: Yeah. I'll never forget that one. Yeah, we were playing Newton, and I was on the kickoff team, lined up. My cousin James Thompson, oh, he could kick. You'd hear the ball go boom, and you'd look up, and when it's coming down, you're flying down the field, rolling, rolling, looking left and right making sure Dwight Thompson's to the right, and I don't know who was to the left, but we were flying. Boom. And I look down. The ball's coming down. The receiver is catching the ball. Boom. That's my target.

Stay in your lane. That's what the coach said. Stay in your lane.

Xenophone Lutz: Stay in your lane.

Tillis Rendleman: Stay in your lane. Stay in your lane. And the next thing you know, the ground came up. Boom. And I was all, "What the crap is this?" And oh, everything was just slow motion, and I'm like, "What in the world?" And I look. My leg was back this way, and I'm like, "Wait a minute. That ain't right." And I'm like, oh, whoa. And everybody was crowded around me. "What's up man? What's going on? Get up, you need to get up." I'm like, oh wow. Oh, I can't get up. John Hodge came up and said, "Man, you need to get up." He called me Red. "Red, you need to get up." I'm like, "I'm trying man." "No, you need to get up."

And I said, "I can't." He said, "You need to. Your grandmother's standing right there. She's getting ready to come on the field." I thought, oh geesh. Ruin a person's reputation, this would do it. The end of T. Rendleman forever. And so they got me up on my feet, and I hobbled off the field. Oh. And she went back to her seat I the bleachers, and I thought, "Oh, lord. Have mercy." But that knee was so sore, they put me behind the players, and Coach Scales got some of that, what was it, red hot? I guess it was called,

Doug: Red Hot? Something like that?.

Tillis Rendleman: Red Hot or something or other, and put it on that knee.

Doug: Hot Stuff. Called Hot Stuff maybe.

Tillis Rendleman: Was it Hot Stuff?

Doug: Balm, yeah.

Tillis Rendleman: Oh.

Doug: Some kind of balm.

Tillis Rendleman: Some kind of balm.

Doug: Salve, balm.

Tillis Rendleman: Whoa. That thing burned right down through the bone, and pretty soon the pain had gone away, and I was hobbling around. And coach said, "Well, we're going to leave you out just a little bit longer," and I thought okay. Okay. And by that time, the game was over.

Interviewer: Now, did you ever get hit like that, where you had a tough time coming back from it? I know you were fast, but still, you probably got hit.

Douglas Bumgarner: Yeah. I got knocked out in Morganton. And this was the first game that my mother came to. She didn't want to come to the games. She didn't want to see her son getting hit. So, I talked her into coming to this game, and we played Morganton, and I can't remember whether I was running the ball or whether I was on defense. I don't remember. But I know I got knocked out, and the first thing I remember was, I was on the sideline, and they was... I think they had something like an AMCap they wave under your nose. It's ammonia, bringing you to. And mother was there looking, and she saw that I was okay, so I got up.

So, we got home. We talked about it, and she's like, "I won't be back to no more games." She said, "That's the last one. I'll just wait until they tell me what happened when you get home." So that was the last one. But yeah, I got knocked out in Morganton. I guess that was their revenge.

Interviewer: Speaking of teams that were gunning for you, Morganton, right?

Douglas Bumgarner: It was one of the main ones, yeah. All of them wanted a piece of the pie, but Morganton really wanted us. We had a rough time with Morganton. When we went to Morganton, they started a fight up there that I think just got out of hand. And we had to wind up getting on the bus, and getting on the floor in other words, to come out of there, because they were throwing rocks. I think they had to call the cops and stuff. They had to come and escort us out. It just got terrible up there. People just stopped playing ball and just started fighting, what it was.

Interviewer: You think it's because they were embarrassed because you were... I mean, I think that one was 32 to nothing, or something like that.

Tillis Rendleman: In the first half, wasn't it? Something like that?

Douglas Bumgarner: I'm not quite sure what it was. I think they were just upset with us, period, and the record that were had had, and they were probably just jealous, envious, and they didn't care whether they'd win or lose. They just wanted to start a ruckus, so hey started it. We finished it.

Xenophone Lutz: Yeah. One of the old sayings of teams like Morganton was, we may not win the game, but we'll win the fight. That was what the guys from Morganton would say. That was their attitude, and so again, during the course of the game when they knew they weren't going to win, there came the fight, and unfortunately they had to call the game. All the players on the field fighting, everybody on the field were fighting. People on the sidelines were fighting. Then finally both sidelines headed for the middle of the field, and the coach got the players off the field, got us on the bus, and-

Tillis Rendleman: Down 40.

Xenophone Lutz: Down 40. Headed out of Morganton. But again, that was the attitude of teams, some of the teams back then. They would start fights during the game and after the games, because they knew they couldn't win the game. So again, they said they would win the fight.

Interviewer: Now, did you all sing the song at Morgantown?

Tillis Rendleman: Oh yeah.

Xenophone Lutz: Before every game, on the bus we would sing songs. On the bus, we would sing songs. I mentioned to I believe Doug and Tillis the other day, one of the songs we used to sing was, when we approached the stadium, it was *I See The Lights*. There was a song back then, I see the lights, I see the party lights. So that's what we used to call the party. I see the lights. (singing, in harmony) *I see the party lights, red and blue, and green. Everybody, won't you come on out? We're going to win this game.* Stuff like that. So again, but singing the songs, and then let's go down and get it over with. We're going to win this game. Yeah, those were before every game. Yeah.

Douglas Bumgarner: Yeah, but when we left Morgantown, we were singing The Lord's Prayer. Get us back out of there. Get us home safe.

Tillis Rendleman: I mean, we all were overwhelmed by them folks. There was a lot of them. But there was a lot of people from Hickory and Catawba County there too. They escorted us out of that place.

Xenophone Lutz: I think that was one of the few times that I was actually afraid something bad was going to happen.

Tillis Rinneman: Yeah.

Xenophone Lutz: So just a normal fight, that's nothing. I've been in fights on the football field a few times that year anyway, but when everything exploded I just felt something very bad was going to happen, when both sidelines met on the field, and that was some growing up opportunity for me right there, to realize just how bad and how some things just didn't really make sense. But like Doug said, on the way back, if we sang anything, it was The Lord's Prayer. We were thankful to get out of there in one piece. But Morganton, yeah. That was some kind of game. Yeah.

Interviewer: Now, what was this thing about being an "altar boy?"

Tillis Rendleman: On the line you've got John Hodge and Joe, and Craig Wilfong, and my cousin, Charles Redman. Big dudes. I mean, they would pound you man. You're like, "Oh, call the hospital." And me, hey, I'll knock you down. (indicating helping them up) "Hey, how you doing brother? It's going to be a good day." He said, "No no. You've got to be one or the other. You've got to be one bad you know what, or you're going to be an altar boy." I said, "I can be both. You just have to turn it on or off." Whatever. And that's how that discussion came up, and that's one of the reasons that we had words. That was bold back in them days. You didn't have no words with Coach Davis.

Xenophone Lutz: Oh, absolutely not.

Tillis Rendleman: Yeah. I mean, I think about that. I'm thinking, what was wrong with me? And then I had words with Mr. Broome, the principal. I was driving the school bus, picking up kids from East Hickory, because our paths would cross as I was taking the kids down 127, and there's all these kids from East Hickory. They have to walk to Ridgeview. And I thought, "Well, why not?" I've got all these empty seats on this bus. We've got to spend money for the gas anyway. Why don't I take them and drop them off, and keep going? Nope, not in the plan. So I had words with them about that, and actually they listened to me, but they couldn't make any decision to change anything.

Interviewer: Do you remember when you got to the point that you said, we can go unscored on the whole season. You remember that point?

Douglas Bumgarner: Yeah. it was pretty much in the mid season I think. We got the feeling that we could go unscored on, but we still wanted to keep our composure and not get too overconfident. But we felt that if we just continued to play the way we were playing that we could do this, and we wanted to do it because it was going to be something that we could say we did, our team that year. And so, I think everybody really buckled down on that. We took everything more serious, training and being on time for practice and stuff, and backing each other up. We always had this thing about when, if a play goes the other way, around the other end, if you're playing this end, well you just don't stand there and let them go. You go over there also in case they miss a tackle or something like that.

Then you can be there to follow up and make the tackle. So we concentrated on covering each other's position to keep from letting anybody slip through the cracks. But it put a lot of pressure on us, but we felt that we could do it. We wanted to do it, and we did it.

Xenophone Lutz: Right, and you know the coaches wanted to do it too. One thing we can say about Ridgeview, particularly on defense, we made a lot of substitutions. Everybody got an opportunity to play, but if a team was say, threatening or looked like they might want to make a move toward the goal line, the coach would put the first team back in.

And we would always come in and back the team back up. So again, the coaches, they cautioned us about going unscored on, but they didn't want to go unscored on as well, and the players didn't. It wasn't the focus, but that was the goal. So yeah. We didn't want anybody to score. Of course, nobody wants anybody to score, but we felt that nobody would

score. And again, we backed that up.
Interviewer: Because if you think about it, I mean, that speaks to your defense. But your offense is scoring 30, 40, 50 points a game. So you had it going on on both sides of the ball.
Xenophone Lutz: Both sides of the ball, yeah. And both complimented each other. The offense put the defense in a good position. The defense put the offense in a good position. So again, we were awesome on both sides of the ball, and I guess that was really the key to the season.
Douglas Bumgarner: Yeah. We were playing against ourselves. Offense defense. Like he said, we were on offense, and we was on defense, so we were just playing against ourselves. It wasn't like you had a new offense and a new defense. You had the same team out there on the field the whole time. For me, that was good because it didn't give you a chance to get cold. Sometimes you get taken out of a game, and it affects some people. Some people it don't. You get taken out of a game for say, ten, five minutes, whatever, you start to get cold, and when you go back in, then you've got to make contact before you start getting loose and limber, get them jitters out. So we were playing both ways. It didn't give you a chance to get dry or whatever. I think that worked out for us.
Interviewer: And you didn't get tired?
Douglas Bumgarner: You got tired, but you had what they call, that second wind. I think all that came from conditioning. It's why we were able to do all this, the conditioning we went through. And another thing about that was, when we started training on August the 15th, some of us guys who had been playing ball, we know, you'd go out there a week before training to get in condition for the training. You just don't go out there on August the 15th like some of the freshman didn't know. They'd be out there. Some of the freshmen was always... You'd go out there August 15th and expect to be running five miles. It's kind of hard. But if you prepare before that, it's not as bad. Conditioning, I think that's what kept us being able to go both ways at full speed.
Xenophone Lutz: Oh, sometimes as early as a month before the training season, the guys would get together and start playing, working out and getting ready to train. So again, that was one of our keys. We were in tremendous condition, and that also enabled us to play both ways. And as far as getting tired, yeah, you would get winded at times playing

both ways, but coach would substitute you every now and then, and you also learned what I call how to pace yourself. Of course, I'm not saying you held back, but you knew how to pace yourself during the game in order to be fresh enough to make a play.

But yeah, I like what Doug said though. Yeah, just playing both sides regular, that kept you in tune with what's going on with both sides of the ball.

Interviewer: I've heard people say before, you guys were a fourth quarter team.

Xenophone Lutz: Yeah. Absolutely, yeah. Yeah. So again, going back to that loss to Lexington Dunbar, well as far as I can remember, we felt we were going to win that game even though they had us on our heels most of the game, but we were coming back. We were so well conditioned, we always knew that we were going to play better than the other team in the last quarter. Last quarter. Last half, we always knew that that belonged to us. And we contributed that to conditioning and confidence and all that stuff.

Interviewer: I want to talk about the Dust Bowl.

Douglas Bumgarner: The Dust Bowl. It was rugged, and there was a lot of dust, but the thing that I hated most of all about that was practicing after you had a rain, and the sun would come out a couple days and dry it all up, and it's just a bunch of tough clay out there, and you had to go out there and practice on it. That's the hardest thing I hated about the Dust Bowl. Any other time, it's okay. But if you had a rain, and a couple days it dried, and the cleat marks and scuff marks made little ridges in the ground, it was hard to play on. And I think Joe mentioned a while back about the strawberries you used to get.

You picked them up during early season in August when training started, and some of them would last you the whole year.

Xenophone Lutz: Skinned elbows and knees, yes sir.

Douglas Bumgarner: You'd keep re-injuring them during training and playing games. You'd always tear the scab off or whatever, the skin. We had donuts that you would put on, a piece of rubber with a hole cut out, and you'd tape that on and just try to keep it from getting infected, and putting stuff on like that, but it was hard to play on when you had that rain, and it turned dry, and you had little ridges in it. And they called it the Dust Bowl, because that's exactly what it was, dust. I think Joe mentioned about how the dust rises up in the air at night when we were playing the game. You could just see it all up in the air.

Tillis Rendleman: It was unbelievable.

Douglas Bumgarner: Probably see it for miles.

Interviewer: How was your field compared to, like when you went on away games?

Douglas Bumgarner: Night and day.

Tillis Rendleman: Yeah.

Xenophone Lutz: If a team had a nice field, that's all we'd talk about at first. "Man, look at this field. Man, this is nice, ain't it man?"

Tillis Rendleman: I always checked out the locker room. Wow, it's got clean floors.

Douglas Bumgarner: They had grass, as opposed to dirt.

Xenophone Lutz: Yeah, grass. Yeah.

Douglas Bumgarner: Yeah. See, I think we were about the only school that we played that had their own field. We had our own field, so we practiced on it, and we played on it. We practiced and we played. It never had time to grow grass in the center of the field, because of all the activities that we had out there. Other places we went, they'd use somebody else's field. I think we went to Shelby one year, and I'm not sure, but I thought it was a cow pasture really. That's what it seemed like to me, the way the grass was all out of it. The other teams had grass to play on. We didn't have grass.

Tillis Rendleman: Yeah, and we played the championship at Lenoir-Rhyne. It was beautiful.

Douglas Bumgarner: Man, wow. I was tripping and falling all over the place.

Tillis Rendleman: It was beautiful. The locker room was clean. It was fantastic. We were like... I was stunned. I'm like, "Whoa, where is this place?" Unbelievable.

Douglas Bumgarner: It can spoil you.

Tillis Rendleman: Oh yeah.

Douglas Bumgarner: Their field is beautiful. It's beautiful. I wish we would have had something like that the whole season.

Tillis Rendleman: Yeah.

Douglas Bumgarner: Unfortunately, we claim the dust bowl.

Interviewer: Now, when you got to that last game, like you say, you

had almost done this the year before. And you had to be thinking about Lexington Dunbar at that point, right? Were you thinking about that?
Douglas Bumgarner: I was just nervous about the game itself. The title that we were trying to uphold, being unscored on, and getting the championship team. It was very tense for me, and that can be dangerous sometimes. My hands get sort of stiff. You know, it's kind of hard to hold on to the ball when I get like that, but we just did what we had to do, and thank God we made it. For me, it was tense. It was a tense game, because we were worrying about the record, the Untouchables, unscored on, and also winning the championship game. We've come this far, and I just couldn't see us going home without it. So there was a lot of pressure on me, and Joe, and the rest of the guys too.
Interviewer: Now, what'd you think about that game? I mean, what kind of pressure?
Tillis Rendleman: Well, my first play was on defense, and I line up, tackle, Charles Redman's over to the right, and then Dwight Thompson. And I line up in front of the guard, and he says, "Rendleman, I've got your number," and I thought what the heck? And I'm like, "What is this?" And boom, we go off, and get in there. We make a tackle, and I'm thinking what in the world? So I said something to John. "Who are these people? Why would they know me?" That freaked me out.

Yeah. And undoubtedly, they had scouted us, and I thought, "Oh wow." The year before, I had number 61, and the last year was number 50. So I thought, well, I don't know what they've done, but they've got me down pat, and so, we told the coach, and I don't know if he made any drastic changes, but he did take that under consideration. We settled down, and we played ball just like we had been playing ball, and we didn't spare the rod.
Interviewer: Of course they took you to a scoreless half, right?
Tillis Rendleman: Yeah. Well, I guess we did make a goal line stand. Yeah, all these guys were in the article. I'm that little one that says in others. I always thought that was cool. My grandma said, "What the Sam hill is that? Others. Is that you?"
Doug: You ain't going to play no more.
Tillis Rendleman: No.
Interviewer: Now, I know you've told me about it a couple times, but that goal line stand.

Xenophone Lutz: Yes sir. But first, let me say that during that game, and any game we played, I had maybe doubts about losing, and that was when I was a freshman, and I wasn't really playing much. I just played a little bit, but from my sophomore year to my senior year, I never really thought about losing or entertained the thought of losing. I never really thought we could lose. Not I, but we could lose. And that's the same attitude I had during the championship game. I never thought about them scoring or them winning, nothing like that.

I just felt that we were going to win this game, and somehow. And during the championship game, at half time, a few minutes before half time, Hamlet had a first down around the five yard line. I blurted out, "Man, you all ain't going nowhere. You ain't going nowhere," and then John Hodge said, "Man, shut up. Play some ball." And so, Hamlet came at us four times, and we stopped them four times. In fact, they were farther away for the goal line, somewhat. I don't know how far, but we'd backed them up. And I said, "Man, I told you. Told you. Told you," you know? And again, that was my attitude, just no score, no win.

You all can't score. You all can't win. And I just felt that we were going to stop them, and I always felt we were going to win.

Interviewer: How did you feel about the name Untouchable?

Xenophone Lutz: I thought that was cool. I thought that was cool. Yeah, so again, during that time, I was a big fan of that Untouchable television series, Elliot Ness and the Untouchables, so I just said, "Man, that's special. I like that, Untouchable." So yeah, I thought that was a great name.

Interviewer: Do you remember when someone first called you that?

Xenophone Lutz: I'm just remembering... I think I first read about it. Somebody said they heard Ellis Johnson said after the game, but I just remember seeing it in print, and putting everything together, so... But shortly after that game, that's when it really rang a bell, that man, Untouchables, I like that. And I kind of forgot about it for about 50 some years, and forgot about it, and then thankfully you brought this thing to life man. I certainly appreciate that. It reminded us of who the Untouchables really were, and that we were the Untouchables.

Tillis Rendleman: You made that other statement famous too. When we'd make a tackle there, you'd see the number, the orange and blue. Poof. And he said, "Oh, there's a whole host of Panthers on that tackle."

Interviewer: Now, do you remember getting labeled as the Untouchables? Do you remember that?

Tillis Rendleman: Yeah.

Interviewer: What was that like for you?

Tillis Rendleman: Like we had arrived, because we had been, not harassed, but teased about some of the old guys that had played ball before us, coming into the field, "Oh, you boys ain't going to play no ball today. Let's go get us a MD 2020, and sit back and relax." And you'd just go like, "What?" And the coaches, "Ah, don't talk down to these guys. These guys have been there, done that. Be respectful." We'd go, "Okay coach. Yes sir. No problem, but they need to get off our case." And I tell you, I thought about that for years and years and years. I thought about that. And I thought about killing a gnat with a sledgehammer, and it all meant something. It meant a lot to the growth of a boy to a man in my case. I learned a lot, a lot of life lessons.

Xenophone Lutz: And let me say that even to this day, there are some former players, and we still haggle or argue a little bit about who was the greatest team ever at Ridgeview, so some would swear on their lives that they were the better team. "Yeah, we did this. We did that. We made you all what you are," you know. But when that word Untouchable comes up, 1964, that separates us from the rest, because we went unscored on, and that goes further than that, further than scoring. It separates us from the other Ridgeview teams. We love those guys, but we were the best. We were the Untouchables, so that speaks for itself.

Interviewer: Now, what do you remember about that first time you heard you being called that?

Douglas Bumgarner: Well, the first time I saw it was in the *Hickory Daily Record*. I think it was on a Saturday morning, and it was one of them wow moments. I said, "Wow, Untouchables," and then it all started clicking together, you know? And as Joe was talking about, the teams, the other guys that liked to joke with us about it, I think Allen put it in perspective, like there's a lot of good teams. There's a lot of championship teams, but there's no perfect season teams. We only got one, and that's what we're labeled as right now, and we just invite them to come onboard with us and just enjoy the victory. I mean, we always do. We're not hating on them. But we got the title, and that's that.

Interviewer: What do you think about the whole arch and all the

artwork that's being done as the public art? How do you feel about that?
Douglas Bumgarner: Oh, that's exciting. That's really exciting. We appreciate all of that. It's going to be a beautiful day, and I like the archway. I like the way everything is made on it. Everything looks good, and talked to Miss Kathy Greathouse. I was talking to her about some little things on it like that, and she was saying, "Yeah yeah. It sounds good too," but I think it's wonderful. I love it. I love it.
Interviewer: How do you feel about being recognized all these years after this?
Douglas Bumgarner: Love that too. I'm pleased with it. I'm happy with it. I am. I really am. It's something that's long overdue, but it's here, and I think we just need to seize the moment and just enjoy it.
Interviewer: And what do you think this will say to folks who've come along after you?
Douglas Bumgarner: Well, that anything's possible. Just try hard enough and keep at it, don't give up on it, do your best in whatever it is that you do, and I guess that's about it. And to never give up on your dream.
Interviewer: What do you think about the 55 plus years after all this happened?
Tillis Rendleman: I think it's fantastic. It maybe should have happened before. I don't know. But at least it's happening, and something for our grandchildren to be proud of. We can be proud of it in our last days. Well, some of these old folks' last days, but yeah, it's fantastic. It's fantastic.
Interviewer: And what do you think this means to history?
Tillis Rendleman: It's going to be a big time bump in history when this comes out to play. It's amazing. It's just amazing. It blows my mind just to think about it. I mean, 55 years. That's a long time. A long time. I think it's going to be something positive for Hickory, something positive for western North Carolina.

When I was in the Army, people would say, "Ah, you a hick from Hickory." Forget it. At that time, we were the best furniture making organization in the world. I said, "You need to go and experience Hickory in the foothills and the Blue Ridge and then come back and tell me what you think."

And of course, they did. Some of them didn't, but I've always enjoyed living around here, and I can't badmouth it, and I'm not going to ever.

Xenophone Lutz: Yeah, guys would say, "Oh, where you from?" "Hickory." "Oh, hickory dickory dock."

Tillis Rendleman: Yeah, that crap too.

Xenophone Lutz: Oh boy, that's something else.

Tillis Rendleman: Yeah.

Interviewer: So what do you think about this thing coming up with the arch and all that and the recognition?

Xenophone Lutz: Man, I think that's... I think it's just great, one of the greatest things that could happen to me, and I think the football team, Ridgeview area, and even Hickory as a whole. It's just one of the greatest things that could happen. There's some sadness. You wish that a lot of key guys that are no longer living, I just wish they could see this and be a part of it, but that's just one of those things. But I'm just thankful that as many as are here now can enjoy it, and again, I think it's great.

I think it'll be a good positive influence for the community, when little children read about it and hear about it and talk about it. Again, they say, "Oh, this is what we did, people from this community did," and a lot of our relatives. "Yeah, my grandpa, my uncle, my so and so, their names are on there." Again, it's a mark in history that I can't ever see being duplicated these days and times, the way sports is, and that record's going to stand.

It's awesome, and I'm just thankful to God, thankful to you Mr. Eller, Ms. Greathouse, Mr. Canipe, and all those who took a part in it, and just seeing that arch. Ridgeview would usually have our school reunions every other year, and we usually do a lot of things over at the gymnasium, and all they have to do is walk down to the field and see that arch and see the names, and they can show it to their children, and children's children. And again, it's something to be proud of.

Ridgeview was something, something special. Hickory is special, so it's a great thing, an awesome thing.

Buffalo Bills Strengthened By Famed Ex-Ridgeview QB

By ELLIS JOHNSON

Ernest (Ernie) Warlick, present "tight" end of the Buffalo Bills of the American Football League, is a former football and basketball star of Ridgeview High school.

Ernie, the son of Brice Warlick and the late Mrs. Edna Warlick, is a 1948 graduate of Ridgeview. In his high school football days he played both quarterback and end. His playing won him the nickname "Hands," pinned on him by his fellow teammates.

Born on Jan. 31, 1932, Ernie grew up in Hickory and became interested in scouting. He rose to the rank of Eagle Scout of Troop 10 and became an aggressive worker in the Friendship Baptist church.

Won Various Honors

From the Ridgeview campus, he attended North Carolina college at Durham. An outstanding student and athlete, Ernie played end on the football team and participated in basketball. He received All-CIAA and All-American honors while playing football.

After graduation, Ernie enlisted in the United States Air Force and was stationed at Bolling Field, Washington, D. C., where he continued his career in both football and basketball as a member of the base teams. Named to the All-Service team, Ernie became known as "Mr. Basketball."

Upon release from the service in 1957, he signed with the Calgary Stampeders of the Western Canadian League as an end. Then, in 1962, Ernie signed with the Buffalo Bills, who outbid other American and National football league teams for his services.

In his first year, the former Ridgeview great was the Bills' leading receiver with 35 catches. In '63 he totaled 24. Before his trade to the Bills, Ernie was named All-Pro twice in the Canadian Football League.

Ernie has two brothers who are also following his footsteps. Thurston was a former Ridgeview great who also played football and basketball. He continued his athletics through college. Before his graduation from Xavier university at New Orleans, La., Thurston was named to the All-Catholic team. He also served in the Air Force and is now a physical therapist at the Veterans hospital in Newark, N. J.

ERNEST WARLICK

Brother Follows Example

Ernie's youngest brother, Bobby, traced the exact steps his brothers had made while at Ridgeview. He attended college at Denver University in Denver, Colo., Pueblo Junior college at Pueblo, Colo., and Peppeidine college at Los Angeles, Calif. He was voted to the All-Tourney basketball team and eventually selected as the outstanding player on the National Junior College Basketball team.

Ernest is married and the father of two children. He wears Number 84 on the Bills uniform and remains stationary at his end position.

A 1948 GRADUATE OF RIDGEVIEW HIGH SCHOOL, AND A FORMER PANTHER FOOTBALL AND BASKETBALL GREAT, ERNIE WARLICK SIGNED WITH THE BUFFALO BILLS IN 1962.

14, 1957

Signs Pro Contract

ERNIE WARLICK

Ex-Ridgeview Star Athlete Inks Pact To Play Canadian Football

By ELLIS JOHNSON

Ernie (Hands) Warlick son of Mr. and Mrs. Brice Warlick of 635 First Street, SW recently signed a professional football contract with the Calgary Stampeders of the Western Canada Football League. Warlick is a Ridgeview High School graduate, class of 1948.

Ernie was an outstanding athlete in High school, stood high in his class, an Eagle Scout and a aggressive worker in the Friendship Baptist Church.

He attended North Carolina College at Durham where he was also an outstanding student and athlete, playing both football and basketball.

Warlick made all CIAA and all American teams. Upon graduating from college he enlisted in the United States Air Force, stationed at Bolling Field, Washington, D. C. He continued his athletic career in both football and basketball at Bolling Field.

Warlick was named to the All Service team and became known as "Mr. Basketball."

Ernie has another brother Thurston who is a member of the United States Air Force at Charleston, S. C., Air Force Base. He too was an outstanding High School Athlete, attended and graduated from Xavier University at Cincinnati, Ohio. Named to the All Catholic team he is now playing with the Charleston, Air Force Base team.

Ernie's baby brother Bobby, a Sophomore at Ridgeview, is presently only playing basketball. Ernie signed as an end, the position he played in college and in the Air Force. He is six foot four inches tall and weights 230 pounds.

Ex-Ridgeview Grid Great, Now Playing With Redskins

By ELLIS JOHNSON

Ozzie Clay a defensive back for the Washington Redskins is a 1959 graduate of Ridgeview High school.

The son of Mr. and Mrs. Johnnie Clay, formerly of Hickory but now of Charlotte. Ozzie scored 25 touchdowns during his last two years at Ridgeview. His greatest year was 1958 as he scored 13 touchdowns to lead all the Panthers.

He placed second in the longest touchdown run department with a seventy eight yard run. He was third in the point after touchdown department with four.

Ozzie was on the all-state team of 1959 and on the All-Northwestern Conference team of 1958 and 1959. He was also a member of the Northwestern Conference Championship team of 1958 and 1959 and the Western District Class AA Champions that lost to Panbar High of Lexington in 1958 in Hickory 48-14, and 12-6 in Lexington in 1959.

Picked Iowa

From the campus of Ridgeview, after considering a large number of Athletic scholarships, which included every major Negro college of the CIAA and University of Indiana, he attended the Iowa State College at Ames, Iowa, on a scholarship. He played on both offense and defense there. He carried the ball 74 times for a total of 311 yards. He threw eight passes and completed four for a total of 63-yards.

Ozzie is six feet tall and weighs 190-pounds. He was born in Hickory Sept. 10, 1941, and became a Redskin on June 30 of this year and was the seventeenth draft choice of the Skins. He wears the number 28 on his uniform.

OZZIE CLAY

His younger brother, Leonard, is a member of Maryland State College Team of Princess Anne, Maryland, of the CIAA conference. He is on a Athletic scholarship. His middle brother Edward is a barber in Charlotte. All three boys are graduates of Ridgeview. Ozzie is still single.

A 1959 GRADUATE OF RIDGEVIEW HIGH SCHOOL, AND A FORMER PANTHER FOOTBALL GREAT, OZZIE CLAY PLAYED FOR THE WASHINGTON REDSKINS.

RIDGEVIEW PANTHERS
Northwest Conference 2A Champions
1964

HEAD COACH	ASSISTANT COACH
Sam Davis	Roger Scales

1964 SCORES		OPPONENT	
RIDGEVIEW	40	Huntersville Torrence Lytle	0
RIDGEVIEW	56	North Wilkesboro Lincoln Heights	0
RIDGEVIEW	22	Lincolnton Newbold	0
RIDGEVIEW	52	Spindale Carver	0
RIDGEVIEW	44	Canton Reynolds	0
RIDGEVIEW	38	Lenoir Freedman	0
RIDGEVIEW	30	Mt. Airy Jones	0
RIDGEVIEW	32	Morganton Olive Hill	0
RIDGEVIEW	36	Newton Central	0
RIDGEVIEW	52	Shelby Cleveland	0

NCHSAC 2A PLAYOFFS

Western Title

RIDGEVIEW	28	East Spencer Dunbar	0

State Title

RIDGEVIEW	16	Hamlet Monroe Avenue	0
Totals	**446**		**0**

Conference record	**7 – 0 – 0**
Regular season	**10 – 0 – 0**
Overall	**12 – 0 -- 0**

Individual highlights:

Lee Douglas Bumgarner -1172 yds, rushing, 21 TDs; Edward Cunningham -12 TDs; Alan Burch -12 TDs; Allen Pope - 4 TDs scored, 7 TD passes; Curtis Cunningham – 3 TDs.

RIDGEVIEW REUNION 2009
CLASS OF 1965 SNAPSHOTS

1964 – 1965 NC State Division 2A Champions

"THE UNTOUCHABLES"

Perfect Season: No-defeats–No–ties–No–opponent scores

Co-Captains: Lee Bumgarner, Edward Cunningham, Johnny Hodge & Xenophone Lutz

Front row (left to right): Lindsey Parks -Trainer (not pictured), Hubbard Morrison, Mitchell Anthony, James Thompson, Xenophone Lutz, Douglas Bumgarner, John Hodge, Allen Pope, Dwight Thompson, Edward Cunningham, Craig Wiltong, Harrison James. ***Second row:***. Coach Sam Davis, Detroit Rhyne, Roosevelt Corpening, Danny Carter, Curtis Cunningham, Charles Thompson, Tillis Rendleman, John Thompson, Louis Collins, Tommy Euby, Coach Roger Scales. ***Third row***: Jerry Johnson, Hamp Davis,Willie Byrd, Carroll Carter, Douglas Thompson, Elbert Morrison, Frank Abernathy, Pete Heard, Ollie Parks, Ronald McKnight-Trainer. (Not Pictured) Edward White, Anthony Parks, Larry Williams, Allen Burch.

1964-1965 STATE 2A CHAMPIONS
"THE UNTOUCHABLES"

Front row (left to right): Lindsey Parks (not pictured), Hubbard Morrison, Mitchell Anthony, James Thompson, Xenophone Lutz, Douglas Bumgarner, John Hodge, Allen Pope, Dwight Thompson, Edward Cunningham, Craig Wilfong, Harrison James. Second row: Coach Sam Davis, Detroit Rhyne, Roosevelt Corpening, Danny Carter, Curtis Cunningham, Charles Thompson, Tillis Rendalman, John Thompson, Louis Collings, Tommy Euby, Coach Roger Scales. Third row: Jerry Johnson, Hamp Davis, Allen Burch, Willie Boyd, Carroll Carter, Douglas Thompson, Elbert Morrison, Frank Abernethy, Pete Heard, Ollie Parks, Edward White (not pictured), Anthony Parks, Ronald McKnight, Trainer (not pictured).

HICKORY DAILY RECORD 1964

Panthers Take State Title, Finish Season Unscored On

By ELLIS JOHNSON

The amazing Ridgeview Panthers of Hickory set a record at Lenoir Rhyne College Field Friday night as they shut out the Monroe Avenue Tigers of Hamlet, 16-0.

The 1960 team went through 11 games but this team has completed 12 games and ended a perfect season. In it they won the Northwestern Conference, District Class AA (District Two and defeated the District One champion) and defeated the District Three champions for the Western Class AA title Friday.

The Ridgeview Panthers became the North Carolina Negro Class AA champions for the second time. In 1962 they defeated Edenton for the crown on College Field (LR). For Coaches R.W. Davis and Roger Scales it was a happy ending to a dream.

Lost Toss

The Panthers lost the toss and had to kick off to the Tigers. It was returned to the Tigers 35-yard line. Deep in their own back yard the Tigers pulled a quick kick on third down. The ball was put in play on the Panthers 29-yard line behind excellent blocking, halfback Lee Bumgarner carried for 27 yards and again behind excellent blocking halfback Lee Bumgarner carried to the Tigers 14-yard line.

At this point Lee Bumgarner was called on again and carried to the four-yard line. The Panthers attempted to score on three tries but were pushed back on fourth down from the three-yard line. A Panther fumble was recovered by the Tigers. The Panthers defense soon made the Tigers kick and the Panthers took over on their own 31. A long penalty forced the Panthers back to their own 16-yard line where the Panthers had to kick. The gun sounded ending the quarter.

Halfback James Thompson got off a fine kick to start the second quarter. It was taken on the Tigers 46-yard line. The Tigers moved the ball well, picking up two first downs. On the Panthers 25-yard line, defensive guard Edward White recovered a fumble. Guided by quarterback Allen Pope, the Panthers moved the ball to the Tigers 45.

Plagued by a 15 yard penalty which set the Panthers back to their own 40-yard line, the stout defense of the Tigers pushed the Panthers back to the 36. Once again the Panthers had to call on James Thompson, their fine punter. The punt was returned to the Tigers 30-yard line. The fine offense of the Tigers began to click, picking up two first downs. The Tigers found themselves on the Panthers two-yard line, first and goal to go. The Panthers defense, led by Captain John Hodge, Xenophone Lutz, Charles Redman, Allen Pope and others, stopped the drive of the Tigers on the one-yard line as the gun sounded to end the scoreless half.

The second half kickoff to the Panthers own 15 yar line. Once again the Panthers were moving as fullback Edward Cunningham carried for eight to the 23, but this fine defense of the Tigers forced them to kick once again. James Thompson's kick rolled dead on the Tigers 14 yardline. The Panthers defense held and forced the Tigers to kick, which was taken on the Panthers 40 yardline.

At this point fullback Edward Cunningham raced fro 15 yards and a face mask penalty give the Panthers a first down on the 10 yardline. The hard hitting Tigers hit halfback Allen Burch, who fumbled the ball on the Tigers six yard line. The happy Tigers moved the ball down to the Panthers 34 yardline and were pulled down from behind.

The Tigers pass was intercepted by halfback Frank Abernethy and a penalty set the Panthers back to the six yardline.

Pass Intercepted

At this point halfback Lee Bumgarner brought the crowd to their feet as he raced for 59 yards behind good blocking. He was pulled down from behind on the Tigers 35. At this point the explosive Panthers called on halfback Allen Burch, who, behind excellent blocking, raced 35 yards to score a dtouchdown. Halfback Frank Abernethy added the two pointer.

The kick was returned to the Tige 30. The Tigers picked up a first down o their own 40 and had another on the Pa thers 45 yardline as the third quarte ended.

In the final period the Tigers wer on the Panthers 31 yardline as a result a 15 yard penalty. Then the Tigers fe back to the Panthers 46 yardline due to fifteen yard penalty. Halfback Fran Abernethy intercepted another Tig pass on the Panthers 38 yardline.

Once again Panthers quarterba Allen Pope got his team rolling as hal back Allen Burch carried for eleve yards after a nine yard loss. Pope h Burch on the Tigers 35, then Pope h Bumgarner on the 10 yardline. An o side penalty against the Tigers w refused. It gave the Panthers first a goal on the 10 yardline where fullba Edward Cunningham, behind excelle blocking, raced ten yards to score. Qua terback Allen Pope added the t pointer.

From this point the Tigers tried score. The Stout Panther defen stopped their drives on the Panthers yardline. Quarterback Pope fumbled the Panthers 46 as the final g sounded. The untouchable Panthe ended a victorious perfect season.

Ridgeview School News

ALJUANA CURRY, GLORIA [illegible] and
JACQUELINE [illegible]

Mr. Touchdown, Mr. Lineman, and Mr. Linebackers have been chosen from the Panther's camp in honor of their outstanding performances throughout the 1964 season.

The honor of Mr. Touchdown goes to Lee Douglas Bumgarner. Douglas has made a total of 1,178 yards rushing, and scored 21 touchdowns. He has also received the honor of first string halfback on the all-conference team.

Douglas, a Senior, is the son of Mr. and Mrs. Cecil Bumgarner of 135 Eight Street Drive, SE. He plans to enter Maryland State next fall.

DOUGLAS BUMGARNER

On District Team

Xenephone Lutz, a Senior, received the honor of Mr. Lineman, not only on the football team but also for the Northwestern District. Lutz, 6'-3" and weighing over 200 pounds, was one of the largest players on the team.

The distinctive honors of Mr. Linebackers were given to Johnny Hodge and Craig Wilfong, both Seniors, who were considered by the coaches as essential links of the line.

XENEPHONE LUTZ

Johnny is the son of Mrs. Amanda Hodge of First Street, SW. He has been placed on the first team of the all-conference team as tackle. He is 6'-3" and weighs 195 pounds. Basketball and football are his favorite sport. Hodge also plans to enter Maryland State next fall.

Craig Wilfong has been placed on the second team of the all-conference team. Craig also is considered a very good basketball player.

To Enter State

Wilfong plans to enter North Carolina college next fall to major in elementary education.

A French club, under the direction of Miss Poole, was formed this week. The purpose of the club is to help the members have better oral communication in French. The officers are: President, Patricia Killian; vice president, Gloria Derr; secretary, Marcenia Brown; assistant secretary, Mary Jett; sergeant-at-arms, Xenephone Lutz; and reporters, Jacqueline Randleman and Sarah Cornwell. Committee chairman are Janice Lutz, social committee; Dorothy Thompson, program committee; and Janet Burke, constitutional committee.

JOHNNY HODGE

Hickory
SAMUEL WILLIAM DAVIS, SR.
MULTIPURPOSE FIELD

Home Economics Mrs. Thompson

Electricity, Learning How To Make A Bell Ring

A. W. Booker, Principal

Taft H. Broome, Principal

A FACTUAL ACCOUNT OF EACH GAME EXISTS IN THE ARCHIVES OF THE *HICKORY DAILY RECORD*. PLAY-BY-PLAY ANNOUNCER ELLIS JOHNSON TOOK THE TIME AFTER EACH GAME TO WRITE AN ARTICLE FOR THE PAPER, PROVIDING VIVID DESCRIPTION OF THE WAY THIS TEAM ACHIEVED ITS FAME. FOR THOSE OF US WHO DID NOT GET TO SEE THE TEAM IN ACTION, JOHNSON'S ACCOUNTS VISUALIZE THE AWESOME POWER OF COACH SAMUEL DAVIS' DEFENSE AND COACH ROGER SCALES' DARING OFFENSE THAT POSTED A SEASON TOTAL OF 446-0.

Panthers Weak Again, Says Conference Champs Coach
HDR, August 25, 1964, p. 8
by John Robinette

Coach S.W. (Sammy) Davis of Ridgeview High School is not known as an optimist and from the woeful tune coming from his Panther camp, he's in his best form in years.

With a "tremendous" loss of five players from his state semi-final team of last season, Davis stated, "Everything we've got is as green as grass, we're going to be hurting just about everywhere."

One thing Davis may be in trouble with for sure, however, is his quarterbacks.

Last year's number one man, William Roland, has vacated the camp via graduation and the stand-in man last season, Allen Pope, according to Davis, "is somewhere in Pennsylvania and I don't know whether he's coming back or not."

To Carry Burden

This leaves the burly, quiet-spoken head coach with only an untried pair of Sophomores to carry the burden at the quarterback slot.

According to Davis, the quarterback role will just about decide the entire situation for the club. "If we find somebody that can throw the ball, we'll be a passing team, but otherwise we'll stay on the ground."

He also stated that the quarterback would be a determining factor in what type of offense the club uses, but in general it will be a multiple offense, with tight and spread T's and wing T formations. "We might even use a little single wing if we can find someone to run it, and someone to run against it."

State Champs

The multiple show has been good to the club the past two seasons, as in the 1962 the club rolled to the undefeated record and the state championship, and in 1963 went through the nine-game regular season undefeated and finally fell, 28-16, to Dunbar High School of Lexington in the Western AA state playoffs.

This year will not be as easy, at least in Davis' estimation, as he expected trouble from just about everyone in the Northwestern Athletic Conference. Pushed a little however, he predicted that Newton, Shelby, Morganton and Canton would probably be the roughest opposition for the Panther 11.

In the backfield to handle the ball carrying end of the offense will be a few outstanding backs, combined with several newcomers.

At fullback, where Davis lost the services of Franklin Derr, will probably be Edward Cunningham, a converted halfback that has seen considerable action for the past two seasons.

Halfback duties will be divided between veterans Donald (sic, Douglas) Bumgarner and Allen Burch, and newcomer Curtis Cunningham. Davis contends that most of his backs are in the 125-pound class, but a feeble glance would indicate that about 25 more pounds could be added without fudging too much on most of the older boys.

Sophs to Play

At quarterback, providing that Pope does not return, Davis is slated to give Sophs Danny Carter and Willie Byrd a try.

Up on the line, experience is a little better with tackle Xenophone Lutz and guard John Hodge heading the list. Opposite Lutz at the other tackle will probably be Craig Wilfong, while manning the other guard slot should be Charles Redmond.

Ends are pretty stable, with vets Hubert Morrison and Dwight Thompson expected to get the starting call. At center, Davis is fairly undecided, but favors Mitchell Anthony at present.

THE SCHEDULE

Date		Opponent	Place
Sept.	4	Huntersville	Home
	11	Wilkesboro	Home
	18	Spindale	Home
Oct.	2	Shelby	Away
	8	Canton	Away
	16	Lenoir	Home
	30	Morganton	Away
Nov.	6	Newton	Home

Xenophone Lutz (left) and John Hodge (right), guard and tackle respectively, on the Panther club, are slated to man offensive starting roles when the Ridgeview boys open Sept. 4 against Huntersville.

Ends Hubert Morrison (left) and Dwight Thompson (right) get a few pointers on pass catching from Ridgeview High Head Football Coach S.W. (Sammy) Davis. Both boys are expected to play important roles in Ridgeview's defense of the Northwestern Athletic Conference title this fall.

Area Grid Teams Open Fall Schedule Friday
HDR, September 3, 1964, Second Section (partial)
by John Robinette

Pads will be popping and footballs flying again Friday night as nearly all Hickory area High schools open their 1964 seasons.

With Hickory's Red Tornados delaying a week, Ridgeview will send its Panthers into the only action in the immediate Hickory area.

The 1964 edition of the Panthers will open its season at the Panther home field against Huntersville, and several new faces are expected to dot the starting lineup.

Coach S.W. (Sammie) Davis will need replacements for tackles Nelson Brockenborough and Edward Rogers and also quarterback William Roland and fullback Franklin Derr, but Davis, who heads the defending Northwestern Athletic Conference championship team, is a past master at coming up with big men in big holes.

Defending Champs

The Panthers won the Northwestern Conference title and Western District playoffs last season before falling to Lexington in the state quarterfinals.

The Ridgeview starting lineup will have Mitchell Anthony at center, Xenophone Lutz and John Hodge at guard, Craig Wilfong and Charles Redmon at tackle, Dwight Thompson and Hubert Morrison at end. Allen Burch and Douglas Bumgarner at halfback, Edward Cunningham at fullback and Allen Pope or Danny Carter at quarterback.

To Lead Ridgeview Band
HDR, September 4, 1964, p. 11

Caption to picture
Mary Cornwell, Patricia Coates, and Betty Foster will lead the high

stepping, 40-piece Ridgeview High School marching band on the field at half time, at a rate of 280 steps per minute, tonight at 8 p.m. This will be a relatively new record for the band. It was stated by A.V. Evans, band director, that the ultimate objective this year is to reach 300 steps per minute. He feels that the band will reach this objective near the end of this marching season. The assistant band directors are Jacqueline Rendleman and Gerald Reid. (Robin Gatwood Photo)

Ridgeview School News

HDR, September 5, 1964, p. 4. (partial)

by Alivana Curry, George Derr and Jacqueline Rendleman

The Ridgeview High School Marching Band, under the direction of A.V. Evans, is off to a very good year. At this time the band is completing all of the half time shows that they will perform this year.

The band, formerly under the direction of T.H. Penn, has received outstanding recognition in the state contest many years. Mr. Evans stated "It is not every day that a young man gets the opportunity to follow in the footsteps of a man who is as talented and versatile as Mr. Penn."

Spirit in the Panther's camp was very high this week, as we faced Torrence High of Huntersville. The team has been looking fair, although the coach is pessimistic about the forthcoming season. With luck and the full support of the team we feel they may be triumphant.

The Panthers have been faced by the loss of a few men since last season begun and this has been a disadvantage on our side. We are having quarterback trouble, however, Allen Pope shows more promise than the others.

In the backfield we feel we are well prepared.

The Ridgeview field can now seat comfortably 2,000 people, so we are now asking full support at every game. Kickoff time is 8:00 o'clock.

There was a pep meeting Friday afternoon. The cheerleaders, Barbara Sadler, Ethel Hector, Judy Dula, Brenda Micheax and Mary Jett together with the student body gave the team a great send off.

Panthers Rip Huntersville, 40-0; Ridgeview Squad Strikes Early for Conference Win

HDR, September 5, 1964, p. 10.

by Ellis Johnson

The Ridgeview Panthers defeated Huntersville, 40-0, on the Panthers' home field Friday evening.

This was the season opener for both schools The Panthers looked like old form as they received good blocking for the scatbacks and played good defensive ball as the Panther line stood out.

The Panthers lost the toss and had to kickoff to Huntersville which received it on its own 10 and returned it to the 32.

For three downs Huntersville could only gain three yards, aided by a penalty, and finally went back to punt over to the Panthers.

A high pass from center was fumbled and recovered by end Hubbard Morrison for Ridgeview on the Huntersville 13-yard line.

Burch Scores

At this point halfback Allen Burch galloped 13 yards to score.

The try for extra point was no good. Once again the Panthers kicked off with ball taken on the Huntersville eight-yard line with the return to the visitors' own 21-yard line where once again the fumble played an important part as tackle Xenophone Lutz recovered a fumble on the Huntersville 13-yard line. Halfback Burch carried to the 11 and halfback Lee Douglas Bumgarner carried the ball in for the score.

Point No Good

The try for extra point was no good. After a series of plays the Huntersville team recovered a Panther fumble on the 45-yard line as first quarter ended, 12-0, Ridgeview.

After a 15 yard penalty set Huntersville back, guard James Heard recovered a fumble on the Panther 24-yard line.

A series of penalties set the Panthers back to the three-yard line. A fake punt by halfback James Thompson and a pass to halfback Lee Douglas Bumgarner on the 40-yard line opened up a 60-yard score standing up. The try for the extra point was no good.

Plays Fall

A series of plays could produce nothing for either team as the half ended, 18-0, Ridgeview. The Ridgeview Panther Marching Band put on a great halftime show for the large crowd.

To start the second half fullback Ed Cunningham took the kickoff and behind good blocking raced 69 yards before being pulled down from behind on the 11-yard line.

At this point halfback Lee Douglas Bumgarner carried the ball in for the score and fullback Cunningham bucked in for the extra point.

Carter Intercepts

After the kickoff, quarterback Danny Carter intercepted a pass and carried for 28 yards to the the 42-yard line of Huntersville. Quick as lightning, quarterback Allen Pope three (threw) a pass which was intercepted, but the Panthers regained control of the ball as the period ended. Score, 26-0.

To start the final period, halfback Frank Abernathy raced 35 yards to score the touchdown. The try for extra point was no good.

After the kickoff to the Huntersville 32-yard line tackle James Heard recovered his second fumble of the evening.

Fail To Score

But the Panthers didn't score at this point. With four minutes left in the game guard Ed White recovered a fumble on the Huntersville 26-yard line. A run and a penalty gave the Panthers a first down on the five-yard line where quarterback Allen Pope got in the scoring act as he went into the end zone behind good blocking. The try for extra point was no good.

Huntersville tried vainly to score but time and a big Panther defensive line were against them. As the final gun sounded the score was 40-0. Ridgeview.

Ridgeview School News
HDR, September 12, 1964, p. 12. (partial)
by Alivana Curry, George Derr and Jacqueline Rendleman

The Panthers felt Friday that they would be triumphant this week as they faced Lincoln Height(s) of Wilkesboro, although Wilkesboro is one of the largest teams in the conference and is considered to have a fairly good team. Results Friday night bear out this punch.

Battle of Panthers Sees Ridgeview on Top, 56-0
HDR, September 12, 1964, p. 8.
by Ellis Johnson

The Ridgeview Panthers defeated the Lincoln Heights Panthers of Wilkesboro 56-0 on the Ridgeview field Friday night.

The Ridgeview Panthers offense and defense stood out like shining armor.

For the second week in a row, the Panthers lost the toss and had to kick to the Lincoln Heights Panthers. It was received on their three-yard line and was returned to their own twenty-one.

After a 5-yard penalty on fourth down, a high pass from center was picked up by the punter in the end zone but he was hit hard by a host of orange jerseys for a safety.

After an exchange of punts, fullback Edward Cunningham carried the punt from his own 40-yard line to the Wilkes 45.

At this point, on first down, Danny Carter hit halfback Allen Burch on the thirty who raced the distance to score, untouched. Fullback Edward Cunningham add the extra point.

Score at this point was 10-0, ending the first quarter.

After holding the Wilkes boys, Fullback Ed Cunningham returned a punt from the midfield stripe to the 15-yard line. At this point Halfback Lee Douglas Bumgarner behind good blocking galloped fifteen yards to score. Try for extra point was no good.

The kickoff was returned to the 30-yard line. In a cloud of dust a fumble occurred and a host of Ridgeview Panthers were in on the play.

Moving the ball down to the four, the Hickory lads drew a long penalty, which set them back to the 19-yard line.

A pass from Quarterback Allen Pope to Fullback Ed Cunningham was good for the touchdown halfback Frank Abernathy added the extra point.

With less than four minutes left in the game a fumble was recovered on a fourth down play by Ridgeview on the Wilkes 19-yard line.

At this point Halfback Lee Douglas Bumgarner raced nineteen yards to score. Fullback Ed Cunningham added the extra point. The half ended with the score Ridgeview 32, Linclon (Lincoln) Heights 0.

Band Puts On Show

After the Ridgeview Panthers Marching Band put on a great halftime show for the fans, Lincoln Heights kicked off to the Ridgeview three-yard line. Burch received it and returned it to the twenty-eight-yard line.

At this point, like lightning, Halfback Lee Douglas Bumgarner, behind excellent blocking, raced 72 yards to score. Try for extra point was no good.

After the kickoff on fourth down a high pass from center gave the Panthers the ball on the Wilkes twenty-five-yard line. Fullback Jerry Johnson raced 25 yards behind good blocking to score. Try for extra point was no good. After a series of plays the quarter ended score Ridgeview 44 Lincoln Heights 0.

To start the final quarter a high pass from center caused a Wilkes punter to be smeared by a host of orange and blue jerseys on the Wilkes 20-yard line. A 5-yard penalty set the Hickory lads back to the twenty-five. At this point halfback Curtis Cunningham, behind good blocking, scored standing up. Extra point was no good.

Returns to 30-Yard Line

The kickoff was returned to the 30-yard line of Wilkes where a fumble was recovered by a host of Panthers amidst the dust that was flying.

Once again the Hickory lads were not to be denied from 30 yards away. The quarterback at this time was Willie Byrd, who tossed to lanky End Detroit Rhyne, Jr., who gathered it in on the 2-yard line and fought his way to the end zone extra point was no good. Hickory was on the move again s End Harrison James recovered a fumble on Wilkes 40. Two plays later the final gun sounded.

Ridgeview School News

HDR, September 19, 1964, p. 4. (partial)

by Alivana Curry, George Derr and Jacqueline Rendleman

Band News

The RHS Band completed its third half-time show Friday night at the stadium. The theme of the show was a trip around the world in music. The band was led by Mary Cornwell. The band will probably be stepping at the rate of 290 steps with a goal of 300 steps per minute. The band will lead the Masonic parade from the lodge house to Morning Star church.

Panther Captains Speak

Xenophone Lutz stated, "Although we made mistakes, we feel we will correct them in future games."

Douglas Bumgarner stated, "The team is in fair condition with things looking better each day. I feel that we are capable of a good season."

Johnny Hodge stated that "We have the potential of a great

season and with the 11 seniors doing a great job in shaping up the team. The team should benefit a great deal from this leadership for a team is no better than its leaders. I feel that we are capable of handling Spindale with luck and the support of our team.

Tillis Rendleman is a new addition to the pack.

Panthers Romp to Easy Win

HDR, September 19, 1964, p. 3.
by Ellis Johnson

The Ridgeview Panthers defeated the Carver High Eagles of Spindale 52-0 on the Ridgeview field here Friday as outstanding Panther line play yielded only 22 yards rushing.

Play began on the twenty-nine yard line as the Panthers kicked off and in three [tries], the Eagles gained only one yard. The punt went out of bounds at the 39 yard line and the Panthers started to roll. Fullback Ed Cunningham carried to the 20, halfback Allen Burch pushed up one yard, and behind good blocking, Cunningham advanced the ball to the 14-yard line.

Set Back By Fumble

After another advance he was set back by a fumble to the eight-yard line. The Ridgeview crew lost the ball to the Eagles on the five-yard line.

Luck rode with the Panthers as Cunningham recovered a fumble on the 10-yard line. A 15-yard penalty nullified a touchdown run by Burch and set the ball on the 25. Allen Burch carried to the 14 yard line and Halfback Lee Douglas Bumgarner went in to score. Quarterback Allen Pope passed to halfback Lee Douglas Bumgarner for the extra point.

After the kickoff to the 18-yard line Tackle Xen(o)phone Lutz downed the Eagle quarterback. who fumbled the ball. Lutz recovered.

From the 11-yard line Cunningham went in to score helped by sensational blocking. The extra point was lost, for a score of 14-0.

The Eagles soon had to kick and the Panthers downed the punt on their own 43-yard line. Quarterback Allen Pope hit Cunningham on a 28-yard pass to end first quarter play.

Pass Intercepted

As second period parted (started) a pass from quarterback Danny Carter was intercepted by the Eagles and returned to the Eagles 41. Penalty flags flew as the Eagles reached the Panthers 35. The Panthers held and took over at their 35.

At this point Burch raced 20 yards to the Eagle 45-yard line. Quarterback Allen Pope then hit Bumgarner who scored standing up. The extra point was no good.

Bumgarner Snatches Pass

The Eagles took the kick off on their own 35, and an Eagle pass was intercepted by Bumgarner at the midfield stripe. Behind good blocking he scored another touchdown standing up. Quarterback Allen Pope hit Halfback Frank Abernathy for the extra point.

With less than four minutes to the play in the half, after the Eagles had punted to the Panthers and their drive was halted by the Eagles, Tackle Craig Wilfong recovered a fumble on the Eagles 30-yard line. Quarterback Pope went back to his 40 and threw a 38-yard pass. The defender tipped the ball, but on second effort by end Hubbard Morrison he gathered it in for the touchdown. Halfback Burch added the extra point.

The gun sounded at kickoff to end the first half. Despite showers, the Ridgeview Marching Band put on a colorful show.

To start the third period the Eagles kicked off to the Panthers. Quarterback Danny Carter took it on the 20 and returned it to the Panthers 34-yard line. On first down Bumgarner behind excellent blocking raced down the field to score. Burch added the extra point.

From this point on most of the excitement was in flags flying.

Late in quarter Tackle John Hodge intercepted an Eagles' pass on the Panther 31 but the Panthers lost the ball as the quarter ended.

The final Panther score came in the fourth quarter with less than four minutes to play.

From the Eagles 40-yard line, the Panthers marched down to the 25. Pope took over and carried the ball to the seven-yard line. Carter returned to carry to the one-yard line setting up for Burch to go over. Carter added the extra point as the game ended.

22-0 Win Over Lincoln Keeps Ridgeview on Top

HDR, September 26, 1964, p. 8.
by Ellis Johnson

The Ridgeview Panthers of Hickory continued their winning ways here Friday night as they defeated the Newbold Panthers of Lincolnton 22 to 0.

It was a hard fought game all the way and the Ridgeview defense was called on several times inside the 30-yard line to hold the home lads.

Hickory lost the toss and had to kickoff. The ball was returned to the Newbold 31-yard line. Two plays later Ridgeview halfback Lee Douglas Bumgarner recovered a fumble on Newbold's 35.

The Panthers rolled down the field and lost the ball on a fumble on the 7. The Lincolnton Panthers could not move as the Panthers defense rose to stop them on the 10 when a host of orange jerseys rained in on the kicker to block the kick, which was recovered by tackle Xenophone Lutz out of the end zone for a safety.

After a series of punts the Ridgeview team got the ball on its own 20. At this point halfback Lee Douglas Bumgarner, behind excellent blocking, raced 80 yards to score the touchdown. The try for extra point was no good. As the first quarter soon ended.

Several Fumbles

Fumbles played a big part in the second quarter as both teams with drives going lost the ball. With less than four minutes left int he half, Panther halfback Lee Douglas Bumgarner intercepted a Newbold pass and raced it back to the Newbold 49. At this point fullback Ed Cunningham went down the field behind good blocking for 22 yards. The halfback Frank Abernathy reeled off yardage to the 5-yard line, where a penalty gave the Hickory lads the ball on the 2 1/2-yard line. From this point Halfback Bumgarner went in to score. The extra point was added by halfback Frank Abernathy as the gun sounded to end the first half.

While the teams were resting from their first-half battle the Ridgeview Marching Band put on another of its fine shows.

Third period play began as the Panthers of Ridgeview got the kickoff and returned it to their own 29-yard line. They promptly fumbled the ball on their own 31. Once again the defensive unit led by Lutz and John Hodge, stopped the Newbold Panthers on the 26-yard line.

From this point it was a battle of punts, fumbles and penalty flags until late in the period when the Ridgeview Panthers took over on the Lincolnton 44. Behind good blocking and a beautiful key block by tackle Rendleman, halfback Allen Burch broke loose down to the 10-yard line. A penalty gave the Ridgeview Panthers a first and goal at the 5-yard line. From this point fullback Ed Cunningham moved down to the one-yard line where halfback Allen Burch went in to score the touchdown. The try for extra point was not good. The gun sounded to end the third quarter.

In the final period the Ridgeview Panthers had several good drives going but were plagued with penalties and fumbles. Tackle Hodge intercepted a pass and returned it to the Newbold 37 yard line. Flags were flying again as a pass from quarterback Allen Pope was intercepted. After stopping the Newbold Panthers the Ridgeview Panthers had their final drive going as the gun sounded to end the ball game. Next week the Panthers of Ridgeview journey to Shelby to battle the Cleveland High Tigers.

Ridgeview, Shelby Game Washed Out

HDR, October 3, 1964, p. 3.

Rain caused the postponement of Ridgeview High school's game with Shelby at Shelby Friday night. Ridgeview, with a full ten-game schedule, does not presently have an opening for the game. As conference rules require that only seven conference games be played, it is not mandatory that the game be made up.

Next Friday night, the Panthers travel to Canton to engage Reynold High School in one of the top games of the season. Reynolds lost few boys last year and should be a tough contender for the title this year.

Hot Ridgeview Panthers Melt Canton Tigers, 42-5
HDR, October 9, 1964, p. 12.
by Ellis Johnson

It was a cold Thursday night at Canton High stadium but a hot Ridgeview High Panthers of Hickory completely smothered the Reynolds High Tigers, 44-0. The Hickory lads went into the game with four wins and no loss record and had compiled a 42.5 scoring average.

As usual this season the Panthers haven't won the toss so far and Thursday evening was no exception. After the kickoff to the Reynolds Tigers the ball was taken on the ten yard line and returned to the thirty-five yard line. The stout Panther defense soon forced the Tigers to punt. The ball was out of play on the Panthers 35-yard line.

Fast Backs Go Into Action

At this point the Panther's fast backs went into action. Halfback Allen Burch reeled off twelve yards then fullback Edward Cunningham came back with nine yards and a fine run to the the Tiger thirty-five. At this point halfback Allen Burch reeled off ten yards to the twenty-five yard line. Quarterback Allen Pope behind excellent blocking raced down side lines for twenty-five yards and a touchdown. The extra point was no good.

Once again after the kickoff the ball was put into play on the thirty-five yard line of the Tigers and once again the Panthers stout defense held and forced the Tigers to punt. The kicker was rushed and the punt was blocked by John Hodge.

The ball was recovered by Tackle Craig Wilfong at the Tigers 10-yard line. From here, halfback Lee Douglas Bumgarner ripped off ten yards to score behind excellent blocking. Fullback Ed Cunningham added the extra point.

After the kickoff the ball was put into play on the Tigers' 35-yard line. Trailing fourteen to nothing the Tigers took to the air and a Tiger pass was intercepted by James Thompson who carried it to the forty-seven yard line. As quarter ended halfback Allen Burch, behind good blocking carried the ball for thirty-five more yards. Ed Cunningham added five more yards.

First Penalty

Then came first penalty of the game. The penalty set the Panthers back to the Tiger 16-yard line. On a third down play, halfback Lee Douglas Bumgarner sc(o)red the touchdown. Quarterback Allen Pope threw to end Harrison James for the PAT. The kickoff play began on the 25-yard line of the Tigers. On a second down play, Panther halfback, Lee Dou(g)las Bumgarner recovered a fumble, Edward Cunningham capitalized on the mistake and galloped twenty-two yards to score. Try for extra point was no good.

A penalty after the touchdown was called, and the Panthers had to kick off from the 25-yard line. Another five yard penalty was called against the Panthers. This time making them kick off front the 20-yard line. In exchange of flags, the ball was placed on the Tigers 10-yard line.

Stout Defense

Once again the Panthers stout defense arose to stop the Tigers, who had to kick from their own end zone. With the onrushing orange jersey, the punter got off a poor kick with rolled out of bounds on the Tiger twenty yard line. A penalty gave the Panthers the ball first down on the ten yard line. At this point halfback Allen Burch, being excellent blocking read in the end zone to score. Quarterback Allen Pope added the extra point as the half ended.

No Score In Third Quarter

The Panthers were held scoreless in the third period although tackle Rendleman recovered a fumble on the Tigers twenty-five yard line as the gun sounded to end the period.

In the final period, after being pushed back to the thirty-five yard line, the Panthers lost yardage by penalties, to the forty-five yard line.

Then halfback Frank Abernethy got off a twenty yard run behind good blocking and Burch carried to the fifteen where fullback Ed Cunningham went in to score. Halfback Curtis Cunningham added the extra point.

Tigers Come Close

In the closing minutes the Tigers got a drive going from their own thirty-five. They moved the ball to the Panther 5-yard line. On first and goal the Panthers drew a penalty, half the distance of the goal. But the Panthers stout defense held and pushed the Tigers back to the six yard line. Quarterback Allen Pope held onto the ball to end the game.

Ridgeview School News

HDR, October 10, 1964, p. 4. (partial)
by Alivana Curry, George Derr and Jacqueline Rendleman

Try as they may, it seems that no team can open a pathway to score a touchdown through our linebackers. These boys act as an impenetrable brick wall.

Their main objective is "an undefeated and unscored on season for the year."

The reason? The linebackers together following their motto. "One for All and All for One" to secure the strength of a robust line.

During the season of 1962 the Panthers managed to obtain and hold an unscored on season. The boys feel they have the material required to obtain this title for the season.

The leaders of the untouchable gang are John Hodge, a six-foot five-incher, and Xen(o)phone Lutz, a six foot two incher, both weighing approximately 209 pounds. Other members of the gang are Craig Wilfong, Dwight Thompson, Edward White, Hubbard Morrison, Harrison James, William Heard, and Tillis Rendleman. Their weights are from 175-209 pounds.

Ridgeview Queen and Court
HDR, October 20, 1964, p. 2.
Caption under Picture

The Ridgeview High School Homecoming Queen Miss Joyce Ann Pope (seated in the center, top row) is a senior. She was crowned at halftime ceremonies during the Ridgeview-Freedman game here Monday night. The Grammar grade queen Miss Theresa Griffith, and homecoming king is Curtis Byrd (above). Mrs. Walter Thompson, Sophomore Mother of the Year (seated directly below Miss Pope) has eight children, seven of whom attend Ridgeview. Others in the photo are members of the royal court. (Photo by Ronald L. Harris)

Coach at Ridgeview Honored
HDR, October 20, 1964, p. 2.
Caption under Picture

Ridgeview Athletic Director S.W. Davis (center) received the football Hall of Fame plaque Monday night during halftime of the Ridgeview-Freedman tilt from VFW post Commander E.T. Moore, Sr., with members of the post looking on. (Photo by Ronald L. Harris)

Ex-Panthers Paid Tribute In Ceremony
HDR, October 20, 1964, p. 2.
by Ellis Johnson

The Eugene Saddler post (9881) of the Veterans of Foreign Wars has instituted the Ridgeview Football Hall of Fame with four being selected as the initial recipients of the honor. They are Guilford McCall Derr, James (Bill) Fisher, James (Mike) Whitener, and Elmore Eckard. The plaque was presented to the school Monday night by Post Commander E.T. Moore to coach S.W. Davis.

Ridgeview High school Panthers were state champions in the school years of '31-'32, '32-'33 and '33-'34 under Coach J.T. Wilson and Derr, Eckerd and Whitener played on those teams. Derr and Eckerd played halfback slots in the single wing, T formation and 'Y' formation (which is known today as the "spread" formation). Whitener was the quarterback. Only teams in the area playing then were Wilkesboro, Shelby, and Morganton. They also played teams from Kingsport, Tenn., Atkins High of Winston-Salem, Price of Salisbury and Monroe. For three years straight they played Lincoln Academy at the Cleveland County fair and was never scored on. Fisher played under coach Jack Faggatt as a 1942 graduate of Ridgeview. He went on and won honors at Johnson C. Smith University, Charlotte, playing end. Fisher was later head coach at Voorhees College at Denmark, S.C., until his tragic death in an automobile crash seven miles from Denmark.

Thomas A. Johnson, treasurer for the Ridgeview Alumni Association presented a public address system system to Panther Coach Roger Scales for the use of the Athletic department during the football season.

Panthers Top Freedman High With Ease, 38 To 0

HDR, October 20, 1964, p. 11.
by Ellis Johnson

Before a large homecoming crowd, the Ridgeview Panthers defeated the Freedman Blue Devils of Lenoir, 38-0 here Monday night.

The big Panther line was outstanding although it had a three-day workout recess. The linemen were Craig Wilfong, Dwight Thompson, Xen(o)phone Lutz, Mitchell Anthony, Tillis Rendleman and Hubbard Morrison, who were playing their last homecoming game for Ridgeview.

The Panthers lost the toss as they have done all season long, and had to kick off. Senior James Thompson got off a fine kick, which was taken on the 10-yard line and returned to the Blue Devils' 26. The fired up Blue Devils began to roll picking up two first downs. However, a 15-yard penalty stopped their drive on the 29-yard line and they punted to the Panther 16 and the ball was returned to the Blue Devils' 46.

At this point the Panthers swung into action, featuring runs by Lee Douglas Bumgarner and Edward Cunningham to the 19-yard line. At this point, fullback Cunningham broke loose for a touchdown behind excellent blocking. Quarterback Allen Pope, playing his last homecoming contest and his finest game of the season added the extra point.

After the kick-off, the Blue Devils, on the move from their 33-yard line, were stopped cold on a brilliant tackle by End Dwight

Thompson on the Blue Devil 26-yard line, as the gun sounded to end the quarter.

To start the second period, a 15-yard penalty against the Panthers gave the Blue Devils a fourth and one-yard situation on their own 42-yard line. At this point, the Panther line arose to the occasion, led by Tillis Rendleman, Charles Redman, Edward White, and William Heard, and stopped the Blue Devils on the 37-yard line.

The combination of Burch, Bumgarner and Cunningham moved the ball to the one-yard line, where fullback Cunningham carried it in for the score. The try for extra point was no good.

The Blue Devils tried to strike back through the air, but were stopped cold on a brilliant pass interception by quarterback Allen Pope on the Panthers' 35 as the half ended.

Halftime Activities

At the end of the first half, with the Ridgeview Panthers leading 14-0, the homecoming ceremonies were held. The high-stepping Ridgeview marching band, under A.V. Evans, director, and drum major Roosevelt Williams, took the field. The theme of the show was "Modern Dancing for the King and Queen."

Miss Grammar department, Theresa Griffith, of East Hickory Elementary School, escorted by Maxson Smith, was the first to be crowned by Panther co-captain Lee Douglas Bumgarner. The homecoming king was Curtis Byrd of the primary department and his escort was Miss Frederick. He was crowned by Panther tackle Craig Wilfong. Miss Eunice Harper, Miss Freedman High, also took part in the royal procession and was given a bouquet of flowers by Panther tackle Xen(o)phone Lutz.

Then came the crowning of Miss Ridgeview, Miss Joyce Ann Pope, a Senior, by Captain John Hodges, also a senior.

In the third period, the Blue Devils kicked off to the Panthers on their own 35-yard line, and returned it to the Panther 45. At this point Bumgarner raced 55 yards behind good blocking to score. The extra point was added by Allen Burch.

After an exchange of punts, the second Panther score of the quarter came late in the period on a brilliant 85-yard run by halfback Allen Burch, behind good blocking. The extra point was added by Bumgarner.

Panthers Score Again

In the final period quarterback Allen Pope threw a strike to Danny Carter on the Blue Devils 31. He then threw to halfback Bumgarner for the touchdown. Halfback Ollie Parks added the extra point.

A defensive battle was then staged by both teams. Once again quarterback Pope made an interception, and Ridgeview held on to the ball as the final gun sounded.

Ridgeview Fullback Crosses Goal Line
October 20, 1964, p. 11.
Caption of Picture

Swift Ridgeview fullback Edward Cunningham scats over the goal line for the first Panther score Monday night against Lenoir. A Lenoir defender (center) narrowly missed bringing him down on the goal line. The game was played at Ridgeview Monday night as a result of a postponed Friday night tilt. (Photo by Ronald L. Harris)

Mt. Airy Falls to Ridgeview by 30-0 Tally
October 23, 1964

The Rampaging Ridgeview Panthers of Hickory did it again Thursday night when they defeated Mt. Airy, 30—0 to maintain their perfect record by not allowing an opponent to score on them this season. The Panthers have not been beaten in a gridiron connotes since 1957.

Scoring honors for the Ridgeview team was performed by Lee Bumgarner, Ed Cunningham and Allen Burch. Onc point after touchdown was added on an Allen Pope pass to Harrison James.

The game was a Panther victory all the way. The score at the end of the half was 22-0. In the second half Ridgeview railed again to score two more touchdowns but one was called back on account of illegal procedure.

Ridgeview High School Band
HDR, October 24, 1964
Caption of Picture

Pictured here are 46 members of the Ridgeview marching band which will perform at the Ridgeview-Olive Hill football game at Morganton next Friday night. The band puts on a fine half-time show that would equal most college bands. (Photo by Ronald L. Harris)

Ridgeview School News
HDR, October 24, 1964, p. 4. (partial)
by Alivana Curry, George Derr and Jacqueline Rendleman

The Panthers added another victory to their undefeated and unscored upon record when they triumphed over Jones High school of Mt. Airy, Thursday night, there.

Due to weather conditions, the Panthers faced two teams this week. They defeated Freedman of Lenoir Monday night, 38-0, and Mt. Airy, 30-0. The team will journey to Morganton, whose team is expected to give the Panthers a struggle for triumph.

Ridgeview Bowls Over Morganton Team, 32-0
HDR, October 31, 1964, p. 12
by Ellis Johnson

Quarterback Allen Pope guided his Ridgeview fastbacks here Friday night to a 32-0 victory over a highly spirited Olive Hill Yellow Jackets team. The victory pulled the rug from under the Yellow Jackets championship hopes.

The Panthers won the toss and received. It was a short kick as the Yellow Jackets tried to keep the ball from the Panthers fast backs, being downed on the Ridgeview 47-yard line. On the first play from scrimmage the Panthers missed a touchdown by inches off the finger tips of Hubbard Morrison. Quarterback Allen Pope then called on his fullback Ed Cunningham, who cracked the line twice, picking up short yardage. Pope picked up the first down behind good blocking to keep the drive alive.

Makes First Down

Pope hit end Danny Carter on a third down play for a first down on the 29 to keep the drive alive. Panthers' Lee Douglas Bumgarner carried down to the 10-yard line where the Panthers too lost the ball after a series of penalties.

The Yellow Jackets got the ball after the Panthers had controlled it for five minutes and twelve seconds. But the Panthers' stout defense soon rose to stop the Yellow Jackets drive and took over on their own 45. Once again the Panthers moved down the field behind the running of the fast backs to the nine-yard line, where a five-yard penalty set them back to the 14. Quarterback Pope threw a 14-yard touchdown pass to end Danny Carter. The try for extra point was no good.

The Yellow Jackets took the kick off on their own 34-yard line as the quarter ended.

Ed Cunningham intercepted an O'Neil pass as the second quarter began. In three plays the Panther fullback carried the ball to the Yellow Jacket 25-yard line. At this point quarterback Allen Pope hit end Harrison James for the first down at the 21-yard line then, like lightning, halfback Lee Douglas Bumgarner raced 21 yards to score behind excellent blocking. Quarterback Pope added the extra point.

The Panthers' hard hitting defense held the Yellow Jackets at bay until the closing seconds when Allen Pope intercepted a pass on the Yellow Jackets 45-yard line. At this point he threw a strike to end Hubbard Morrison, who gathered it in on the 10-yard line and went on to score, standing up. The extra point was no good with ten seconds left and the Panthers kicked off.

Many Penalties

In the third period play was plagued with penalty flags until late in the quarter, fullback Ed Cunningham returned a punt to the Yellow Jacket 36-yard line. Once again the amazing speed of halfback Lee Douglas Bumgarner behind excellent blocking raced 36 yards to score. The extra point was no good. Then the rest of the quarter was once again plagued by the penalty flag.

Early in the final quarter the Panthers were once again knocking on touchdown's door, thanks to a 39-yard run by halfback Lee Douglas Bumgarner and the quarterback Allen Pope's amazing 15-yard run to the 11-yard line. At this point halfback Curtis Cunningham fought his way in to score. The extra point was no good.

The rest of the quarter was good hard hitting football and resulted in fumbles. One was recovered by Frank Abernathy and another by Ed Cunningham. Panthers were moving as the final gun sounded - score 32-0 and the "Untouchables from Hickory" had remained untouched.

Ridgeview, Central Clash Slated Here Friday Night

HDR, November 5, 1964, p. 18

by Ellis Johnson

The Ridgeview High School Panthers are set for the most important football game - at least to them - of the season this week. On it rides the Northwestern Conference Championship and the Western North Carolina District II championship.

Last week the Panthers defeated the Olive Hill Yellow Jackets of Morganton, 32-0. The Yellow Jackets were the Western North Carolina District I Champions and had a good chance at the Northwestern conference championship until the Panthers went to Morganton and pulled the championship rug from under them.

While the Panthers were at Olive Hill of Morganton the Central High Hornets had their hands full trying to stay undefeated as they barely got by Reynolds High of Canton, 16-13 (Earlier reports had the score reversed). It seems that the Hornets were overlooking the Reynolds Tigers and pointing to this Friday's clash with the Panthers in Hickory.

The Panthers have won the Northwestern Conference Championship every year since 1958 and went through the regular 1960 season undefeated and unscored on. The Panthers have not lost a regular season game since 1957.

Ridgeview and Central score since 1958:

Ridgeview 54 - Central 8	1958
Ridgeview 38 - Central 0	1959
Ridgeview 46 - Central 0	1960
Ridgeview 30 - Central 0	1961
Ridgeview 24 - Central 14	1962
Ridgeview 24 - Central 14	1963

The Ridgeview Panther's four running backs are as follows, (This (does) not include the quarterbacks).

	Total Rushing	Touchdowns
Bumgarner	1177	29* (printed error, should be 19)
Burch	658	7
E.Cunningham	689	8
Abernathy	151	1

Total of four backs rushing, 2,576.

Total touchdowns for the four, 35.

Panthers Net Championship
Ridgeview Wallops Undefeated Central High

HDR, November 7, 1964, p. 10
by Ellis Johnson

The Ridgeview High school Panthers defeated Central High Hornets on Ridgeview field 36-0. There was an overflowing crowd on hand to watch the two undefeated powers of Catawba county. The Panthers lost the toss and had to kick off. The Hornets returned the kickoff to their own 29-yard line. After trying to crack the stout Panther line, quarterback Kennedy tried a pass which was intercepted by Ed Cunningham. He got excellent blocking and scored on a 35-yard run. Halfback Lee Douglas Bumgarner added the extra point.

Hornets Pushed Back

The Panthers kicked off to the Hornets which was returned to the Hornet 20-yard line. After a penalty the Hornets were pushed back on terrific defense play by end Dwight Thompson.

Neither team could move and exchanged punts. Fullback Ed Cunningham was pushed back to the Panthers 30-yard line for a loss of five yards as the first quarter ended.

Good, Hard Football

In the second period it was good hard football that is always displayed when the two county rivals get together. With less than four minutes left in the first half the Panthers were on the move as Lee Bumgarner carried for six yards to the Hornet 20. At this point quarterback Allen Pope hit halfback Allen Burch on the 5-yard line for a first and goal.

Plagued by penalty flags, the Panthers were set back to the ten yard line by offside infraction. At this point halfback Allen Burch carried to the seven yard line. Fullback Ed Cunningham behind a terrific block as Captain John Hodge went in to score from (the) 7-yard line for his second touchdown of the evening. Quarterback Allen Pope added the extra point.

Once again the Panthers kicked off to the Hornets as the half ended.

"Showboat" Band

The Central High Band displayed a showboat style playing hit numbers of present and past. The high stepping Ridgeview Panther Band also put in a "big show" as they played hit tunes from the past as well as the present.

In the third period the Hornet's kick-off to the Panthers was taken by fullback Ed Cunningham on the Panther 35-yard line. Ridgeview couldn't move and soon lost the ball as quarterback Pope was hit hard and fumbled on the Panther 21.

Pass Interception

Pope intercepted a Hornet pass on the 5-yard line and carried it back to the ten yard line of the Panthers to stop the threat. Soon the Panthers had to kick to the Hornets. The ball was downed on the Hornets 36 yard line. The Panther stout defense held and forced the Hornets to kick.

Halfback Lee Douglas Bumgarner took it and raced it back to the Hornets 30-yard line and aided by a personal foul, gave the Panthers a first down on the Hornets 15-yard line. Halfback Allen Burch carried behind excellent blocking to the one-yard line, where quarterback Allen Pope carried it in for the touchdown. The try for extra point was no good.

60-Yard Run

Late in the quarter Edward Cunningham picked off a Kennedy pass and with a terrific block from John Hodge and Charles Redmond raced 60 yards to score his third touchdown of the evening. The try for extra point was no good. The Hornets were back on their ten yard line as the quarter ended.

Early in the fourth quarter Lee Bumgarner picked off the fourth pass interception for the Panthers and carried it back to the Hornets 30 yard line. At this point quarterback Pope's passes fell incomplete and the Hornets took over on their own 29.

Several Fumbles

End Danny Carter threw Kennedy for a 9-yard loss to the 20-yard line. The punt was fumbled by halfback James Thompson on the Hornets 43 and recovered by the Hornets at that point. The Panthers recovered a Hornets fumble on the 40-yard line. The Hornets got the ball back on a fumble recovery then filled the air with passes.

There was another fumble in the Hornet backfield which was recovered by guard White for the Panthers on the Hornet 30. Halfback Curtis Cunningham carried the ball to the 15-yard line. At this point Pope's pass was intercepted to stop the Panthers drive.

The Panthers' pass defense hero picked up his third pass interception of the evening and carried the ball to the Hornet 30-yard line, where halfback Curtis Cunningham raced behind good blocking to score the touchdown. The extra point was added by Jerry Johnson.

Conference Champs

The Panthers kicked off to the Hornet 25-yard line. The final gun sounded and the Panthers were the Northwestern Conference Champions once again. Ridgeview will end the regular season Thursday evening against the Cleveland High Tigers. This game was postponed some time ago due to a hurricane.

Panthers Top Shelby, 52-0
Remain Undefeated, Unscored On
HDR, November 13, 1964, p. 10
by Ellis Johnson

The Ridgeview High school Panthers of Hickory romped over the Cleveland High Tigers here Thursday evening, 52-0. For the lads from Hickory, it ended a perfect regular season with 10 wins and no losses, with no one crossing the Panthers' goal line.

The Panthers lost the toss and kicked off to the Tigers to their own twenty eight yard line. Unable to move through the Panther defense, they tried a third down pass which was picked off by fullback Ed Cunningham on the thirty five of the Tigers for a touchdown behind good blocking. The try for extra point was no good.

The kick off was short and returned to the Tigers 40-yard line. From there the Tigers moved the ball on fine runs fashioned with several long penalties to the Panther 8-yard line, but the hard hitting Panthers line made the ball carrier fumble, and it was recovered by Panther end Dwight Thompson on the 10-yard line. The Panthers lost five yards due to a missed signal. At that point halfback Lee Bumgarner brought the ball out to the thirteen. Then like lightning, with a couple of key blocks, halfback Allen Burch galloped 87 yards to score. Quarterback Allen Pope added the extra points, and the Panthers moved to a fourteen to nothing lead.

After the kickoff the gun sounded to end the quarter. To start the second quarter, the Tigers had to punt. It was taken by fullback Ed Cunningham and returned to the Panthers 40-yard line. At this point the Panther fullback rolled for thirty yards. The the Panthers flashy halfback, Lee Bumgarner raced thirty yards to score behind good blocking. Quarterback Pope hit end James in the end zone for the extra point. After the kickoff Panther fullback, Frank Abernathy recovered a fumble on the Tiger 49-yard line. At this point Lewis Collins went in as quarterback. Between halfbacks Allen Burch and Lee Bumgarner, they moved the ball to the 19-yard line, where behind good blocking, halfback Burch went in to score. The try for extra point was no good.

After the kickoff play began on the Panther 36-yard line. After losing four yards fullback Ed Cunningham intercepted a pass and returned it to the Panther 42-yard line. A long penalty set the Panthers back to the 27-yard line. At that point halfback Frank Abernathy, behind excellent blocking, raced 73 yards to score. Quarterback Pope threw to end Morrison for extra points.

Kickoff was returned to the Tigers 17-yard line as the half ended.

During the half the fans were entertained by the Cleveland High Band and the Ridgeview Marching Band.

The Tigers kicked off to the Panthers to start the second half with Ridgeview leading thirty-six to nothing at this point. The kickoff was returned by Abernathy to the Panthers 37-yard line. At this point, halfback James Thompson got off his first punt of the night, a fine one that carried sixty yards in the air. The Tigers put the ball in play on their own 16-yard line. The Panthers pushed them back to the 11-yard line where tackle Xenophone Lutz recovered a fumble on the 12-yard line of the Tigers. At this point quarterback Allen Pope carried it in for the score. The try for extra points was no good.

After the kickoff play began on the Tigers 13-yard line, where the Panthers held and forced a punt. A high pass from he center rolled out of the end zone for a safety. The Panthers were on the move as the quarter ended. The Panthers final touchdown came midway (in) the period on a back, Ed Cunningham behind excellent blocking. Quarterback Allen Pope added the extra point.

Panthers were again on the move as the final gun sounded, score Ridgeview 52, Cleveland High 0.

Ridgeview Meets Dunbar In Playoffs
November 19, 1964, p. 14.

Ridgeview travels to East Spencer Friday night to engage the Dunbar High school football, champs of District 3 at 7:30. Ridgeview represents District 2 and District 1 was eliminated previously by the Panthers.

Ridgeview coach, S.W. Davis describes this game as a "must", and he comments that the team's going "all out for this one."

The team itself is in fine shape, Mentally and physically. Coach Davis comments that his passers and runners are moving the ball well.

Dunbar High school has a big team with a big line and some big backs. They run from a variation of the T and can throw the ball as well.

Providing Hickory wins, the winners will return to Hickory for the North Carolina State championship game.

Panthers Set to Do Battle with Dunbar
HDR, November 20, 1964, p. 10.
by Ellis Johnson

The Ridgeview Panthers are set to battle with the Dunbar High team of East Spencer on the Dunbar field tonight at 7:30 o'clock.

The two teams' records are as follows

Dunbar
Dunbar 30, Belmont 6.
Dunbar 22. Monroe 0.
Dunbar 24, Statesville, 0.
Dunbar 12, Annapolis 0.
Dunbar 8, Lexington 38 (3A)
Dunbar 30, Salisbury 6 (3A)
Dunbar 36, Mt. Airy 0.
Dunbar 2, Thomasville 0.
Dunbar 2, Asheboro 0.

Ridgeview

Ridgeview 40, Huntersville 0.
Ridgeview 56, Wilkesboro 0.
Ridgeview 52, Spindale 0.
Ridgeview 22, Lincolnton 0.
Ridgeview 44, Canton 0.
Ridgeview 32, Lenoir 0.
Ridgeview 36, Mt. Airy 0.
Ridgeview 32, Morganton 0.
Ridgeview 36, Newton 0.
Ridgeview 51, Shelby 0.

Starting Lineups

Ridgeview	Pos.	Dunbar
Morrison	RE	Jefferies
Thompson	RT	Neal
Hodge	RG	Alexander
Anthony	Center	Turner
Lutz	LG	Faulkner
Wilfong	LT	Noble
Carter	LE	Oakley
Pope	QB	Lanear
Bumgarner	LH	Washington
Cunningham	FB	Jackson
Burch	RH	Sifford

Panthers Romp
Ridgeview Explodes Again, Defense Still Unscored On
HDR, November 21, 1964, p. 10
by Ellis Johnson

The highly explosive Ridgeview Panthers defeated the Dunbar High Tigers here Friday night, 28-0, for the Western North Carolina State AA championship.

The Panthers lost the toss and kicked off. The return was to the Tiger 25-yard line. On second down from the 27-yard line tackle John Hodge and halfback Lee Bumgarner recovered a fumble on the Tiger 27. The Panthers with the fast backs moved down to the 10-yard line where quarterback Allen Pope hit halfback Lee Bumgarner for the touchdown. Halfback Allen Burch added the extra points.

Defense Holds

The kick-off was returned to the Tigers' 30 where the stout defense of the Panthers held and forced the Tigers to kick. The poor punt was taken on the Tigers' 47-yard line. After a five-yard gain Lee Bumgarner behind excellent blocking raced 42 yards for a touchdown. The extra point was no good.

After the kickoff the Tigers were on the move but was stopped as John Hodge, the Panther captain, recovered a fumble on the Panther 40-yard line. The Panthers moved down to the Tigers' 37-yard line as the quarter ended. A fine run by fullback Ed Cunningham gave the Panthers first down on the 13-yard line of the Tigers, but a costly penalty moved the ball to the 28. The Tigers soon took over on their own 15-yard line.

The Panthers took over on downs on the Tigers 29 and moved down to the 13-yard line, where on fourth down the Panthers' quarterback, Allen Pope, hit his halfback Allen Burch for a touchdown. The extra point was no good.

Late in the quarter a blocked Panther punt was recovered by the Tigers on the Panthers' 15-yard line, but the Panther defense arose to stop the Tigers on the 14-yard line. At this point halfback Lee Bumgarner raced out to the Panther 35-yard line as the gun sounded to end the half.

The exciting play of the third quarter was a 70-yard pass and run play from Pope to Lee Bumgarner to the Tigers 11-yard line. Plagued with penalties, the Panthers soon lost the ball. During an exchange of punts late in the quarter, a bad pass from center and the Tigers took over on the Panther 22-yard line. Aided by a long penalty and fine defensive play, the Panthers got out of trouble.

Intercepts Pass

In the final period, after exchange of the football, quarterback Allen Pope intercepted a pass to stop the Tigers' drive. A costly 15-yard penalty backed the ball to the Panther 19-yard line. A blocked punt was recovered by the Tigers on the Panthers 15-yard line, but a costly penalty and the fine defensive play got the ball from the shadows of the Panthers' goal. The Tigers' drive was stopped on a fumble recovery by tackle Craig Wilfong.

Late in the quarter the Panthers were on the move and drove down to the 20-yard line, where quarterback Allen Pope hit halfback Allen Burch for the touchdown. Pope added the extra points. The gun soon sounded the end of the game.

Ridgeview faces Hamlet in Hickory Wednesday night for the State AA Championship.

Panthers To Battle Hamlet On College Field for Title
HDR, November 24, 1964, p. 12.
by Ellis Johnson

The state AA Championship between Ridgeview High school and Monroe Avenue High school will be played on the Lenoir-Rhyne College Field here Wednesday evening at eight o'clock. For the Panthers this is their dream come true as they have mowed down foe after foe to reach this point.

The Panthers worked long and hard Monday in preparation for this final big one. Ridgeview's defensive unit will lean heavily on such boys as tackle Craig Wilfong, who has been outstanding all year in both the offense and defense. He is noted for his hard hitting tactics. Dwight Thompson, who moved from end to tackle, has really found a home in plugging up holes on offense as well as defense and had played a rugged game all year. Frank Abernathy, one of the defensive backers, has been one of the unsung heroes of this Panther team this year and is an offensive bomb with his speed.

Allen Pope, the Panthers Number One signal caller, has really come into his own this season and has been a terror at the defensive halfback slot and has come up with several key interceptions. With his speed of a halfback, Pope will also run from his quarterback slot. Charles Redmond, a big Panther tackle came into the Panther lineup in the latter half of the season and has turned in a fine job as a defensive tackle.

Tillis Rendleman, another quiet, but hard hitting guard, has been a terror on the Panther defensive unit that boasts a clean slate.

There are a few of the unsung heroes on this explosive Panther team this year.

Panthers in State AA Title Game Friday
HDR, November 25, 1964, p. 15.
Caption of Picture

The Ridgeview High school Panthers, who will play Hamlet Friday night at eight o'clock on College Field in Hickory to determine the winner of the North Carolina AA Championship crown, completed the regular season undefeated, untied, and unscored upon. The game, originally set for tonight, was postponed due to inclement weather.

Members of the team are (left to right): First Row - William Heard, Ollie Parks, Willie Byrd, Allen Burch, Edward White, Frank Abernathy, Jerry Johnson, Charles Thompson, and Hamp Davis; center row - Edward Cunningham, Hubbard Morrison, Xenophone Lutz, Harrison James, Dwight Thompson, Douglas Bumgarner, Johnny Hodge, James Thompson, Craig Wilfong, Mitchell Anthony and Allen Pope; back row - Coach Samuel Davis, Bobby Bivens, trainee, Eddie Corpening, Lewis Collins, Detroit Rhyne, Danny Carter, Charles Redman, John Thompson, Douglas Thompson, Jimmy Shade, Larry Williams, Tommy Yearby, Anthony Parks, Curtis Cunningham, Elbert Little, Tillis Rendleman and Coach Roger Scales.

Undefeated 11 Hopes to Set Mark Tonight
HDR, November 27, 1964, p. 19.
by Elias Johns

The Ridgeview High School Panthers with the best balance(ed) team in years with a perfect record also can set history tonight at Lenoir-

Rhyne College if they can shut out the Monroe Ave. High School team of Hamlet, N.C.

Ridgeview, who have been in (the) playoffs since 1958, lost to Dunbar of Lexington, N.C. for the Western NC Title in '58, 48-14 and lost the Western title in '59 again to Dunbar by a score of 12-6. In 1960 the Panthers had a perfect record going, defeating Kannapolis 12-0 and Wadesboro 36-0 to advance to state championship finals, then was smothered by a fine Lincoln High of Chapel Hill team 38-8. Since then the Panthers lost a state bid to Lincoln High of Chapel Hill and then in 1962 the Panthers won their first state championship by defeating Edenton, N.C. here on college field.

In 1963 the Panthers lost the Western title to Dunbar High of Lexington, 28-22. Now the Dunbar High has moved up to 3A. Last week the Panthers with ten straight wins took on the Dunbar Tigers of East Spencer for the Western State 2A title. (The) scores was 28-0 and the Panthers perfect record was intact.

Hamlet fields a fine team rolling over R.L. Vann High school of Ahoskie 20-0 last Thursday in a game played in Hamlet.

RIDGEVIEW RECORD
Ridgeview 40, Huntersville 0.
Ridgeview 56, Wilkesboro 0.
Ridgeview 52, Spindale 0.
Ridgeview 22, Shelby 0.* (teams transposed)
Ridgeview 44, Canton 0.
Ridgeview 32, Lenoir 0.
Ridgeview 36, Mt. Airy 0.
Ridgeview 32, Morganton 0.
Ridgeview 36, Newton 0.
Ridgeview 51, Lincolnton 0.*
Western AA Championship
Ridgeview 28, East Spencer 0

OFFENSIVE LINEUP

Hamlet	Pos.
Albert Ingram	LE
William Fisher	LT

Robert Ratliff	LG
Levi Mims	C
Edgar Morrison	RG
James Deberry	RT
Maurice Stuart	RE
Robert McCaskell	LHB
Nelson David	RHB
Winslow Ellerbee	FB
James Newton	QB

Ridgeview

Danny Carter	LE
Dwight Thompson	LT
Xenophone Lutz	LG
Mitchell Anthony	C
John Hodge	RG
Craig Wilfong	RT
Hubert Morrison	RE
Lee Bumgarner	LHB
Allen Burch	RHB
Edward Cunningham	FB
Allen Pope	QB

MONROE AVE. RECORD 9-1

Mon. Ave. 28	Wadesboro 0
Mon. Ave. 42	Rowland 8
Mon. Ave. 38	Clinton 12
Mon. Ave. 10	Siler City 0
Mon. Ave. 36	Mor. Train. 16
Mon. Ave. 24	Dunn 8
Mon. Ave. 0	Lumberton 2
Mon. Ave. 22	Monroe 12
Mon. Ave. 16	Trenton 0
Mon. Ave. 20	Ahoskie 0

Tribute to H.S. Teams
HDR, November 28, 1964
Editorial

Teams representing Hickory High School and Ridgeview H.S. in Hickory, are deserving of editorial tribute for the excellent football records which enabled them to participate in championship contests, Friday night.

Here at College Field, the Ridgeview Panthers in a game with the Monroe Avenue Tigers, of Hamlet, kept their perfect record by remaining unscored on all season, as they emerged from a fierce contest with a 16-0 victory. For the second time in a two-year period, Ridgeview has won the North Carolina Negro Class AA title. Their first State crown was won in 1962 when the Panthers defeated Edenton in the final game of the season - also at College Field here.

Going into its game at Blanton Memorial Stadium, in Shelby, against Thomasville H.S. for the WNCHSAA crown, Hickory H.S. Tornadoes sprung a great surprise by scoring two touchdowns with the first few minutes of play. It required the second and third quarters before the surprised and stunned Bulldogs could go ahead with a one point margin. Another Thomasville touchdown in the final period of play resulted in a final score of 20-13 in favor of the Bulldogs. It was only after a valiant stand by the Tornadoes who have been rated as underdogs, that the championship crown was surrendered.

Certainly, the two teams representing Hickory's two High Schools are entitled to well-earned salutes.

Panthers Take State Title, Finished Season Unscored On
HDR, November 28, 1964, p. 10
by Ellis Johnson

The amazing Ridgeview Panthers of Hickory set a record at Lenoir Rhyne College Field Friday night as they shut out the Monroe

Avenue Tigers of Hamlet, 16-0.

The 1960 team went through 11 games but this team has completed 12 games and ended a perfect season. In it they won the Northwestern Conference, Western District Class AA (District Two and defeated the District One champions) and defeated the District Three champions for the Western Class AA title Friday.

The Ridgeview Panthers became the North Carolina Negro Class AA champions for the second time. In 1962 they defeated Edenton for the crown on College Field (LR). For Coaches S.W. Davis and Roger Scales it was a happy ending to a dream.

Lost Toss

The Panthers lost the toss and had to kick off to the Tigers. It was returned to the Tigers 35-yard line. Deep in their own back yard the Tigers pulled a quick kick on third down. The ball was put in play on the Panthers 29-yard line behind excellent blocking, halfback Lee Bumgarner carried for 27 yards and again behind excellent policing halfback Lee Bumgarner carried to the Tigers 14-yard line.

At this point Lee Bumgarner was called on again and carried to the four-yard line. The Panthers attempted to score on three tries but were pushed back on fourth down from the three-yard line. A Panther fumble was recovered by the Tigers. The Panthers defense soon made the Tigers kick and the Panthers took over on their own 31. A long penalty forced the Panthers back to their own 16-yard line where the Panthers had to kick. The gun sounded ending the first quarter.

Second Quarter

Halfback James Thompson got off a fine kick to start the second quarter. It was taken on the Tigers 46-yard line. The Tigers moved the ball well, picking up two first downs. On the Panthers 26-yard line, defensive guard Edward White recovered a fumble. Guided by quarterback Allen Pope, the Panthers moved the ball to the Tigers 45.

Plagued by a 15-yard penalty which set the Panthers back to the 36. Once again the Panthers had to call on James Thompson, their fine punter. The punt was returned to the Tigers 30-yard line. The fine offense of the Tigers began to click, picking up two first downs. The Tigers found themselves on the Panthers two-yard line, first and goal to go. The Panthers defense, led by Captain John Hodge, Xenophone Lutz, Charles Redman, Allen Pope and others, stopped the drive of the Tigers on the one-yard line as the gun sounded to end the scoreless first half.

Halftime Show

The Ridgeview band put on a dedication show to the school's principal, Panther coaches and football team and to the many fans for their support this year. Halfback Allen Burch returned the second half kickoff to the Panthers own 15-yard line. Once again the Panthers were moving as fullback Edward Cunningham carried for eight to the 23 but the fine defense of the Tigers forced them to kick once again. James Thompson's kick rolled dead on the Tigers 14-yard line. The Panthers defense held and forced the Tigers to kick, which was taken on the Panthers 40 yard line.

At this point fullback Edward Cunningham raced for 15 yards and a face mask penalty gave the Panthers a first down on the 10 yard line. The hard-hitting Tigers hit halfback Allen Burch, who fumbled the ball on the Tigers six yard line. The happy Tigers moved the ball down to the Panthers 34 yard line and were pulled down from behind.

The Tigers' pass was intercepted by halfback Frank Abernathy and a penalty set the Panthers back to the 6-yard line.

Pass Intercepted

At this point halfback Lee Bumgarner brought the crowd to their feet as the raced for 59 yards behind good blocking. He was pulled down from behind on the Tigers 35. At this point the explosive Panthers called on halfback Allen Burch, who, behind excellent blocking, raced 35 yards to score the touchdown. Halfback Frank Abernathy added the two pointer.

The kick was returned to the Tiger 30. The Tigers picked up a first down on their own 40 and had another on the Panthers 45-yard line as the third quarter ended.

In the final period the Tigers were on the Panthers 31-yard line as a result of a 15-yard penalty. Then the Tigers fell back to the Panthers 46 yard line due to a fifteen yard penalty. Halfback Frank Abernathy intercepted another Tiger pass on the Panthers 38-yard line.

Once again Panthers quarterback Allen Pope got his team rolling as halfback Allen Burch carried for eleven yards after a nine yard loss. Pope hit Burch on the Tigers 35, then Pope hit Bumgarner on the 10-yard line. An offside penalty against the Tigers was refused. It gave the Panthers first and goal on the 10 yard line where fullback Edward Cunningham, behind excellent blocking, raced ten yards to score. Quarterback Allen Pope added the two pointer.

From this point the Tigers tried to score. The stout Panther defense stopped their drives on the Panthers 35-yard line. Quarterback Pope fumbled on the Panthers 46 as the final gun sounded. The untouchable Panthers ended a victorious perfect season.

COACH ROGER J. SCALES
ONE OF THE MEN BEHIND THE SCENE OF "THE UNTOUCHABLES"
BY JOANN M.SCALES AND JOSEPH M. SCALES

Who was this man fondly referred to as Coach Scales? Most who knew of the football team at Ridgeview High, Hickory, NC, knew him as one of the men behind the scene during its epic season of 1964… the season the Panthers' football team would become the undefeated, unscored upon, State Champions known as the "Untouchables."

To know, and have an appreciation for Coach Scales, and his philosophy about coaching, one only needs to look at who he was as a person. A native North Carolinian, born in Mt. Airy, NC, during a time when Jim Crow laws governed, he was the youngest of thirteen children, born to a Primitive Baptist minister. Strong Christian values, high expectations, hard work, honor, respect, resourcefulness, and helping others were familial norms. Coach Scales attended segregated public schools and graduated from J.J. Jones High School with honors and having lettered in several sports. As a teenager he worked many jobs, including picking tobacco, driving the school bus and caddying at a local white only golf course, a job he walked away from because of excessive exposure to profanity. These formative years, rich with experiences, would provide an invaluable foundation and beginning framework for how he would view others, his community and the world. More importantly, they would influence his thinking regarding his personal direction in life and how he might have a positive impact on individuals like himself, and the community.

Coach Scales attended Fayetteville State University, on an athletic scholarship, and graduated with a degree in Elementary Education and Physical Education. Following graduation, he enlisted in the army, hoping to travel overseas but was assigned stateside duty with the Personnel Dept, at Fort Bragg, NC. His formal teaching and coaching duties immediately followed two years of service in the U.S Army. His pursuit of excellence and quality performance would continue with his completion of the Masters' degree in Education at Indiana Univ., and additional study in Guidance and School Administration.

In 1960 when Coach Scales was initially employed by the Hickory School District, it was to teach junior high school classes and coach varsity football and varsity baseball. After three years he would serve as an assistant principal along with his coaching duties, fully invested in giving his all in each capacity. To his credit he had an uncanny ability to relate to colleagues and others in his work environment, and the community with professionalism and integrity.

To the team, Coach Scales was especially relatable, as he had traveled a similar path and brought an array of skills. Not only was he a young, talented athlete, he was mature and disciplined. He also was a teacher, motivator, counselor, father figure and consultant. Finding joy in ongoing learning and development, he remained a student of the game, studying playbooks, attending clinics, and collaborating with others on key aspects to share with the team and aid in building a stronger, more sophisticated football team.

Being greatly influenced by his life experiences and perspective, Coach Scales' involvement with the Ridgeview community far exceeded the boundaries of the classroom, administrative office and field. Intrinsically, he knew and felt that, as a black man in a pivotal position, working with African American youth especially, he had a unique responsibility of ensuring that students received positive affirmations and the support needed to be successful in life. He particularly, did not want any student giving credence to stereotypical impressions projected onto them or the Black community, directly or systemically. The field, the classroom and the administrative office provided an opportunity for him to demonstrate a broad range of skills as a professional and role model. Regarding the players, his focus was on assisting in molding men who would be well prepared for life. It was important to him that his players were confident in who they were as young black men and their ability to be successful on the field and in life despite racial injustice and the disparities which existed (in our education, health and economic systems) and which they endured daily.

From many conversations and dialogues of Coach Scales about his involvement with Coach Davis (Head Coach), and the Panthers football team, it was very clear that their love for the game was exceeded only by their expectations of themselves and the players, which were unquestionably high. Behind the high expectations were guiding principles and concepts that were germane to players' ongoing development and meeting expectations. These principles and concepts would prove invaluable on their journey in football and beyond.

Some are noted here:

1. Mental Preparation and having a positive mindset. Setting the tone for their engagement through prayer; relationship building- team above self.
2. Knowing your craft and understanding the fundamentals of the game. Familiarity with your role and others. Receiving/accepting the knowledge and resources of team leadership.
3. Physical Preparation and Conditioning. Being willing to push the limits, challenge themselves and teammates; Performing exercises and drills to reach desired results. Developing and maintaining a healthy regiment.
4. Mastering & Executing plays as designed. Applying critical thinking skills, demonstrating flexibility, playing dual roles, adapting to play changes
5. Ongoing Assessment. Critique individual and team performance. Evaluating strengths and weaknesses, revising goals, developing new strategies as tools.
6. Celebrating achievements with appreciation, honor and humility. Being clear of their "brand,"- who and what you represent. Readying oneself for the next chapter.

These concepts were intended to enhance and maximize player performance on the field and provide a road map for ongoing learning, development and pursuit of other goals. The success of the Panthers as a winning team was seen as a residual effect of the bond between coaching staff and players and their commitment to hard work, determination and ownership of ascribed principles.

Coach Scales was a very humble man who was described at his retirement celebration as a "gentle giant." He was deeply honored and grateful for the opportunity to serve along with Coach Davis at Ridgeview HS. He was even more grateful for the opportunity to work with a great group of aspiring young Black men, sharing life experiences and giving voice and confirmation to who they were and could aspire to become. He ascribed to and frequently quoted, "To Whom Much is Given, Much is Expected." He appreciated and relished the idea of coaching and teaching, and was relentless in his support and efforts in building a solid team of young men whose family, school and community could be proud of and embrace as model students, athletes and human beings. Coach Scales left Hickory in 1965, but returned in 1966 as

Administrative Assistant to the Superintendent of Schools and taught Adult Education Classes at Catawba Valley Technical Institute. He would continue teaching, coaching and administrative roles for many years. He met his wife Joann Morgan while at Livingstone College as Dean of Men and Offensive Coach. They have one son Joseph M. Scales. Coach Scales passed in 2010, but his legacy lives on in the many lives he touched during his lifetime. The joy that he found in being a part of the Ridgeview family was immeasurable and left an indelible mark on his heart.

To God be the Glory for the achievement of 1964 coaches and football Team of Ridgeview High School. May you be granted your rightful place in History.

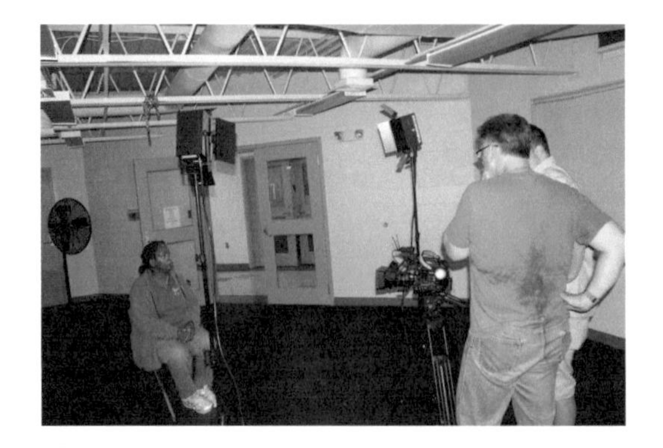

Readying for interviews. A stand-in from the Recreation Center assists with sound and light check.

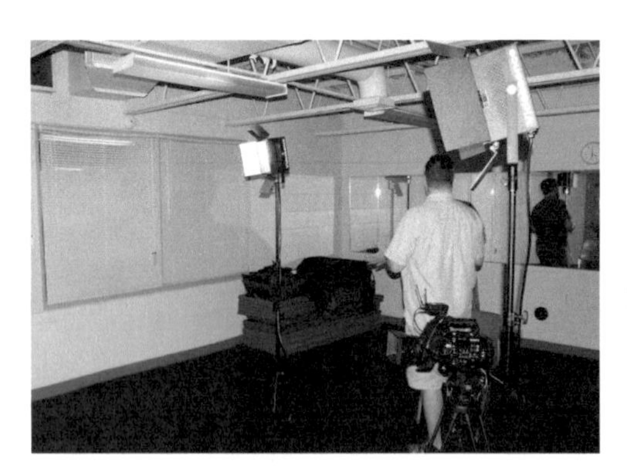

Adjusting the lighting before the players arrive.

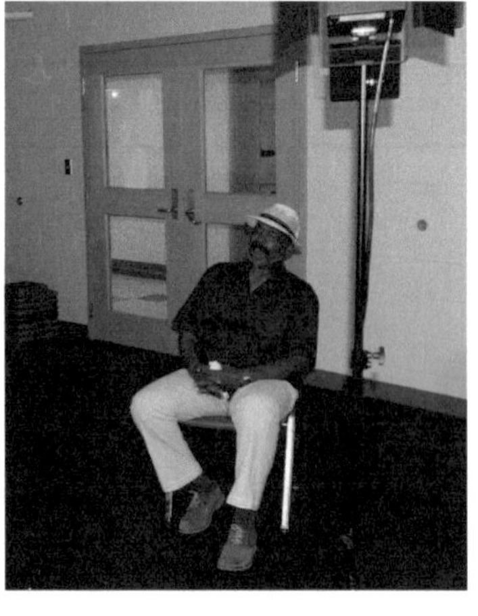

The Reverend Xenophone Lutz waxes eloquently about the amazing 1964 season.

Douglas Bumgarner takes it easy between interview sessions.

Made in the USA
Columbia, SC
05 February 2024

30998682R10139